"Dorothy Leeds gives you the courage to ask and the power to assess. Buy it, read it and gain the competitive edge!"
— Lori Burgess, publisher of *Mademoiselle*

"A sincere, intelligent question can make the difference in your life, your work and with all of your relationships. Learn the art of questions, and see how much richer your life will be. Dorothy Leeds will show you the way in *The 7 Powers of Questions*."
— Terrie M. Williams, author of *The Personal Touch: What You Really Need to Succeed in Today's Fast-Paced Business World*

"Finally, the essence of win-win communication! Why didn't I learn these brilliant insights and strategies early in my career?"
— Dr. Denis Waitley, author of *Empires of the Mind*

"It is age-old advice: 'Ask and you shall receive.' But that leads us to some very important questions: 'What do you ask for?' and 'How do you succeed in getting what you want?' Read *The 7 Powers of Questions* and find out."
— Michael LeBoeuf, Ph.D., author of *How to Win Customers and Keep Them for Life*

"At last, a book that addresses the real secret of how to win friends and influence people—you've got to ask the right questions. Dorothy Leeds shows you how to do it."
— Robert L. Shook, author of *It Takes a Prophet to Make a Profit*

"At Ziff Davis Publishing, we know that the better our questions the easier it will be to succeed with our clients in the Information Age. We should all be 'wired' into *The 7 Powers of Questions*. Read this book and benefit immediately."
— Jim Spanfeller, executive vice president, publishing director, Ziff Davis Publishing

"In a time when just about everyone you meet thinks they know all the answers, Dorothy Leeds teaches us that what we really need are the questions and the ability to listen."
—Dr. Alan Altman, assistant clinical professor at Harvard

"Working a room and building conversation requires the appropriate questions to engage colleagues, associates, clients, and potential friends. Dorothy Leeds provides the ultimate guidelines and unleashes the power of questions so you can shine in any room."
—Susan RoAne, keynote speaker and bestselling author of *How to Work a Room* and *What Do I Say Next?*

"In an age of information overload, Dorothy Leeds has raised important questions and produced persuasive answers in *The 7 Powers of Questions*. Her stories and quotes are compelling. Her guidance is to-the-point and practical—both at work and at home."
—Dr. Rick Kirschner, coauthor of *Dealing With People You Can't Stand* and *Life by Design*

"Bravo! For everyone who was taught that it is bad manners to ask too many questions, I say this is a godsend! We can all be empowered by reading this book."
—Marianne Howatson, senior managing director, ScreamingMedia.com

"The most effective arrow in any communicator's quiver is the astutely aimed and incisively phrased question. The single most authoritative archer is Dorothy Leeds! Her *7 Powers of Questions* hits the bull's-eye."
—George Walther, author of *Power Talking: 50 Ways to Say What You Mean and Get What You Want*

"After reading Dorothy Leeds's book *The 7 Powers of Questions*, I have only one question: Why wouldn't everybody want to buy this book to improve their communications?"

—Leil Lowndes, motivational speaker and author of *Conversation Confidence*

"To keep ahead, we all need to fix things before they get broken. *The 7 Powers of Questions* will help prevent things from getting broken and enable you to communicate more clearly, creatively, and effectively."

—Robert Kriegel, Ph.D., author of *If It Ain't Broke . . . BREAK IT!* and *Sacred Cows Make the Best Burgers*

"Salespeople are looking for one thing: Answers. The only way to get those answers is one word: Questions. Dorothy Leeds's book *The 7 Powers of Questions* will lead salespeople to the knowledge that they need to gain more sales."

—Jeffrey H. Gitomer, author of *The Sales Bible* and *Knock Your Socks Off Selling*

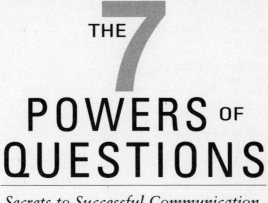

THE 7 POWERS OF QUESTIONS

Secrets to Successful Communication
in Life and at Work

Dorothy Leeds

A Perigee Book

A Perigee Book
Published by The Berkley Publishing Group
A division of Penguin Putnam Inc.
375 Hudson Street
New York, New York 10014

Copyright © 2000 by Dorothy Leeds
Author photograph by Cliff Lipson
Book design by Carolyn Leder
Cover design by Liz Sheehan

First edition: September 2000

Published simultaneously in Canada.

The Penguin Putnam Inc. World Wide Web site address is
http://www.penguinputnam.com

Library of Congress Cataloging-in-Publication Data

Leeds, Dorothy.
    The 7 powers of questions : secrets to successful communication in life and at work /
Dorothy Leeds.—1st ed.
        p. cm.
    Includes bibliographical references and index.
    ISBN 0-399-52614-5
        1. Interpersonal communication. 2. Questioning. I. Title: Seven powers of questions.
II. Title.

P94.7.L44 2000
302.2—dc21

                                                                                        00-034655

Printed in the United States of America

10   9   8   7   6   5   4

What did I do right in this world to have such a delightful child in my life?
To this very special gift, my new granddaughter, Talya:
May you always maintain your inspiring curiosity and seek the answers to your questions.

CONTENTS

Foreword   xi
Preface   xiii
Acknowledgments   xix

1 Why a Book About Questions?   1

2 Power Number One:
  QUESTIONS DEMAND ANSWERS   15

3 Power Number Two:
  QUESTIONS STIMULATE THINKING   36

4 Power Number Three:
  QUESTIONS GIVE US VALUABLE
  INFORMATION   61

5 Power Number Four:
   QUESTIONS PUT YOU IN CONTROL   89

6 Power Number Five:
   QUESTIONS GET PEOPLE TO OPEN UP   110

7 Power Number Six:
   QUESTIONS LEAD TO QUALITY
   LISTENING   131

8 Power Number Seven:
   QUESTIONS GET PEOPLE TO
   PERSUADE THEMSELVES   157

9 Sell, Lead, Think:
   USE QUESTIONS TO TRANSFORM
   YOUR ORGANIZATION   169

10 Closer Knit Than Ever:
   HOW QUESTIONS CAN DRAW
   FAMILIES TOGETHER   216

11 Rediscover Questions:
   Recapture and Redefine the Essential You   244

12 The Fifty Smartest Questions   271

   Suggested Reading   280
   Postscript   284
   Index   287

FOREWORD

Gaining a clear understanding of the value of questions is probably the single most dominant factor in my overall success in business and in life. As a sales trainer and the author of ten books on the subject of selling, including *How to Master the Art of Selling*, I have always been a believer in the value of questions. I teach this premise in all of my seminars: When you are *talking* you are only covering what you already know. The only way to learn what the other person needs (and what you don't already know) is to ask questions—over, under, and all around the topic of conversation—and then listen to the answers. People who ask questions in business and in life are more respected and, usually, more wealthy. If you doubt this, think of people like Barbara Walters, Oprah Winfrey, Art Linkletter, Larry King, and the other great interviewers of our time. Their careers revolve around their ability to get people talking and they accomplish this by asking questions.

Personally, I am thrilled that Dorothy Leeds has created a whole book on this subject because I truly believe it is so critical to one's personal development that it merits solitary study. It took someone with Dorothy's inquisitiveness and talent to present the information with an innovative focus in an accessible format.

Everyone picking up this book can benefit from reading it by learning how to ask questions that will build relationships. Relationships are built on shared information. Your sex, age, or profession does not matter. You can benefit from this book!

- As a grandparent you can learn to ask your grandchildren good questions that get them talking and asking questions in return.

- As a parent you can grow closer to your kids without seeming intrusive.

- As a friend or spouse you can learn tactful ways of asking questions in uncomfortable situations.

Dorothy explains why communication often breaks down or does not work and how questions can help us. There is great power in learning to use questions effectively. I believe this is the most important communication book you can own because asking questions can change your life.

Asking the right questions will take you to great places. Look where it took Dorothy . . . she questioned me into writing this foreword!

Tom Hopkins,
author of *How to Master the Art of Selling*

PREFACE

I have a passion for questions.

When I was sixteen I had the great privilege of accompanying Dean Dixon, a well-known orchestra conductor, to Israel and Europe. He and his wife, Vivian, were giving concerts with all the major orchestras and the three of us had an incredible trip. In Paris the night before I returned home, Dean and Vivian took me out to a lovely café for a farewell dinner. Dean leaned over to me and asked, "What are you going to do with this wonderful experience you have had traveling?" Before he asked me that question, the thought had never entered my mind to do something with this trip. All night I thought about his question, and I decided I would give talks at my high school and to organizations who were interested in a teenager's view of Europe and Israel. Although I did not become a professional speaker until 1979, that question was the start of all those unconscious yearnings for this special career.

In looking back on my life I have become more conscious of how questions have made me who I am today. Dean's question was arguably the most important. Without my willingness to ask questions I would not have met and become friends with so many different and interesting people all over the world. I would not have the successful career I have today if I had not asked, "What can I do to achieve the goals I envision for my company?" My curiosity about other cultures has led me on trips to India, the Galápagos Islands, Morocco, Nepal, and Egypt—trips that have shaped how I think about myself and the world in which I live.

But questions were not always such a great influence on my life. I did not grow up in a home where my parents asked me questions about what I liked, felt, or thought. They were definitely *tellers*, not *askers*. My parents always assumed that I believed what they believed, whether about politics or just everyday situations. As a result, I had little confidence; I felt that my opinions did not count and that I did not control my own life. My parents loved to read, however, and from them I learned to love to read. Even now, decades later, I am always reading several magazines and at least one book at the same time. My search for knowledge and my interest in everything comes to me from my parents. They gave me that very special gift, but I have made it my own by becoming a questioner. Every time I feel depressed, challenged, or inspired, I ask myself, Why? I seek answers. Whether we do this consciously or not, our lives are guided by the questions we ask.

And sometimes a question can save our lives. In 1982 I was diagnosed with breast cancer. Unfortunately, the doctor who diagnosed me did not have the best bedside manner—or really, any bedside manner at all. After my biopsy I remember lying in the hospital bed feeling that nothing was wrong with me. I thought that everything would be okay. However, this doctor had different news for me. When he walked into the room I sat up and looked at him expectantly. I was ready to hear the good news and, once having heard it, to get up from the bed, get dressed, and go home to my family. He looked at me sternly and his voice boomed, "Your tumor is malignant." With that he turned and left the room. Needless to say, I was quite scared, but I was determined to get through this, no matter what it took.

When I sat down with the doctor later and asked, "What are my options?" I was disturbed to hear from him that I had none. I was to have a mastectomy and that was the only way to save my life. Only, something deep down inside of me told me that was wrong. There are always options, aren't there? I was unable to accept his answer. So I went to see more doctors. I went from office to office, armed with only my will to win and a question: "What are my options?" If it hadn't been for my gut feeling, I probably would have had a mastectomy. But I decided to keep asking the question and until I heard an answer that was acceptable to me. It took effort and persistence, but eventually I was able to find that answer. I had asked the question to what seemed like hundreds of doctors in the metropolitan area before I finally found a doctor who agreed: I had options. I am happy to say that I was cured of my cancer—with a lumpectomy and radiation. In 1982 this was not standard treatment as it is now.

I suppose that with my question I was ahead of my time. To this day I am thankful that somewhere deep inside me was the questioning instinct. I am grateful that I did not let my fear paralyze me. I am grateful that there are almost always options and people to exercise them. I am grateful that I asked that question.

Many of the major events in my life have been the result of a question asked. The more I pushed myself to find the answers and the more I kept asking the questions, the better the results. As is the case with many people, I did not find my perfect career from the start. I have done many things—I used to teach in the New York City public school system, for example. I enjoyed teaching very much and I liked my integral role in the learning process, but at the same time I felt as though something was missing. While I was enjoying my work, I wasn't enjoying it as much as I wanted. I felt there was something more out there for me. "What is it that is missing?" I kept asking myself.

Before teaching I had been an actress and, again, I had loved acting. But, again, it did not give me the fulfillment I had been pursuing. In search of the perfect career, I kept asking myself the question, "What career will make me happy?" All of the careers I had—advertising executive, knitwear designer, business owner—were good, but none of them was right for me. Then I started to ask myself even more questions: "What do I like to do?" and "What have I done in the past that has made me happy?" and "What are my talents?" After this long and sometimes difficult questioning process I realized that my talents lay in teaching and entertaining. Fortunately, not only was I talented in those areas, I really enjoyed the correlated roles. So, I asked myself, "How can I combine those two talents?" The career that I came up with is not one your guidance counselor tells you about—a professional speaker. What is that? While I may never have guessed that I would become a professional speaker, now I cannot imagine being anything else. I feel fulfilled—I'm using my talents to my full potential and loving every minute of it. How did I get to the point of finding a great career that makes me feel so good? By asking questions, of course!

It takes energy to follow the questioning path, but I have never regretted doing it. Often the results are surprising and much better than we get without questions. The thing about questions is that you do not realize how much better your life can be by using them. As a teenager and young adult I gave little thought to the power of questions, even though I was reaping the benefits of asking them. As I got more actively involved with business I began to see their great value not only in the business world but in every aspect of our lives—from the humdrum day-to-day events to the momentous occasions that change our lives.

That is the beauty of asking questions: the benefits apply to everyone. I know I could have benefited much earlier in my life from asking them. When I was first married I let my husband pick out our first apartment. The day we moved in was the first time I saw the place—it turned out to be a dark basement apartment. I had let my husband take care of the search and did not ask him questions about the kind of apartments he was looking at because I simply wasn't curious—I had never learned how to exercise the questioning muscle. A few years ago I alienated a good friend because I lost my temper and did not stop to ask myself, "Do I really want to say this? Is winning this argument worth losing a friendship?"

I spent most of my life as a brunette because I hadn't asked, "How would I look as a redhead?" (By the way, the answer is *great*.)

From hair color to careers, questions rule our lives. My purpose in writing this book is to get you to see the power questions hold and how we can harness that power to improve our lives. Without that power, we are like travelers on a road without a map. With the power of questions, however, we can take control and make decisions about which roads to take in life. Imagine how you would feel if you were able to ask more of others, more of yourself, and more for yourself. Can you imagine how much better your life would be?

ACKNOWLEDGMENTS

Having written several books, I know that researching and writing a book is always a team effort. The team that made this book possible is extra special—all Olympic gold medalists. My thanks and gratitude to Tim R. Fredrick, Sharyn Kolberg, Caroline Giordano, Susan Leon, Karl Webber, and Sally Arteseros.

Heartfelt thanks to all the generous and supportive people I interviewed who graciously shared their thoughts and passion for questions: Debbie Allen, Beth Althofer, Michael Bloomberg, Ronda Dean, Lodewijk de Vink, James Fergason, Stephen Gale, Rabbi Gewirtz, David Golomb, Jaakko Hintikka, Tamar Howson, Janice Leiberman, Anthony Lewis, Sharon Livingston, Doug Melton, Dale Moss, Jim Murphy, Mamie Murray, George Priest, Bob Shook, Jon Strauss, Larry Wilson, and Mark Wind. And a special thanks to Tom Hopkins for the contribution of his ideas, and most importantly, his foreword.

To my literary agent, Jane Dystel, for her belief in me and this project, and, of course, to my publisher, John Duff, for his patience and understanding throughout. Thanks also to Hillery Borton, whose editing expertise helped make this the excellent book it is.

To my husband, Nonny Weinstock, the best grammarian I know, and my children, Laura and Ian Weinstock, who have always inspired me with their questions.

My inquisitive and supportive extended family—Rachel Pray, Sanja Kabalin, Grace and Dickson Chin, and Wilson Morales.

And finally to all the companies, organizations, salespeople, and executives who have, through the years, believed in me and in the value of questions. You have all made this possible, and I thank you.

1

Why a Book About Questions?

A question. Since before your sun burned hot in space and before your race was born, I've awaited a question.

—THE GUARDIAN OF FOREVER
"City on the Edge of Forever"
Star Trek, April 6, 1967

CHANGING FOR THE BETTER

Every time you open your mouth to speak you have two options: Make a statement or ask a question. Asking questions can change your life. In fact, it is the act of questioning that causes us to go deep inside and examine our emotional selves and questioning that causes us to take actions that turn our lives around.

We all want to believe that we have the power to change our

lives. In reality setbacks, failures, and frustrations all take their toll. We end up focusing on the negative and asking ourselves unanswerable questions like, "Why does this always happen to me?" or "Why can't I ever do anything right?" These kinds of questions always lead to negative answers like, "You're too stupid," or "You only get what you deserve—obviously you don't deserve to do better."

Often we ask questions of others that put them in the same negative position—"Why do you always do this to me?" or "How could you be so thoughtless?" It is almost impossible to provide rational, positive answers to questions like these.

Learning to change your questioning habits can also change the focus of your life. The right questions can help you move forward and get you through the rough times. Better questions provide better answers, and better answers give you better solutions. Improve your questions and you will improve your relationships, at home and at work.

This book will take an in-depth look into questions, an essential communication tool that as a culture we have stopped appreciating. It will also show you how to redirect the power of questions to expand your potential in every area of life. In the first section, each chapter concentrates on one of the seven powers. The second section focuses more specifically on how to use questions and their powers in business, with your family, and in your personal life. Although you will find questions throughout this book, the last chapter contains fifty of the most effective questions you can ask.

Also appearing throughout the book are sections headed by the letters *IQ*. That stands for either "interesting quote" or "intelligent question." Each section contains words of wisdom on the subject of questions.

IQ Inquisitive people who are not ashamed to ask questions invariably wind up knowing more, and there is a high degree of correlation between knowledge and the ability to make good decisions. There is also a high degree of correlation between people who have the information and people who succeed.

—Michael Bloomberg, founder and CEO, Bloomberg L.P.

Many of these quotes and questions are from people like Michael Bloomberg who were kind enough to share their time and wisdom for this book. I interviewed dozens of people who are *questioning professionals*: salespeople, doctors, lawyers, journalists, psychologists, law enforcement experts, inventors, and clergy. Questions are crucial to all of these people in their professional lives and, as they came to realize while they were being interviewed for the book, in their personal lives as well. In fact, the more people I interviewed, the more I realized just how important questions are to each and every one of us.

IQ Questions set off a processional effect that has an impact beyond our imagination. Questioning our limitations tears down the walls in life—in business, in relationships, between countries. I believe all human progress is preceded by new questions.

—Anthony Robbins, *Awaken the Giant Within*

A WHOLE NEW DIRECTION

Are you getting everything you want out of life? Are your relationships focused and heading in a positive direction? Are you satisfied with the way your career is progressing? Do you feel as if you are reaching your highest potential?

If your response was no to any of the preceding questions, you've just answered the most pertinent one of all: "Why should I read this book?"

My goal in this book is to create a mental and emotional turning point, to get you to start thinking in new and different ways, to help you reach a greater understanding of the situations you encounter every day. The only way to do this is through questioning—through asking more of yourself and more of others. You can make small changes in your life that make a world of difference; you can create a turning point just by asking more questions.

Even the slightest turn can point you in a whole new direction. A turning point doesn't have to be 180 degrees. Imagine yourself at the center of a circle. If you walk straight ahead, you'll end up at point A. But if, starting from the same center point, you move your feet just a few degrees, you will set yourself up to head down an entirely different path.

If you increase the quantity and quality of the questions you ask by a little bit each day, you can move your life in a new direction. You can get more of what you want and need. In fact, you can get more out of everything you do when you develop the asking habit.

You will learn to stop concentrating on what you should *say* next in every situation and instead start thinking, "What should I *ask*?"

THE PROGRESS OF COMMUNICATION

Human progress has often been defined in terms of how we communicate. In the past one hundred years, our world has progressed almost beyond recognition. Now that we are in the twenty-first century, we can only imagine what lies ahead for us.

How much faster will we be able to do business? Will it be possible to have dinner in India and then teleport to New York for coffee and cake?

If we have learned anything in these past one hundred years, it is that anything is possible and that everything is speeding up. We are trying to make our world more efficient through advances in technology; however, it is essentially up to us as individuals and organizations to make the technology work. It is not enough just to be able to use a computer. As Picasso once said, "Computers are useless. They can only give you answers." And as Neil Postman, author, linguist, and chairman of the Department of Culture and Communication at New York University, claims, "Learning to use a computer isn't nearly as important as learning how to ask smart questions." All of the technology in the world will not help us if we are not able, at the core, to communicate with each other and build strong, lasting relationships.

With all the ways to communicate these days and with all the ways that are yet to come, in the end we are still sending messages back and forth. If you think about the evolution of the human race, most of our major advances have involved changes in methods of communication. Perhaps our greatest advance was the development of speech, which separates us from other animal species. When we began using signs and symbols to communicate, the written word was born. Centuries later Gutenberg invented movable type, and the ease with which the printed word—and the ideas it conveyed—could be spread around the world improved exponentially.

In the twenty-first century the telegraph, typewriter, and telephone are disappearing or morphing into computerized connections our ancestors could never have imagined. Yet there is one incredible communications tool that has existed since the beginning of language, one that we take for granted even though we use it every day.

This book was written to help you harness the strength of this incredible tool: the simple question.

THE QUESTION IS THE ANSWER

As we swim through oceans of facts, news, and advice that we receive on a daily basis, we struggle for a way to stay afloat. We exist in a media-saturated, information-overloaded world. To succeed, personally and professionally, we must harness the power of questions.

Questions are a powerful yet simple means to achieve a great deal:

- Find specific or necessary information.

- Establish strong relationships.

- Persuade and motivate others.

- Think more creatively.

- Create meaningful changes in our lives.

Traveling the congested information highway, it is becoming much more difficult to communicate clearly, concisely, and comprehensively. We are missing the mark, at home and at work. Our increasing ability to speed up communication (and our attachment to that speed), meant to make our lives easier, has only served to make life more complicated.

Due to the fast pace of our busy world our attention spans appear to be shrinking. We do not even seem to have the time to talk to each other, despite the fact that we have more methods of communication than ever before: fax machines, answering machines, voice mail, e-mail, cordless phones, cell phones, pagers that transmit through a wristwatch, cameras the size of a pinhole, and who-knows-what kind of technology coming tomorrow. These innovations give us greater opportunity to connect interpersonally. They also allow us to miscommunicate and misunderstand each other even more often.

This was dramatized in an underrated 1995 movie, *Denise*

Calls Up, about a group of telecommuting New Yorkers who stay in touch with each other exclusively by fax, phone, and computer. Characters create and destroy relationships without ever meeting one another. Now we do the same thing almost daily over the Internet. It is getting easier to live our lives without ever leaving the house.

In a *Harvard Business Review* article, "The Human Moment at Work," psychiatrist Edward M. Hallowell decries the disappearing *human moments* at work—times where two people interact face-to-face. "The irony is that this kind of alienation in the workplace derives not from lack of communication but from a surplus of the wrong kind," writes Hallowell.

In the face of all this, what can we do to understand each other better?

We can ask questions. Questions bring us back to human contact.

> IQ We are always awaiting the new magical pill that will enable us to eat all the fattening food we want, and not gain weight; burn all the gasoline we want, and not pollute the air; live as immoderately as we choose, and not contract either cancer or heart disease.
>
> In our minds, at least, technology is always on the verge of liberating us from personal discipline and responsibility. Only it never does and it never will. The more high technology around us, the more the need for human touch.
>
> —John Naisbitt, *Megatrends*

Why do we need this human touch? Because no matter what the changes in the *way* we communicate, *why* we communicate remains the same. We need information. In order to get that information, we have to know what questions to ask and the right way to ask them. Because knowledge is power.

IQ They say that our neocortex—the newest part of our brain—is only about two thousand years old. When people say we're only using 5 percent of our brains, that's the part we're using. Our old brain, the brain stem that's been around for millions of years, is the part that runs by instinct. That's the part that animals have. They don't ask questions. The purpose of our "new brain" is to override and challenge our old brain, and we do that by asking questions.

—Larry Wilson, founder and vice chairman, Pecos River Division, AON Consulting

THE POWER OF QUESTIONS

In the information age, he who has the most information wins. Never before has getting the right information at the right time been so crucial, nor has building better relationships (the means to getting better information). We talk about the empowerment of the individual and, at the same time, about understanding our essential differences. In this new age, communicating has become a challenge. That challenge can be met by relying on the power of questions.

The art and skill of asking questions can benefit everyone, from the CEO of the largest corporate conglomerate to the high school senior trying to figure out, "What do I do now?"

Knowing how to ask the right questions can help you solve problems faster ("Are we looking for the *right* solution or just *any* solution?"), make better decisions, and get more out of life. It will help you understand yourself, comprehend why you do some of the things you do ("Is this really worth my effort at this time?"), and focus on what you can do to change the things you want to change. It will help you learn what's important to those around you ("Can you share with me why this particular issue bothers you so much?") and how you can help them get what they need as well.

I started my career as a communications consultant working with managers. Most were intelligent, motivated individuals who were having problems communicating with their teams. I kept asking myself, "Why aren't they as effective as they want to be?" The answer came back loud and clear—they were telling, not asking. They possessed a lecture mentality. They assumed that telling someone to change his behavior would get the job accomplished, but that method was not working. I recognized that these managers needed more effective tools to help them communicate and to encourage team support, involvement, and commitment. They needed to ask questions like, "Will this be a growth experience for my employees or merely more work?" and "Do my employees know specifically what I expect from them?" and "What are my options?" and "Is this particular problem part of a larger problem?" As I worked more with this technique, I began to realize that the missing link to their success was questions. This knowledge inspired me to write my first book, *Smart Questions: The Essential Strategy for Successful Managers.*

We are all managers in one way or another. We manage our own lives and we manage our relationships with others. And for all of us, in all aspects of our lives, questions are the missing link to success. Over the past twenty years I have conducted extensive research on the role of questions and their role in communication and I have found that questions hold seven very specific powers:

1. **Questions demand answers.** When someone asks us a question we are compelled to answer it. This feeling of obligation is what I call the *answering reflex.*

2. **Questions stimulate thinking.** When someone asks a question it stimulates thinking in both the person asking and the person being asked.

3. **Questions give us valuable information.** Asking the right question can give us the specific and relevant information we want and need.

4. **Questions put you in control.** Everyone feels most comfortable and confident when he or she is in control. Because questions demand answers, the asker has the power position.

5. **Questions get people to open up.** There is nothing more flattering than being asked to tell your personal story or to give your opinions, insight, and advice. Asking questions shows others that you are interested in who they are and what they have to say—and when that happens, even the most reticent individuals are willing to share their thoughts and feelings.

6. **Questions lead to quality listening.** As you improve your ability to ask the right question, the answers you get become more pertinent and focused, making it easier for you to concentrate on what's important to the situation.

7. **Questions get people to persuade themselves.** People believe what they say, not what you say. They are more likely to believe something *they thought up*, and a well-phrased question can get their minds headed in a specific direction. The question is the most overlooked tool in the art of persuasion.

WHY DON'T WE ASK MORE QUESTIONS?

If questions are such a powerful tool, why don't we make better use of them? Why do we often shy away from asking even the simplest question? Why do we find ourselves, time after time, walking away from an important confrontation or negotiation saying, "If only I had asked." There are several reasons for this phenomenon.

The first is that we are afraid to question authority. This is probably the most common reason for not asking. When you perceive that someone has more *power* than you have, fear and insecurity begin to take over. It sometimes seems easier simply to accept the word of someone you fear, rather than face a confrontation. However, the need to ask questions is often greatest when you are most vulnerable:

- When you are angry or upset and not thinking clearly.

- When the person you are dealing with is your boss or supervisor, and you fear for your job.

- When you are in trouble or feel victimized.

- When you are frightened, especially when you are in physical or emotional pain.

- When you are in the presence of someone with specific knowledge—such as a doctor or lawyer—and automatically you think that they know best.

- When you think that you do not know enough to make an informed decision, so, rather than ask a question, you prefer to let somebody else take charge.

Many times when we find ourselves in these vulnerable positions, we do not know what questions to ask. When faced with difficult situations we often remain mute, less out of fear than confusion. We think we have to ask the most intelligent questions on the spot and feel ill equipped to do so. This may be true. You may be better off to go home, think calmly about the situation, perhaps do some research, write down any questions that come to you, and then request another meeting. There is no law that says all questions must be spontaneous.

Another reason we do not ask is that we think asking questions makes us appear vulnerable and puts us in a submissive position. It seems to me that men, more than women, face this trap—think of the old but true cliché of men not asking for directions while driving. But this is not the case when you ask thoughtful, focused questions. Asking the right questions can get other people thinking in the direction you would like them to go, which puts you in a position of power and strength.

Sometimes people assume that we know more about a particular subject or situation than we actually do. When that happens, we are usually reluctant to let them know they are wrong. We are afraid to look stupid. We are afraid that asking questions will make us look ill informed or unintelligent. Unless people are terrible snobs, they usually admire people who ask about what they do not know.

One of the best stories I know about the power of questions involves Barbara Bush. When George Bush was first running for president, she had to choose an issue to promote, should she become First Lady. She describes in her autobiography, *Barbara Bush: A Memoir,* how, after much thought, she finally realized that her issue should be literacy—that everything would be better "if more people could read, write, and comprehend."

"So the campaign was told that literacy was my interest—but we forgot to mention that I knew absolutely nothing about the subject, at least not yet." One day, on a campaign stop, she was led into a meeting where her hostess said, " 'We are so excited about your visit. I have collected literacy experts from all around Milwaukee, some forty-five of the most informed people . . . we can't wait to hear what you have to say.' "

"I was lucky," writes Mrs. Bush, "for it suddenly came to me what to do. After saying a very few words, I asked them a question: 'If you were married to the President and had the opportunity to really make a dent in the field of illiteracy, what one thing would you do? How would you go about it?' " Needless to say, the room came alive with excellent suggestions.

"I certainly did learn something there," she concludes. "People would rather hear themselves talk than someone else. So when in doubt, keep quiet, listen, and let others talk. They'll be happy, and you might learn something."

A recent article in the *New Yorker* by Karissa MacFarquhar described a rising young star who publishes a magazine that has become the heartbeat of New York's growing Internet industry. This young man, Jason Calacanis, grew up in the streets of Brooklyn. At first, Calacanis was reluctant to question what he didn't know. But he soon changed his attitude: "Now when people drop some name I'll ask, 'Who's that?' And they'll say, 'You don't know who that is?' And I'll say, 'No.' And they tell me, 'He's a poet from the eighteenth century,' and I'll say, 'OK, now I know.' "

We think that the best way to seem smart is to know all the answers, when in fact the best way to seem smart is to ask the right questions. People admire others who show that they are willing to learn what they do not know.

Sometimes we think that asking questions is rude. Some people have been brought up to think that asking questions means probing into another person's life, and that "nice people" don't ask too many questions. And there is always the problem of too much of a good thing. A string of questions, one after the other, can seem more like an interrogation than a conversation. Especially if you don't listen to the answers. In most cases, your objective is to establish a dialogue—which means a give-and-take—in each situation.

This leads us to the final reason we don't ask more questions: We never learned how. All through school, from kindergarten through graduate school, we were encouraged to know the answers, not the questions. In some cases, we were discouraged from asking, as this was seen as being disruptive. In *Questioning and Teaching: A Manual of Practice*, J. T. Dillon states that in the twenty-seven classrooms he observed, questions were asked by only eleven students. "Questions accounted for over

60 percent of the teachers' talk and for less than one percent of the students' talk," says Dillon. "The overall rate works out to eighty questions per hour from each teacher and two questions per hour from all the students combined."

There do appear to be some bright spots, however. The best teachers invite questions and recognize their importance to the learning process. And in New York State, new standardized math tests don't require simply the correct answer. Students must follow each problem with a short explanation of the methods they used—in other words, what questions they asked themselves to come up with the answers.

As you can see, these reasons for not asking questions are based on misconceptions and unfounded anxieties.

Kids naturally and naively ask the most important questions, questions that grab at our jugular. When I started teaching the day school, the previous teacher told me, "You'll get questions like, 'Why are there big chairs in the sanctuary?' and 'What does the microphone sound like?'" And I thought, I can deal with that. When it was time for questions, many eager hands went up. I picked a little girl sitting in the front row, and she asked a simple question.

"Rabbi," she said, "who made God?"

—Rabbi Matthew D. Gewirtz, Congregation Rodeph Sholom

2

POWER NUMBER ONE

Questions Demand Answers

In the beginning, God was on his way to his meeting on the Mount with Moses to deliver the eleven Commandments. He was running late and rushing. In his haste, one of the tablets fell and shattered into many pieces. God went on to give Moses the remaining commandments (needless to say, Moses was pleased with the ten he got). But God was curious and went back to see which of the powerful commandments had been left behind. He patiently picked up the shattered fragments and pieced the tablet back together again.

What was the eleventh commandment?

"THOU SHALT ASK QUESTIONS—AND ANSWER THEM, TOO!"

THOU SHALT ANSWER QUESTIONS

When I was a young girl I went to the doctor every six months for a routine checkup. The doctor would sit me up on the examination table, my legs dangling over the edge. Then he would pull out a rubber-tipped hammer and tap my leg just below the kneecap. My foot would shoot out straight in front of me, barely missing the doctor.

The doctor was checking my reflexes. The hammer would hit a tendon, which would stimulate the nerves, which would prompt an automatic reflex, which would cause my foot to shoot straight out. That reflex, like all reflexes, was an involuntary response to a stimulus.

We experience hundreds of different kinds of reflexes every day, including pulling our hands away from hot objects, blinking at a loud noise, and the one I call the *answering reflex*. The stimulus that causes this reflex is, of course, a question.

A question is very much like a reflex hammer; it stimulates the nervous system, gets the brain cells working, and—before you know it—out pops an answer! An answer is not quite as involuntary as our knee-jerk response. We can't stop our knee from jerking, but we do have the ability to stop ourselves from answering. However, our initial impulse is to answer—in fact, we feel compelled to do so. This gives the asker an enormous advantage.

Haven't you found yourself telling someone you do not know an intimate secret, just because he or she asked? Watch any news program or talk show and you will see people from all walks of life—rich, poor, blue-collar, famous, or infamous—fall under the spell of the person asking the questions. You will see the richest and most powerful people—politicians, CEOs, celebrities—succumb to the power of the asker. The person who is asking is probably less powerful in terms of money or position, but the politicians and celebrities answer anyway (and when they do not answer, we assume they are being evasive).

When we ask a question, we expect an answer. Until that question is answered, we feel a certain amount of tension. In *The Questioning Presence: Wordsworth, Keats, and the Interrogative Mode in Romantic Poetry,* Susan J. Wolfson writes,

"Questioning is an active power of dislocation. . . . [The] event of an unanswered question retains a disruptive effect."

When a question is asked, we must reply. Even if we do not answer out loud, we say the answer in our minds. More often than not, though, we do actually answer. The answering reflex is so strong, and so important to the art and science of communication, that it is the basis of each of the other six powers of questions.

THE ANSWERING REFLEX

Where does the answering reflex come from? It is something we are taught in the first few years of our lives, at the same time that we are learning to speak. When we begin to speak, how do we practice? By answering questions. Doting parents proudly show off this ability at every opportunity. "Johnny, tell your aunt Sheila—what does the cow say? What's your brother's name? What color is that car? Can you count to three?" The better your answers, the bigger the hug you get as a reward.

Another year or two go by, and we learn to verbalize our own questions and to demand answers from others. "Why is the sky blue? How does the rain fall? Where do dreams go in the daytime?" As our demand for answers increases, so does our knowledge of the world around us.

Part of that knowledge has to do with manners and etiquette. We are taught early on that it is rude to ignore questions we have been asked. Linguist James L. Fidelholtz, professor at the Instituto de Ciencias Sociales y Humanidades in Mexico, says that as we acquire language we also acquire rules about how to use that language. "Specifically, there are rules about being cooperative," he says. "If we hear a question, we know the person is looking for an answer from us, and our normal response is to try and be cooperative."

The other day, sitting in a neighborhood restaurant, I could not help but overhear the conversation of a group of people sitting behind me. Two mothers and their kindergarten-aged children were having dinner when one of the women asked, "Tiffany, how was your day at school?" The child did not respond. The young girl's mother quickly said, "Tiffany, don't be rude. When someone asks you a question, you should answer."

PROGRAMMED TO ANSWER

This admonition to answer questions follows us through life. In school we have to answer teachers' questions and questions on tests and quizzes. If we do not answer—or worse, are unable to answer—we are embarrassed and feel we have failed in some respect.

What happens when a teacher asks a question? The people who know the answer raise their hands and practically jump out of their chairs to get the teacher to call on them. They are thrilled to be among the smart elite. The rest of the students cringe in their seats, hoping (because they don't know the answer) that they might suddenly turn invisible. If the teacher does call on one of these students, and he or she gives the wrong answer, the other students often laugh. This kind of experience affects how we feel about questions for the rest of our lives.

So early on, questions affect our identity and self-esteem, how others feel about us, and how we feel about ourselves. Fear of questions can stop us from learning. I know this from my own experience. Although I was usually a good student, I took a course in logic in college. I had great difficulty understanding the subject. I was so afraid of the questions being asked in the course and on the test, I skipped the midterm altogether (although by some miracle I suddenly understood the subject the day before the final exam, and I passed the course).

As a teacher, coach, and trainer, I have to both ask and

answer questions all the time. When I started out as a teacher in the New York City school system, I had some very bright kids in my classes. I would study and prepare extra hard for my classes with them, because I knew they would ask me difficult questions and I was expected to answer them.

But it is not only in school that questions are powerful. Our entire legal system is based on the premise that questions must be answered. Perry Mason, the famous fictitious lawyer, won every case (except one) by grilling a witness with so many questions that he or she finally confessed to the murder, usually right on the witness stand, in a torrent of tears. These people confessed because they had to answer his questions.

We've all seen courtroom dramas in which the witness is being grilled by a prosecuting attorney. If the witness remains silent, the judge will lean over and state sternly, "You must answer the question!" If the witness still refuses to answer, he may even be jailed on charges of contempt of court.

IQ When the Court questions a witness, the witness is not permitted to reply, "Let's not go there."

—Judge admonishing a witness,
from a D. Reilly cartoon, the *New Yorker*

Of course, in our country, we have the privilege of taking the Fifth Amendment. But what is the result of choosing this option? Suspicion—there must be more to the story. I've sat on juries. The judge instructs the jury that guilt (or innocence) is not to be inferred just because a defendant chooses not to testify. Intellectually, that point is made very clear. But emotionally, one cannot help thinking, "Why won't this person answer the questions? What has he got to hide?"

These principles of law are all based on the fact that we believe we have a right to know all about what concerns and affects us. But the power of questions is even stronger than the power of law. The truth is we do not have a right to know everything about another person; there are some things that are private and confidential. But the question is such a powerful instrument, it often compels us to voluntarily divulge information we would just as soon keep to ourselves.

How many times have you answered survey questions over the telephone? Legitimate companies conduct most of these surveys, but there are also scam artists out there who rely on the power of questions to get information. First they ask you innocent questions about what soft drink you prefer or what kind of vacation resort you would be likely to visit. Then they go on to ask about your age, marital status, if you live alone, your yearly income, your credit card number. . . .

When you're aware of the fact that questions demand answers, it is easier to keep yourself from getting caught in a manipulative use of this power. And, of course, there are ways that you can use this power to your advantage.

NOT GETTING THE RIGHT ANSWERS? CHANGE THE WAY YOU ASK

How can you use the knowledge that this power exists to help you communicate? You can use it to change the way you ask questions so that you get the answers you want.

Since questions demand answers, you have enormous power when you are doing the asking. That power is defined by the words you use, how you phrase the question, and even your tone of voice. Exactly what question you ask, along with the way that you ask it, can dramatically affect the answer you get.

Pollsters know this. In *The Art of Asking Questions,* Stanley L. Payne cites an example of a poll that asked two questions. The only difference between the two was one word.

1. Do you think the United States should allow public speeches against democracy?

2. Do you think the United States should forbid public speeches against democracy?

Since these questions are exact opposites, Payne says that the percentages should be exact opposites, as well. In other words, if 25 percent of the people answered yes to the first question, then 25 percent should have answered no to the second. However, this was not the case. A much higher percentage of people answered no to the second question. The word *forbid*, which is stronger and more negative, prompted a stronger, more negative response. Payne concludes, "Evidently there is something very forbidding about the word *forbid*. People are more ready to say that something should not be allowed than to say it should be forbidden."

Every word makes a difference. Take, for instance, the two little words *could* and *should*. When it comes to asking questions, we sometimes use these two words as synonyms. Yet the distinction between the two produces different answers. At first glance, there might not seem to be much difference between these two questions:

1. Do you think anything *should* be done to curb the rise of HMOs in this country?

2. Do you think anything *could* be done to curb the rise of HMOs in this country?

Or these:

1. Do you think you *should* eat five servings of fruits and vegetables a day?

2. Do you think you *could* eat five servings of fruits and
   vegetables a day?

There is only one word's difference in both sets of questions, yet
they would likely elicit very different responses.

The wording of a question can be extremely important, and
the judicial system provides a perfect example. Mamie Murray
is the president of Atlantic Forensic Investigations and Consultants, a Canadian company specializing in polygraph tests,
hypnosis, and statement analysis. Questions given during a
polygraph, or lie detector test, must be carefully worded to fit
the situation.

"An examiner must be cautious about inaccurate information, language differences, and the mental elements involved in
each test," says Murray. For example, she says, it may be quite
proper to ask an individual if she "caused the death" of another
person if the cause, the body location, or other facts are
unknown. It would be the wrong wording in many cases, however, because it is open to interpretation. Suppose a baby-sitter
killed a child, for example. If you were to ask the mother, "Did
you cause the death of your child?" she may answer yes. In her
mind, the fact that she hired the baby-sitter in the first place
makes her the one who caused the death.

"I recall once asking a man if he had sexually assaulted his
granddaughter," says Murray, "which he vehemently denied."
When the question was changed to ask if he had done anything
at all to his granddaughter, he freely admitted, "I lick her and
she licks me, but I never touched her." In the initial question,
Murray assumed that she and the grandfather used the same
definition of sexual assault. His second answer, however,
revealed that was not the case. When Murray rephrased her
question, she got an entirely different answer.

Your tone of voice also influences the type of answer you get.
Imagine two different scenarios in which you are getting ready

to move into a new house, and you'd like to take two personal days off from your job to finish packing. In the first scenario, you go into the boss's office, explain the situation, and then add tentatively in a quavering voice, "I'll finish the Johnson project on, uh, Wednesday, I guess, and, uh, I was kind of wondering, maybe I, um, could have, um, well, maybe two days off at the end of the week?"

In the second scenario, you approach the boss, explain the situation, and end on a calm, even note by saying, "I'll have the Johnson project completed by Wednesday—a week ahead of schedule. It would mean a lot to me to have two days off at the end of the week. Is that possible?"

The boss in the first scenario would have a more difficult time taking your request seriously. She might not think the two days off were that important to you and, because of your tentative tone, she might not even be sure you would finish the Johnson project on time. The boss in the second scenario, however, would be inclined to consider your request and would probably grant it. So, although questions do demand answers, unless you ask them carefully, you might not get the answer you want.

DO YOU REALLY WANT TO KNOW?

The fact that questions demand answers can sometimes create a "be careful what you wish for" situation. If you ask, "Do I look fat in this?" you have to be prepared for the answer you've demanded—even if it's not the one you want to hear.

In a scene in the film *Gypsy*, Mama Rose and her daughter, Gypsy Rose Lee, are having an argument. Gypsy has become a star (as a stripper) and is leaving her mother behind. Rose asks, "All that scrimping and saving. All that figuring out how we could all eat on a buck. What did I do it for? You tell me, what did I do it for?" Her daughter turns and says softly, "I thought you did it for me, Mama." It is not the answer Rose was expecting; it is a touchingly painful moment for her, and for the audience as well.

Some of the questions we ask ourselves we don't really want answered; some simply cannot be answered. If tragedy strikes, it does no good to keep asking, "Why me?" There is no answer to that question. Bad things, unfortunately, do happen to good people. No matter how strongly or how often we demand to know that answer, it will not come. It is better to recognize this situation and to move on to questions that can be answered, such as, "What can I do now to get on with my life?"

QUALITY QUESTIONS GET QUALITY ANSWERS

> To find the exact answer, one must first ask the exact question.
>
> —S. Tobin Webster, clergyman

You not only have great power because questions demand answers, you have a great responsibility as well. It is up to you to formulate a good question. In order to do that, your question has to have a specific purpose behind it. A clear purpose helps you get closer to the answer you need and want.

Before you ask an important question, ask yourself, "Why am I asking?" Define your purpose by asking the following questions of yourself first.

1. **Exactly what do I want to gain with this question?** Do I want help, advice, information, commitment? Do I want to open a discussion, develop new ideas, bring out opinions or attitudes? Do I want to achieve agreement or suggest an action, idea, or decision?

2. **Who am I asking?** Someone I know well, someone I do not know at all, someone in authority, someone on my staff?

3. **What is the right time or occasion to ask?** Timing is everything. You don't want to ask your boss an important work-related question at the Christmas party or a personal question at the board meeting.

4. **What will the impact of this question be?** Questions can be asked in many ways. Before you ask a question of someone else, consider: If I phrase the question this way, what possible answers will I get? Is there a more specific way to phrase this to get a more specific answer?

John is a clothing designer who told me this story about the benefits of defining his purpose. After several attempts, he had finally arranged to have a face-to-face meeting with a manufacturer who seemed interested in producing and distributing his clothing line. But the manufacturer kept postponing the meeting. John was anxious to get the deal confirmed, and he kept thinking about what he could say to convince the manufacturer to go ahead with the deal. He even wrote out his ideas until he had several pages of material.

Now what was he going to do? Send the written pages to the manufacturer? Read them to him over the phone? John knew he could not do either of those things, so he tried a different approach. He asked himself these questions:

- **What is my purpose?** Answer: To get the manufacturer to produce and distribute my clothing.

- **Who am I asking?** Answer: The vice president of marketing, who has the authority to take on new designers.

- **What are our common denominators or grounds for agreement?** Answer: To make a good match between the designer and the manufacturer so that we both make money.

- **What are the key benefits of my line that match the manufacturer's goals?** Answer: My clothes are made of natural fibers, which he supports. They are a known quantity in the markets he is trying to reach and they have won the awards he values. His main competitor has had big success with my line.

Then John called the manufacturer. Instead of reciting a monologue about the merits of his designs, he asked these questions:

- "What do you need to know about a new designer before you take on his line of clothing?"

- "What do I need to know about your company, goals, and timetable to be best prepared for our meeting?"

- "When can we get together to see if my designs and your company are a good match?"

John not only got the answers he needed, he helped the manufacturer clarify his own thinking. He did not need pages of reasons to convince the manufacturer to meet with him; he only needed a few well thought-out questions.

WHAT KIND OF ANSWER DO YOU WANT?

IQ Just before she died, Gertrude Stein asked, "What *is* the answer?" No answer came. She laughed and said, "In that case, what is the question?" Then she died.

—Donald Sutherland, *Gertrude Stein:
A Biography of Her Work*

A question is a question is a question—right? Of course not. Questions are as complex as human speech and as wide-ranging as human thought. When we ask a question, we're usually looking for specific information. But our questions are often so broad and unspecific, any answer we get will likely be wide of the mark.

When I first started writing this book, I made a list of people I wanted to interview. Then I made up a list of questions I thought would give me interesting answers. After I had interviewed three or four people using this basic list, I realized something was wrong. I was not getting interesting answers at all! I was getting vague answers, difficult to apply to anything specific. One of my original questions was: "What do you think are the advantages of questioning as a communication style?" Answers to this question were basically the same: "It helps me get the right information and connect better to people."

I knew I had not clearly defined my purpose. What I wanted to know was how these people actually and specifically used questions in their lives and jobs. So I had to go back to the drawing board and create a new list of questions specific to the discipline of each person I interviewed. Of lawyers, I asked, "What is the Socratic method? How is it used in law school and in practice?" Of a clergyperson, "How is religion and the development of religion through the ages based on questions and a questioning process?" And of an investigative reporter, I asked, "When you are questioning someone, what triggers your desire to probe deeper?" Needless to say, rewriting my questions was a lot more work, but it got me the kind of interesting, useful information I needed for the book.

Whether we realize it or not, we can affect the answers to the questions we ask. We can limit the other person's response, assume preexisting conditions, and imply an answer with the actual question. We can get a lot of information or a little, a broad answer or a narrow one, depending on just what we ask and how we ask it.

There is a saying in the computer world, "Garbage in,

garbage out," meaning that computers can go only so far. If you program them badly, or ask them to perform functions for which they have not been designed, you will not get the information you are seeking.

Computers are limited by the way they have been programmed and by their ability to handle only certain types of questions and answers. This was beautifully illustrated to me by my seatmate on a recent trip on the Long Island Rail Road. When I asked this interesting gentleman what he did, he revealed that he was a computational linguist. He must have observed my lack of comprehension, for he quickly shared this excellent explanation: "If I were to ask you if you want to go to dinner with me on Thursday night and you replied, 'I'll be in Chicago Thursday evening,' this would clearly be a refusal on your part. Even a ten-year-old would understand this. Since you have not verbalized a 'no' or a 'can't,' the computer would not understand the refusal." This is just one of many limitations that make searching for information on the Internet so frustrating. Suppose you want to research what your grandfather's turn-of-the-century gold pocket watch is now worth. You could start by typing in the word *antiques*. You'll find millions of sites that contain that word. Type in *pocket watch* and you narrow the search somewhat, but you still won't get the information you need. It isn't until you type in *antique gold pocket watches* that you may even get close to your answer.

Human communications are not so different. People, too, are limited by the information they possess and by their ability to understand the question you are asking. So if you are not getting the kinds of answers you are seeking, you might need to make some changes in the kinds of questions you are asking.

In order to control the answers you get, you can change your questioning style by using a variety of questions. The following pages give a sampling of the kinds of questions available to you.

1. Closed- vs. open-ended questions: Most questions fall into these two broad categories. The closed-ended question is one that extracts a piece of information, but precludes further discussion. Closed-ended questions can be answered with a yes or no or with a simple statement of fact. They are good for getting information in a hurry. Some examples:

- What time does the meeting start?

- How many widgets do you need?

- Have you finished the report?

- Can you drive me to the doctor's office?

- Do you want fries with that?

Since closed-ended questions are so easy to answer, they usually give you the information you need. They can also be used to steer an undirected discussion or conversation back on course:

- Didn't you tell me you had already made your decision?

- Is it possible to purchase this now and return it if it doesn't match?

Closed-ended questions can also be useful when you want to confirm an agreement:

- Are we agreed then?

- When would you like to sign our agreement?

Closed-ended questions will not serve all your needs, however, because—you guessed it—they close the conversation. They do not stimulate thought in either the asker or the answerer. They do not lead anywhere. Try asking several closed-ended ques-

tions when you first meet someone and you will see how unproductive, and annoying, this can be.

- Where do you live?

- What do you do for a living?

- Didn't you like the deviled eggs?

- Did you see the lead story in the paper today?

All these questions can be answered in a word or two, and they
certainly will not get a conversation going.

If you want to open up a conversation, use open-ended questions. These get people to think; they encourage discussion and
opinions. They allow the other person to become involved and
to participate in an exchange of ideas.

An open-ended question requires a more in-depth response
than a yes or no answer or a simple statement of fact. Here are
some examples of open-ended questions:

- How do you know our hostess?

- What are you enjoying at this party?

- What duties did you perform on your last job?

- What do you know about our company?

- What can we change to make this work better?

- How did you come to that decision?

Open-ended questions create a more conversational tone. They
eliminate the sense of interrogation that usually follows a series
of closed-ended questions. People love to talk about themselves,
their feelings and opinions, and open-ended questions invite
them to express all of these.

Why aren't open-ended questions used more often? Because

we have not been trained in the art of asking questions, and we do not think about the kind of question we're asking.

We all get into patterns of communicating. Therefore, we have become accustomed to asking questions in a certain way. In my gathering workshop we play the "Who Am I?" game. A volunteer is given the identity of a famous person, but is not told who that celebrity is. The purpose of the game is for the volunteer to determine his or her own identity. They do this by asking questions of the audience members, who have been clued in. I give the volunteer instructions that they can ask questions to get short, factual answers, not just yes or no. But, without fail, every participant starts off asking yes or no questions. This happens because they are used to asking close-ended questions and playing the "Twenty Questions" game. That's how easily communication patterns are established.

It also takes more effort to come up with open-ended questions—and to pay close attention to the responses. However, it is really not difficult to turn closed-ended questions into open-ended ones. This can be done by adding one or two important words, such as *how, what,* and *could.*

Closed: Can I help you?
Open: How can I help you?

Closed: Didn't you finish that assignment?
Open: What problems did you have finishing that
            assignment?

Closed: I've told you that before, haven't I?
Open: What could I have done differently to help
            you understand the situation?

2. General vs. specific questions: If you want to get more specific answers to the questions you're asking, you have to ask more specific questions. There are times when you want broad, general answers and times when you are looking for a narrower response. The way you word your questions determines how specific the answer will be. For example:

General question:	Do you like your job?
More specific:	What do you like about your job?
Most specific:	What are the three most challenging aspects of your job?

If you were a manager conducting a job interview, you would probably start off with the ever-popular general question, "Tell me about yourself." Although this is technically a statement, it is in reality an implied question—"Will you please tell me about yourself?" Most managers like this general question because they can learn a lot from what the job candidate chooses to tell them.

However, this general approach is not particularly helpful to you if you are the job candidate. The general "tell me about yourself" question is usually asked at the beginning of the interview, before you have been able to get much information. You would do well to ask a question that narrows the scope. Say: "There is so much I can tell you, but I want to focus on what is important to you. What specifically do you want to know?"

Questions can work the other way, too. If you ask a specific question and do not get the answer you need, you might try a more general approach. This is a method used by Janice Leiberman, consumer editor of *Good Morning, America*. If someone cannot or will not answer her first question, Janice will try another way of asking it.

"You can't say to someone, 'How come you can't tell me that?' You have to be nice about it and say, 'Can you help me out some other way?' " says Leiberman. "For instance, I might say, 'I understand that, for legal reasons, you can't give us the name of the company, but can you tell me some of the claims they were making?' Or if you ask a question about a person's salary, and he won't answer, you can say, 'If you can't tell me the salary, can you tell me the range?' "

3. Multiple-choice questions: Multiple choice and either/or questions are useful for limiting the response you get. You are asking someone to answer only within given parameters. When you ask, "Was the woman you saw blond or brunette?" you are leaving out the possibility that she was a redhead. Multiple-choice questions are often used to help make decisions—"What would you like for dinner, chicken or fish?" or "Which tie do you like better, the red or the blue?" Children often respond better to limited choices like, "Would you rather go for dinner at McDonald's or Chuck E. Cheese?" than to an unstructured choice like, "Where would you like to go for dinner?" They sometimes find it difficult to answer, "What do you want to do today?" and may respond better to, "What would you like to do today, go to the zoo or see a movie?"

4. Assumptive questions: These questions assume or accept as fact something that is embedded in the question. If you ask, "Why are our taxes too high?" you are taking as fact that they are too high, which may be true, but "too high" is relative. Salespeople are often trained in the art of asking the assumptive question. For instance, before a prospect has made an actual agreement to buy, the salesperson might ask, "Would you like your car in red or black?"

5. Leading questions: George Priest, John M. Olin Professor of Law and Economics at Yale University Law School, says that a leading question is "one where you lead the witness to give you the answer you want." This is a technique used not only by lawyers, but by teachers and salespeople as well.

A leading question—"Why do you feel this is a good solution?"—suggests its own answer. In this example you've asked only for good points; that's what you will get.

An open-ended question—"What do you think of this solution?"—leaves the person free to say whatever is on his mind.

In the jargon of the polygraph expert, a leading question is known as a *contaminated* question. Contaminated questions contain information that is often picked up by the person answering.

If a police investigator asks a witness, "Did you see the assailant driving a red car?" the witness will unwittingly pick up some of this information and spout it back in the answer. If the witness says yes, she saw him in a red car, it's less reliable than if the investigator had asked, "What color was the car he was driving?"

6. Indirect questions: My mother was a master at indirect questions. We would be sitting in the living room watching television and she would say, "Isn't there something else on?" This was her subtle way of asking if we could watch a different program. Or, instead of coming right out and asking, "Could you get me a glass of water?" she would ask, "Wouldn't you like to get me a glass of water?"

This is not the best way to get willing cooperation. This was vividly demonstrated to me recently when I witnessed a scene in a major department store. A cashier and a salesperson were standing at the register where I was making my purchase. They were making small talk while the cashier rang up my order. A supervisor walked by, saw that the cashier was busy and the salesperson was not, and said to her, "What are you doing now?" The salesperson, obviously annoyed by the way the question was stated, said in a sharp tone, "Nothing. Is there something you would like me to do?" The supervisor then told her to fix up some disheveled clothing racks. It was apparent that the salesperson would rather have been asked the direct question, "Would you please go clean up those racks?"

We use questions in many different ways every day. The best way to use a question depends on what we want to accomplish. Below are some examples.

Objective	Example
To open a discussion	What is a conference?
To call attention to a point, an idea, a fact, or a situation	Why do you think John found it difficult to accept this challenge?

To get information	What is the best way to get there from here?
To uncover causes or relationships	In what ways is your job affecting your grades this semester?
To test ideas	Suppose we did it this way . . . what would happen?
To keep a discussion to the point	Can we go back to the problem of your part-time job and your grades?
To summarize or end a discussion	What is the major point that has been made here?
To bring out opinions and attitudes	How do you feel about the mega-mall being built on Highway 12?
To bring out reactions to a point made	How do you feel about the point John made in his presentation?
To suggest an action, idea, or decision	What do you think the results would be if Barbara told her boss he's made a mistake?

As you grow more aware of the ways questions work and the powers behind them, you will discover how to use questions more fully to benefit yourself and others around you. Observe people asking questions. Listen to everyday conversations. Watch professional interviewers and journalists. Take note of who has the power, and how that power shifts, depending on who is asking the question.

All the answers we ever get are responses to questions.

—Neil Postman, *Crazy Talk, Stupid Talk*

3

Questions Stimulate Thinking

No problem can withstand the assault of sustained thinking.

—VOLTAIRE, author

THE MOTHER OF INVENTION

In 1943, Edwin Land was walking along the beach, his young daughter in tow. He stopped and began snapping photos with his Brownie camera. Impatient to see the results, his daughter asked, "Daddy, why can't we see the pictures right away?"

Approximately twenty years later, Arthur Fry was singing in a church choir when he noted that several of the choir members had marked their places in their songbooks with small strips of paper. Every time they opened their books to a new page, the slips of paper would fly out. "How can I make a bookmark," Fry asked himself, "that would stick to the page without tearing the paper when I want to move it somewhere else?"

36

From Edwin Land's daughter's innocent question came the development of the Polaroid Land camera and the ability to see a photograph seconds after it was taken. From Art Fry's inquisitive wondering came the invention of the ubiquitous Post-it Note and the ability to fill your home and work space with semi-permanent reminders of all the little tasks that need doing.

What those two inventions have in common, of course, is that they both started with a question. In fact, it seems safe to say that every invention or discovery is the result of stimulated thought in response to a question.

"If birds can fly, why can't I?" ————————▸ AIRPLANE

"What makes one human
   being distictly unique from
   any other human being?" ————————▸ DNA

"How can I drink a beer if
   I don't have an opener?" ————————▸ POP-TOP CAN.

ASK YOURSELF, ASK OTHERS

Of course, inventors and scientists aren't the only ones whose thinking is stimulated by questions. We all are—both by the questions we ask of ourselves others and by the questions we ask of others. These are the two types of thought-stimulating questions.

The first type are the ones we ask ourselves in order to help us figure out who we are, how we relate to others, and how we can solve particular problems in our lives.

IQ Of course, the very important questions, "Where do I want to be?" and "Am I on track?" are frequently recurring thoughts. But every day, on my way home from work, I ask myself, "What did I accomplish?" and "What could I have done better?"

—Lodewijk J. R. de Vink, president, chairman, and CEO, Warner-Lambert

The second type are the questions we ask other people to help them think more creatively about themselves. These include questions like, "If you were not doing the work you are now doing, what would you do?" or "If money was no object, how would you solve this problem?"

When you find yourself in a sticky situation, take time to think of the questions you need to ask, of yourself, and of others.

Sometimes our questions are personal and profound ("What do I really want to do with my life?"), and sometimes they are practical and perfunctory ("What would you like for dinner tonight?"). No matter what the question, however, it stimulates thought. A question, then, has great power because it can get you (or anyone else you ask) thinking in a whole new direction.

A QUESTION OF FOCUS

We've all heard some variation of the old saying, "You become what you think about." But in doing research on questions for all these years, I have begun to think that you become what you *ask* about. People who are most successful in life do not get to the top because of what happens to them; they get to the top because of how they react to what happens to them.

Why is it that two people of equal talent and ability don't

always achieve equal success? How come some people in such diverse areas as athletics, business, publishing, science, psychology, television news, law, and philosophy can rise above rejection, hardship, and failure? What is the common denominator that puts these people in the category deemed successful?

I believe the answer lies in the questions these people ask themselves and others about their experiences. Unsuccessful people ask, "Why me?" Successful people ask, "How can I use this? What can I learn from this experience?" In his play *Back to Methuselah,* George Bernard Shaw wrote, "Some men see things as they are, and say, 'Why?' I dream of things that never were, and say, 'Why not?' "

If you ask a negative, unanswerable question, you will get a negative, impractical answer. The question you ask determines the focus of your thinking, your focus determines your attitude, and your attitude determines your ability to take action.

If you want to change your focus, you must ask yourself a different question.

Many years ago, I was diagnosed with breast cancer. Fortunately, it was discovered early and I was cured. At first, though, my doctor recommended that I get a mastectomy. When I asked, "What are my options?" he said, "None." But even then I had too much of a questioning nature to take him at his word. I began to ask many people no end of questions and did my own research. I chose a nonsurgical route for treatment, and it was the right choice for me.

But the whole experience made me reevaluate my life. I began to ask myself some tough questions: Was I happy with the way my life was going? Was I doing work that was satisfying and fulfilling? Was I doing everything I could to improve my relationships with family and friends? I really had to think about the answers to these questions, and the answers I got forced me to make major changes.

Questions get other people to change their focus as well. It can happen as quickly and easily as asking this question: "What would you do if you had only one month to live?" This gets people to ponder what is really important to them. The answer can be revealing, because this kind of question makes people actually picture themselves in that situation. With one simple question, you can focus people's thinking in the direction you want them to go— and that direction may take them where they want to go.

Last month I met a friend for lunch. She had been planning to go into business with a colleague, who had backed out at the last minute. My friend spent the early part of the meal asking negative questions like, "How could she do this to me? Doesn't she realize how much work I've already put into this? How can I afford to do this on my own? I've told everyone I know about this business. How can I now tell them it's not going to happen?"

I listened sympathetically, and then I asked her a question. "Is there anything positive about this situation?"

"Well," said my friend after a few minutes of thought, "she and I had slightly different visions of what our business should be. I bet if we had gone ahead we would have been fighting a lot. It's probably better that we ended it now."

I asked her another question. "How would you run your business if you had to do it by yourself?" She proceeded to tell me her ideas, which were exciting and creative. That conversation started her thinking about ways she could get her business off the ground herself. Of course, she did not solve all her problems over that one lunch, but the few questions I asked her were enough to shift her focus in a more positive direction.

You can use questions to help other people shift their focus in just about any situation: when you are trying to solve personal problems, when you are speaking with your children, when you are trying to make a sale, or when you are coaching an employee. Managers are always saying they want their people to think more, yet they do not always encourage them to do that. That is because most managers think they have to have all the answers, rather than most of the questions. If you consistently tell people what to do, you foster the *telling* culture most organizations display and you stifle their thinking habits.

Instead of giving people solutions to problems, encourage them to think about their own solutions. Ask questions like, "What do you think is the real problem?" or "What do you feel are your options here?" or "If you proceed in that direction, what are the possible consequences?"

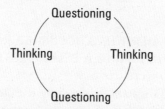

Questions necessarily provoke thought, at least if they are good questions. If we hesitate to answer, barring privacy or personal reasons, usually it is because we recognize the complexity of the possible answers.

—Beth Althofer, psychologist

THE QUESTION/THOUGHT CONTINUUM

```
                Questioning

        Thinking          Thinking

                Questioning
```

If you examine the act of thinking, you are naturally led to the act of questioning. Our thought processes, like our conversations, are rarely made up of one statement after another after another. When we are thinking we are conversing with ourselves. Even our inner monologues are dotted with questions, whether or not we expect anyone to answer.

I go running every morning in a park near my home. As I run, I am exercising not only my body, but my mind as well. I am conducting a persistent internal dialogue that moves back and forth through all the different areas of my life, from "What am I going to wear for work today?" to "What do I need to do to prepare for my three o'clock meeting?" to "How can I help my daughter find a new house?" I do not always find answers to the questions I ask, but I do think about each of them.

To think means to ponder, to analyze or examine, to reflect upon the matter in question. We look at the problems and challenges in our lives and try to find ways to solve them. We look for reasons, motives, and hidden meanings. We question everything we have done, everything we are about to do, and everything we might do. There is probably no thought that is not quickly preceded or followed by a question.

This *self-questioning* is essential to our growth, because it helps us examine ourselves. Self-questioning cannot only help us determine our successes and failures, but it can help us understand the reasons behind those outcomes. Think about yourself and the people you know. You'll notice that the people who are most successful and happy in their lives are those that examine their lives. In other words, they ask themselves self-questions.

NOTHING OF ANY MERIT HAS OCCURRED IN THIS WORLD WITHOUT SOMEONE ASKING A SELF-QUESTION

When Thomas Edison was inventing the electric lightbulb, he failed twelve hundred times before he finally got it to work. A journalist asked him, "How did you deal with twelve hundred failures?" Edison replied, "I did not fail twelve hundred times. I was successful in finding twelve hundred ways the lightbulb didn't work."

If Edison had accepted his 1st failure, or his 100th failure, or his 1,119th failure, you might be reading this book by candlelight. Instead, each time he tried and failed, he went back to the question/thought continuum. He asked himself, as all scientists do, "What was it that I expected to work that didn't? What false assumption did I make?" Once you start questioning your assumptions, you end up changing them. You may even end up with a totally different idea from the one you began with.

James Fergason, inventor of liquid crystal technology, says that before he even begins working on a new idea, he asks himself several questions that must be answered first: "Is this project worth doing? Will the results yield new information, a new product, or a lasting benefit? If the results are completely as anticipated, will it justify the resources and expenses of carrying it to completion?"

As the process continues, Fergason continues to ask himself questions, including: "Do the answers I am getting continue to justify the program? Are there any results that would indicate a reevaluation of the program? Are there any unexpected results that should be pursued? If there are unexpected results, are they more important than the original quest?"

And then, upon completion, Fergason asks himself one final question:

"Am I satisfied with the result?"

ASK A POSITIVE QUESTION, GET A POSITIVE ANSWER

You can use the same sorts of questions in your daily life. Suppose you have an argument with someone who owes you money, and you are thinking about taking him or her to court. Ask yourself, "Is this argument worth pursuing? If I get the result I'm after, will it justify the time, effort, and money I have to put into it?" Then, as the process continues, ask yourself, "Is it still worth it to me? If I get the money back, will that solve the problem? Is there something about this relationship that is worth saving? If so, is that more important than trying to get the money back? What happens if I take this person to court and fail to get the money back?"

The fact that an experiment fails is not as important to a sci-

entist as the questioning process that follows the failure. Most
of us are conditioned to see our failures as personal, as proof
that we are bad or wrong or stupid. Instead, we can use the
questioning process the same way scientists do: we can ask specific questions that move us on to the next step.

Suppose, for example, that your supervisor asks you for a
report on the feasibility of opening a new store in a particular
area of town. You hand in the report and the supervisor returns
it later, saying, "I'm disappointed. This report does not tell me
what I need to know. Please do it again."

You now have three options. You can wallow in self-
deprecating, unanswerable questions like, "Why am I so stupid?" or "Why can't I do anything right?" Or you can get
defensive and ask yourself, "How does he expect me to do a
good job if he doesn't give me the right information?"

Or you can treat the report like an unsuccessful scientific
experiment that needs fine-tuning. Then you can ask yourself
tangible, answerable questions like, "What do I want this report
to accomplish? Did I understand the task? Do I need clarification from my supervisor? Which parts of the report were well
done? Which parts need improvement? Is there anyone I can ask
for help or guidance?"

It is not possible to ask yourself a question like, "Why am I
so stupid?" and come up with an answer that will improve the
report. That kind of question only leads to depression and inac-
tion. It is possible, however, to improve the report by asking
questions that lead to thoughtful action.

On the negative side, this constant question/thought continuum can turn into worry. Worry is the uneasy or anxious feeling we get when our questions cannot be readily answered. We
go over past events and ask ourselves, "Why did I say that?" or
"Why didn't I do that?" We think about our loved ones when
they're not around and wonder, "Why hasn't he called yet?" or
"When will she be home?" or "Has something horrible hap-

pened?" The broader the question ("Why am I so unhappy?" or "What should I do with the rest of my life?"), the more difficult it is to answer and the more anxiety it produces.

Rabbi Matthew D. Gewirtz of Congregation Rodeph Sholom in New York City says that people take drugs like Prozac and Xanex too easily because they are afraid to ask themselves questions. "If you're not taking these drugs in combination with therapy, you're just swallowing the answers, you're not asking the questions," he says. He tells the story of a friend who went to therapy because he thought he had cancer. His tests were negative, but every week for six months he went to therapy and said, "I have cancer." The therapist would say, "No, you don't." Finally, the therapist said, "I can't do this anymore. I need you to ask questions about yourself. I need you to find out why you think you have cancer when all the tests say you don't." And the man said, "I don't want to. What I want you to do is tell me every week that I don't have cancer. I don't want to go through the burden myself."

"The therapist wanted him to ask himself what was driving this," says the rabbi. "But he just wanted to know he wasn't sick. He didn't want to ask questions to find out about the *real* sickness that was deeper inside."

IQ Human reason has this particular fate . . . it is burdened by questions which, as prescribed by the very nature of reason itself, it is not able to ignore, but which, as transcending all its powers, it is also not able to answer.

—Immanuel Kant, philosopher

What can you do when these impossible-to-answer questions crowd out rational thinking? You can stop and ask yourself more logical, pertinent, and answerable questions, such as:

- Is this a legitimate concern? Is there a real, tangible reason to be anxious—for example, is the fact that a sixteen-year-old is fifteen minutes late a legitimate reason to panic?

- Is this something that *might* happen whether I worry about it or not?

- Are there steps I should be taking to prepare for this eventuality, instead of imagining possible scenarios?

- Am I dwelling too much on the past? Am I doing this to avoid confronting present problems and taking immediate action?

- Is this problem really worth the amount of time I'm spending on it? Are there more important issues I should be concentrating on?

- Is there any way I can turn this problem around and find a hidden opportunity?

- Is there anyone I can ask for help?

GETTING BEYOND BASIC THINKING

Recently, I was having a discussion with a friend who is also an author. We were both ready to start new projects and were asking ourselves, "What do I want to write about now?" That opened up a conversation on what we think about to stimulate new book ideas.

My friend is a very successful business writer. When he wants to write a new book he carefully studies current business practices. He asks himself, "What are the hottest business trends today? How can I tap into the market for these trends?" He then comes up with ideas that will capitalize on these trends and writes a book on the subject. He has made a lot of money using this somewhat clinical approach to finding a new topic.

I ask myself a very different question when I want to start a new book. While I have nothing against making a lot of money, it is not my highest priority. My first question is typically, "What do I feel so passionate about that I want to write a whole book on the subject?"

Obviously, he and I have two very different approaches and thought patterns. One is not better than the other. The difference lies in the questions we ask ourselves. If I had asked myself his question, I might be writing a very different book, and the same applies to him.

The questions we ask determine what we think about. This goes back to the first power of questions—questions demand answers. If you get stuck in a particular pattern of thinking, it is often because you keep asking yourself the same question. Change the question, and you just may come up with a more practical answer.

For instance, I have a friend who was always missing deadlines for important projects. This kept her from getting promoted in her job, and once it even got her fired. One night over dinner she told me she had just been given an important assignment at work, and she was worried that she would blow it again. She said, "I ask myself over and over, 'Why do I always wait until the last minute to start a project?' " She had spent a lot of time, and a lot of therapy, searching for the answer.

Although it is probably a good idea for her to find the underlying causes of her bad habit, I suggested that she ask herself a different and more immediate question. I told her not to think about why until the project was completed. Instead, as soon as she receives a project assignment, she should ask, "How can I break this project down into small, achievable steps? What one step can I take today to move forward on this project?" That way, the task would not seem overwhelming. She would not have to solve the riddle of her life in order to do a good job. She only had to ask one simple question, and then take one step at a time toward her goal.

GETTING TO THE HEART OF THE MATTER

Not every question stimulates profound thought. If I ask, "What is your name?" you don't have to search for the answer. There are deeper questions, however, and sometimes the first question we ask does not get to the heart of the matter; it does not stimulate the kind of thought necessary to provide the best answer. Then it is time to ask either a *clarifying* or *probing* question.

Clear communication depends on the fact that all the people involved are using the same language and understand the same terms. It is not just that everyone is speaking English, for example, but that everyone is on the same page and thinking in the same direction. Therefore, it is frequently necessary to ask a *clarifying* question.

To clarify means to make clear or intelligible, to free from ambiguity. We are sometimes reluctant to ask a clarifying question because we think we should know what the other person means—that it is some fault of ours not to be able to understand. But that attitude can have serious consequences. If a doctor tells you, "These pills may make you drowsy," do you know what that means? Does it mean that you should stay home from work? or that you shouldn't drive a car?

I once lost a plum assignment because I did not ask a clarifying question. The president of a large company had spent a half hour with me on the phone discussing the possibility of my doing several programs for his company, on a variety of topics. He suggested that I put together a special program for his company, and at the end of our conversation, he said, "Why don't you jot down some ideas for this program, fax them to me, and then we'll talk again."

I did just that. I thought about the program and faxed him a page of several one- or two-line bulleted ideas. I assumed that we would go into detail about them over the phone. I had never met this man, nor had I worked with him before. I didn't know that when he said he wanted me to "jot down some ideas," what he really meant was a full-fledged outline of everything the program would contain. He was not happy with my bulleted list and decided not to use my services.

That did teach me a great lesson, however. Now when I work with people for the first time, I am especially cautious about areas of possible misunderstanding. I always ask clarifying questions like, "What specifically do you mean by that?" or "How exactly would you like that done?"

This not only helps you meet the expectations of others; it often helps them clarify their own thoughts and demands.

Another way to be sure you are thinking along the same lines is to ask *probing* questions. To probe means to go deeply into a particular issue, to examine thoroughly or to question closely. Probing questions can be useful not only for getting more information, but for getting people to be more open and expansive in their thinking.

Probing questions can be particularly useful in the sales field. I do many sales seminars for the pharmaceuticals industry, and I advise the salespeople, who call on doctors, to use simple probes (those that begin with *who*, *what*, *when*, *where*, *why*, and *how*), such as, "How do you decide which drug to prescribe?" or "Why do you prescribe one drug over another?" or "What type of patient normally receives this drug?"

I also suggest that the salespeople probe even further, using words that encourage the doctors to think a little deeper and expand on what they mean. For instance, rather than using the question, "How do you decide which drug to prescribe?" they may ask, "Can you describe the process you use in deciding which drug to prescribe?" The word *describe* is more powerful; it gets potential customers to indulge in more active thinking. Some other words and phrases you might use in probing questions include:

explain   elaborate
clarify   tell
shed light on   help me understand
enlighten   construct
show   teach
analyze   disclose
expand   translate

These active verbs get people thinking on two levels: facts
and feelings. It helps them discover what they know about a
subject, as well as what they feel about it, which means they
have to think with both sides of their brain.

LEFT BRAIN/RIGHT BRAIN

Those who have studied the human brain have long known
that it has two hemispheres, and that each performs specific
functions. The right side of the brain controls the motor functions of the left side of the body and vice versa. Each side of the
brain also processes specific thinking functions, such as those
listed below.

Left Brain Processes	Right Brain Processes
Language	Pictures
Mathematical formulae	Spatial manipulation
Logic	Forms and patterns
Numbers	Musical appreciation
Sequence	Imagination
Linearity	Daydreaming

Words of a song	Tune of a song
Academic pursuits	Intangible ideas such as love, loyalty, beauty

People who are dominated by their left-brain functions are usually described as rational, analytical, judgmental, detail-oriented, and objective. They may grow up to be accountants, architects, and mathematicians. Right-brained people are more intuitive, creative, subjective, and tolerant. They may turn out to be musicians, artists, writers, and salespeople. Of course, these are gross generalizations. No one is totally left-brained or right-brained. Music, for instance, is closely related to mathematics, and architecture is extremely artistic.

Research has proven that people learn and remember more when both the left and the right brain are engaged. A whole field of study, called accelerated learning, is devoted to this. Through its findings, the old-fashioned model of how we learn best, which was authoritarian, linear, and single-tasked (learning one thing at a time from someone who tells you what to do) has given way to one that is participatory, nonlinear, and multi-tasked (you learn by experience, by processing many things simultaneously).

If you want to change the focus of thinking—yours or someone else's—it is a good idea to ask questions that stimulate both right- and left-brain thinking. A left brain question might be, "Can you tell me how you did this, step by step?" A right-brain question might be, "How did you feel about that?"

You can often use right-brain questions to get people to open up more and explore their emotions. Therapists use this technique all the time; when a patient narrates the facts about an event in his or her life, the therapist will often reply with the question, "How did that make you feel?" Of course, not every right-brain question has to include the word *feel*. Sometimes we just want people to be less literal so that we can get a better idea of what they are talking about. So if someone is reciting a list of facts to you, you might ask, "Can you give me an example of what you mean?" That way, you encourage the person to focus on the bigger picture.

The opposite also holds true; you can sometimes use a left-brain question to contain a volatile situation. I was once sitting in on a meeting in a CEO's office. He was upset with a manager who, he felt, had mishandled the firing of another employee. The manager was getting extremely emotional and defensive about his actions. The CEO then asked, "Can you list for me the facts that caused you to take this action?"

The manager then had to focus his thinking away from his emotions and onto the sequence of events. This helped him get himself under control, and he was able to present a rational explanation of his actions.

IQ It is the nature, and the advantage, of strong people that they can bring out the crucial questions and form a clear opinion about them. The weak always have to decide between alternatives that are not their own.

—Dietrich Bonhoeffer, *Resistance and Submission*

THE CULT OF THE RELUCTANT THINKER

Why do we have to ask questions to get people to think more? Do we spend less time thinking than previous generations did? In certain ways, since we live in a much more complicated world, we have more to think about. On the other hand, this complicated world presents us with many distractions and less time for the "assault of sustained thinking" Voltaire advocates. We're so busy running from one task to the next, we barely have a moment to pose a question or solve a problem.

We're hardly ever left to our own devices—we're accompanied by sounds and images all day. To relax, we watch television or go to the movies. We have CD players in the car; we jog with headphones attached to our ears. We read in the bathroom. We take the cell phone to the garden. We interact with our computers rather than with each other. We may be lonely, but we are never alone. We have joined the cult of the reluctant thinker.

> **IQ** [E-mail] is a refuge when you don't want to grapple with something else, but it also works the other way. Whenever I have a free moment now, I turn to e-mail. It's probably taken away the last few minutes in my life that were available for pure reflection.
>
> —Andrew Hayward, president, CBS News,
> "Going Postal," by Tony Schwartz, *New York* magazine,
> July 1, 1999

Several other reasons help account for our poor thinking habits:

- **We may come up with information and answers we wish we didn't know.** Recently, I was consulting for a biotechnology company that was experiencing complications in its sales and marketing department. Every week more mistakes were discovered, some of which cost the company hundreds of thousands of dollars. These were mistakes that could easily have been avoided. When I asked, "Why do you think these mistakes were made?" I got generic answers: "We aren't double-checking our numbers." "We're not working efficiently." These things were true, but they would not lead to solving the problem. Then I asked, "When did these problems begin?" It turned out the problems began when the department was restructured and a new sales manager was named. The new manager was well liked by his staff more than his predecessor had been. Unfortunately, although he was a biotech and marketing genius, he didn't have much management experience. He was so busy trying to make friends with his new staff, he was not concentrating on business.

If the staff members had been willing to ask themselves a few questions deeper than simply, "What are we doing wrong?" they would not have needed me to help them. But because they liked the director, and because they did not really want to know the answer, they did not delve into the problem.

• **Original thinking is not always rewarded.** Despite recent management gurus telling us that change is good for business and chaos is the order of the day, many organizations cling to a more conservative corporate culture. If things are working reasonably well, they see no reason to make *unnecessary* improvements. In a place like that, if you question the way things have always been done, you run the risk of being seen as a troublemaker instead of an innovator. You are discouraged from developing a questioning attitude and encouraged to maintain the status quo.

IQ ─────────────────────────────
Five percent of people think; 10 percent of people think they think; and the rest would rather die than think.

—Anonymous

• **In our "just do it" society, thinking is not viewed as being productive.** Some salespeople I know have told me that when they request time to go to workshops to improve their listening or closing skills, to spend time learning and thinking of ways to improve, their man-

agers give them grief. "You should be out in the field selling!" is a common refrain. These managers obviously do
not value the long-term benefits of learning time.

Imagine that your supervisor has requested that you
make a presentation in an important meeting that is only
two days away. Your boss walks past your office and
sees you working at your computer. He or she has no
idea what you're doing, but thinks, "Good. Smith is
hard at work on this presentation." A few minutes later,
your boss walks by again and sees you sitting quietly at
your desk, staring into space. What does he or she think?
"I can't believe Smith is sitting there daydreaming when
that presentation is due in two days."

The supervisor, like many other people, worries when
there is not enough activity going on. In *The Magic of
Dialogue,* Daniel Yankelovich says that this "rush to
action" is distinctively American. "In a typical discussion, almost as soon as a problem surfaces, someone is
bound to say, 'Well, what are we going to do about it?'
End of dialogue about problem; beginning of a rush of
ideas for leaping into the fray and doing something . . .
as long as it smacks of taking action."

The supervisor in our example, worried about the
department's performance, wants action. This person
does not value time for thinking. The supervisor is part
of the nonquestioning culture, making judgments only
on what he or she perceives as a productive use of
employee time.

IQ Only active thinking is regarded as productive. . . . Yet
many of those whom our society admires as icons of creativity and wisdom have spent much of their time doing nothing. Einstein, it is said, would frequently be found in his office
at Princeton staring into space. The Dalai Lama spends

hours each day in meditation. Even that paragon of pene-
trating insight, Sherlock Holmes, is described by his creator
as entering a meditative state "with a dreamy vacant
expression in his eyes."

—Guy Claxton, *Hare Brain, Tortoise Mind*

• **Thinking takes time and energy.** In the very beginning of
the movie *Gone With the Wind*, Scarlett O'Hara is asked
if she will attend the barbecue at Ashley Wilkes's Twelve
Oaks plantation the next day. Scarlett replies, "Why, I
hadn't thought about that yet. I'll think about that tomorrow." That philosophy follows her throughout the movie.

It is easier not to think, and, because the result of
thinking is often change, and change can sometimes be
painful, we believe it is easier to fall back on the tried
and true and simply do what was done before. However,
when we try to use a cookie-cutter solution, and fail to
question whether or not it is the best one for the situation, we usually find we have created more problems
than we have solved.

> **IQ** If you do what you've always done, you get what
> you've always gotten.
>
> —Anonymous

• **We stop thinking when we get out of school.** Remember
when you were in college? After spending all day in
class, you and your friends would gather in one of the
dorms. You would order in a pizza. One of your friends
would bring up an issue that had been discussed in a
class that day, and the group would spend hours in deep
philosophical discussion. Or, over tacos and beer, politi-

cal arguments would continue long into the night, with every candidate and issue discussed and dissected.

For most of us, that kind of prolonged discussion ends with graduation. We don't have a ready-made group of thinkers to hang around with every night, nor do we have teachers stimulating our brains by asking questions every day. We are no longer given classroom assignments that require sustained thought and a well-written conclusion. And we have all the responsibilities of adult life that intrude on our thinking time.

- **There are too many distractions.** Even for those with the best intentions, there are many distractions. A few weeks ago, I was working on an important speech I was scheduled to deliver. I had set aside a few hours to really think about what I wanted to say, when a friend called with an extra ticket to a Broadway show. I quickly made the decision to give up my thinking time and go out to see the show. Sound familiar? In our harried, hurried world, we can't wait to get home and settle down in front of the TV. There is just so much that has to get done, who has time to think? If we do have problems, we look for instant solutions and quick fixes. Although we're willing to go to the gym to build up our physical strength, we do not want to take the time to build our mental muscles.

  We're tired, we just want to *veg out*. We want to see action movies where people pummel each other or horror films where teenagers are pursued by psychotic killer monsters. This kind of escapism is a fine thing once in a while, and we all need a break from our daily stresses. But the more we avoid thinking, the more we get out of the thinking habit.

- **We don't believe we are smart enough.** Whether other people have put us down or we have done it to ourselves, we all sometimes suffer from low self-esteem. Every human being thinks, but we tend to see some people as "thinkers"—people like Aristotle, Plato, Freud, and Einstein. True, these people were very smart. But they all started with the same tool—the question—which is available to each of us. You do not have to be a genius to be a thinker; you just have to be willing to ask yourself interesting, challenging questions and be willing to struggle through the answers.

IQ Dumb questions real lawyers have asked:

"Was it you or your brother who was killed in the war?"

"How far apart were the vehicles at the time of the collision?"

"You say the stairs went down to the basement. Did they go up too?"

—Common Lawyer Jokes

IS THERE A PROBLEM HERE?

Regardless of the reasons we have become reluctant thinkers, we cannot stop thinking all together. We are all required to solve hundreds of problems every day, ranging from the relatively minor, such as, "What should I have for dinner?" to the most important, like, "Which treatment option is most effective at curing this disease?"

Questions, obviously, can help you get to the bottom of a problem. But asking the *right* questions will get you to the best solution. The first question inventor James Fergason asks himself is not, "How can I make this idea into reality?" Instead it is, "Is this project worth doing?" Once he has established to his satisfaction that the answer is yes, he can go about solving the problem.

IQ The person who controls the definition of a problem controls its solution.

—Anonymous

In *Smart Thinking for Crazy Times,* Ian Mitroff states that individuals and organizations often run into trouble when they solve the wrong problem. An example would be a McDonald's in Germany, which placed its famous golden arches on a sign leading tourists to the infamous Dachau concentration camp. The company was apparently solving the problem of how to get the most exposure for its ad. The managers should, however, have asked themselves first whether it would be appropriate to place their advertising on that sign at all.

Sometimes the best way to discover the solution to a problem is to work backward. Ask yourself first:

- What do I want to happen?

- What don't I want to happen?

- What is the worst thing that could happen?

- What is the best thing that could happen?

Then use questions to help you brainstorm with yourself or with others, and remember that brainstorming means no criticism:

- What are all the possible ways to approach this problem?

- If I had all the money in the world, how would I solve this problem?

- If I had all the time in the world, how would I solve this problem?

- Assuming I do not have all the time or money in the world, how can I scale down those solutions to work within my limitations?

Finally, when you've come up with a solution, ask questions that will help determine if it is, indeed, the best solution:

- Did I choose this solution to please someone else (my colleague, boss, spouse, teacher, mother, father)?

- Did I choose it because it is what other people expect?

- Did I choose it because it is the way everybody else would do it?

- Did I choose it because it is easy?

Focused, creative thinking enriches our lives and improves our world, both within and without. How much time do you spend thinking? How much do you encourage other people to think? Life is more interesting when people are thinking. And it is the questions we ask, of ourselves and of others, that nurture the thinking process and bring us to the heights of human creativity.

Increased creativity is the natural byproduct of increased questioning and increased thought. But, in today's world it is action that counts. Every organization and every individual is seeking positive change and positive change is the result of meaningful thought brought about by insightful questions.

IQ

Rob: "Why am I not happy?"

Laura: "Because you're the same person you used to be."

—from the movie *High Fidelity*, 2000, based on the novel by
Nick Hornby

4

Questions Give Us Valuable Information

There are only two major ways to get information: by watching and reading and by asking questions and listening.

NO QUESTIONS ALLOWED?

What would happen if you couldn't ask questions?

In my seminars, I often conduct what I call the "paper-tearing" exercise. Each person is given a blank sheet of paper. I ask everyone to close his or her eyes. Then I fold and tear my own sheet of paper six times, giving participants verbal instructions as I go. The goal is to have them come up with the same design I do. Since their eyes are closed, they cannot see what I am doing. And they are not allowed to ask questions.

No one gets it right. They do not have enough clues; their information sources are cut off. For instance, if I say, "Fold the paper in half," they have to guess whether I mean vertically or

61

horizontally. If I say, "Now make a small tear at the corner," they have to decide which corner, and interpret the word *small*. It is possible someone could end up with my design, but not likely.

I then ask them to do the exercise a second time, sitting back-to-back with a partner. One partner (the sender) gives the instructions, and the other (the receiver) must follow. Receivers are still not allowed to watch, but they can ask questions. So if the sender says, "Make a small tear at the corner," the other person can now ask, "Which corner?" or "How small?" This time, at least 50 percent of the people come up with matching designs.

Just by asking questions, participants have increased their chances of getting the right result to 50 percent.

This exercise is a visual representation of how questions can make a difference in getting the information you need.

FILLING THE VACUUM

A statement sets forth facts, observations, or opinions. In other words, it supplies information.

A question, on the other hand, is by its very nature missing some information. The word *question* derives from the word *quest*, which is a search or pursuit undertaken to find or obtain something. So a question is voiced in order to obtain that missing piece of information.

Here is a simple example: "What color is your new jacket?" To answer this question, you would figuratively fill in the blank—to supply the missing information—"My new jacket is brown." A question such as, "What can we do to improve productivity in the Canadian plants?" requires research, opinion, and insight in order to provide an answer. In fact, the bigger the missing piece, the harder it is to answer the question, and the more thought is required. The hole in our information can be as simple as the color of a jacket or as complex as productivity in Canada. Yet it is in our human nature to want to fill that hole, no matter how complex. Nature abhors a vacuum, and so we ask the question.

There is a reason a question arises. First, we perceive something. Then we compare what we have perceived with other similar things we have perceived. If everything seems right—if what we have perceived seems to be the way it should be—we accept it and go on. If you leave your keys on the table in the dining room, for example, you expect them to be on the table when you return. If they are, then everything is fine.

If our perception—what we see, hear, or feel—doesn't match our expectation, we experience perplexity. This is what happens if you leave your keys on the table and they're not there when you return. You may not even realize that the keys are missing, you just know something is wrong with this picture. Your intuition tells you so, and you have to respond. You have to find some way to resolve your feeling of perplexity. The tool you have is the question.

IQ Perplexity is an organismic experience, felt in the body as well as the mind. . . . We display some unease, restlessness or discomfort . . . ; a furrowed brow, a scratched head, a purse of the lips; we might bite fingernails and tear out hair. These and all manner of "body language" signal above all to the self that over *some* matter, pressing or fleeting, one is experiencing *a degree* . . . of doubt, wonderment, ignorance, bafflement, incomprehension, uncertainty, puzzlement—perplexity. Only in that perplexed condition can a question arise.

—J. T. Dillon, *Questioning and Teaching*

INFORMATION, PLEASE

Who will succeed in the information age? The people with
the power. And who will have the power? The people with the
best information. Now that information is so readily available
to us, it's not good enough just to be well informed. You must
have the *best* information, the most relevant facts, the latest
news, the broadest database, the most complete knowledge. . . .

Whether you are buying a computer or selecting a mate,
searching for a new home or negotiating a raise, you need information. The better your information, the greater your chances
of success.

In *Bargaining for Advantage,* G. Richard Shell asks the question, "What do skilled negotiators do that average negotiators
do not?" His answer? They ask more than twice the number of
questions that average negotiators ask. They ask questions with
a definite purpose, designed to elicit specific information. In
fact, a study that monitored the behavior of English labor contract negotiators showed that "skilled negotiators spend 38.5
percent of their time acquiring and clarifying information—as
compared with just under 18 percent . . . by average negotiators."

Although we may not frequently find ourselves in formal
labor negotiations, we always need information. Getting good
information is always important, but there are certain times
when getting the right information is paramount (choosing a
nanny, finding a good contractor, hiring the best employee,
deciding on a course of treatment for an illness, choosing a college—the list goes on).

If you are at a job interview, for instance, aren't you more
likely to get the job if you know what the employer is looking
for? Won't you get ahead faster, whatever your job, if you know
how to get the information you need? Aren't you going to be a
better parent if you know what your kids are thinking and feeling? Won't you have a more successful relationship if you know

whether you and your mate are really compatible? If you are in sales, won't you be more successful if you know what your prospects and customers really want and need?

The answer to all of these questions is yes. And how can you get the information you need to make decisions; learn something new; understand yourself and others; be a more valuable employee; gain the advantage; know what it is you need to ask?

By asking questions.

> IQ   I never learn anything talking. I only learn things when I ask questions.
>
> —Lou Holtz, former Notre Dame football coach

It would be a wonderful world if the information we wanted was automatically handed to us on a silver platter. Unfortunately, most information is buried in stacks of snail mail, e-mail, reports, and idle chatter—not to mention that all the messages are obscured by the thoughts and emotions of other people. Somewhere deep in this sea of facts, figures, and feelings is the one bit of data we actually seek.

So we make decisions based on a hunch and a prayer and hope that we will be proven right in the long run. We hurt ourselves in so many ways by not getting the right information:

- We waste time.

- We cannot separate the information we need from irrelevant data.

- We miss opportunities.

- We follow false leads.

- We are misled by our own assumptions.

- We misjudge people's motivations.

- We do not get what we want.

- We do not give others what they want.

Seems hopeless, doesn't it? But it is not. You do not have to be Albert Einstein to be smart in the information age. In fact, you may be better off in this fact-filled frenzy if you are more like Sherlock Holmes. With the right clues you can piece together the big picture; with the right information you can go as far as you like.

BECOMING A QUESTIONING DETECTIVE

"Sometimes, in order to solve a problem, you have to introduce the dog," says Jaakko Hintikka, a professor of philosophy at the University of Helsinki. He is referring to a Sherlock Holmes story he tells his students as an example of the mechanics of solving problems. The story, called "Silver Blaze," involves a stolen horse and a slain stable master. It is, as usual, a puzzling situation that the police are unable to solve.

When Holmes comes into the picture, he immediately deduces that the stable master was involved in the theft of the horse. How does he do it?

When the local police inspector asks Holmes, "Is there any point to which you would wish to draw my attention?" Holmes answers, "To the curious incident of the dog in the nighttime." The inspector says, "The dog did nothing in the nighttime," to which Holmes replies, "That was the curious incident."

Holmes is trying to help get the inspector come to the same conclusion at which he arrived—that the stable master himself had to be involved. This conclusion was reached by asking himself three questions: Was there a dog in the neighborhood when the horse disappeared? (Yes, there was a watchdog.) Did the dog bark when the horse was stolen? (No, the stable boys slept through the night.) Who is it that the dog won't bark at in the middle of the night? (Of course, the stable master himself.) When you ask the right questions, the answer is . . . elementary!

IQ Ask a clever question, get a clever answer.

—Jaakko Hintikka, philosophy professor,
University of Helsinki

Everyone loves a mystery. We follow every move the detective makes, picking up clues, adding suspects to the list. Finally, just one step ahead of the detective, using our own incredible deductive powers, we come to the inevitable conclusion that sends the bad guys to jail and leaves everyone else to live happily ever after. That is the way it is in fiction, anyway.

In real life, it is not always so easy to get the information we need. We often find ourselves in situations where we are missing one piece of vital information without which we cannot complete a task, or because of which we miss an opportunity or even suffer dire consequences. We take on an assignment at work and fail to ask the date of the deadline. Suddenly we discover that it is due in one week, yet we have two other projects to complete. We take a prescription from the doctor and do not ask if it is all right to drink alcohol at the wedding we plan to attend next week. It is not until we end up in the emergency room after one glass of wine that we realize one little question might have made the difference.

Even journalists, those people we depend on for much of our information, do not ask enough questions. A few years back, NBC was criticized for airing an inaccurate story about the effects of clear-cutting forests in Idaho. The highly regarded network showed two separate scenes of dead fish floating in water, claiming the fish died as an indirect result of the deforestation. It was later discovered that in one of the scenes, the fish weren't even dead. In the other, the stream was not in Idaho.

The mistakes were made because the reporter was unable to attend the editing session, and no one questioned him or his crew to verify the story. In a *New York Times* article, an NBC News staff member said, "It was a stupid mistake. It could happen to anybody. But what we learned from this is to question everybody about everything."

SOLVING THE "CRIME" OF MISCOMMUNICATION

We must all become questioning detectives. Think of Columbo. He always solved his crimes by asking (in his famously offhand way) one more question: "One last question, sir, I don't mean to bother you, but . . ." We must be willing to be like Columbo— to ask that extra question and to probe and clarify until we are sure that we understand what we need to do. We are looking for the same answers detectives seek: Who is involved? Where are they? When can we speak with them?

Who, where, when, what, why, and how are the most basic questions we can ask. When we leave out the basics, we leave ourselves open to the crime of miscommunication. Following are some questions you can ask to provide basic clues to what you may be looking for.

Who

At some point, all novice salespeople make the mistake of selling to the wrong person. The scenario usually goes like this: The salesperson is thrilled to get an appointment to speak to Bob Jones at Acme Manufacturing. He spends forty-five minutes telling Mr. Jones all about his Wonderful Widgets, and how they would be a perfect fit in Acme's Whatchamacallits. Mr. Jones smiles and seems interested throughout the presentation. Finally, the salesperson says, "So Mr. Jones, is there any reason why we can't go ahead with this sale today?" to which Mr. Jones replies, "Oh, I have to take this up with my supervisor first. I can't make this kind of buying decision."

That's forty-five minutes of wasted time. The salesperson really should have asked if Bob Jones was the person with whom he needed to speak.

We all make this kind of assumption, even if we are not in sales. How many times have you called a doctor's office and started talking about what was wrong with you—and then five minutes later you find out you have been talking to the answering service? And all they do is take your name and number. Ask questions to find out if you are speaking to the right person:

- Are you the person I need to speak to for information on this subject?

- Is there anyone else, besides yourself, who can give me the information I need?

- Who has the authority to sign off on this?

Where

For some reason, human beings have problems with directions. Men hate to ask directions. Women ask, but often do not get specifics. If you get the address, you do not get the room number. If you get the room number, you do not get the cross street. When you are getting directions, picture yourself traveling step by step from your starting point to your destination. Have all the steps been explained? The following may not contain the word *where*; that is what you are trying to determine. To cover all bases, ask questions like:

- What is the exact location?
- What floor is that on?
- What is the room number?
- How far is it from here?

When

Everybody is so busy these days, it is becoming more and more important to get places on time. I am a punctual person. I like to know when I am supposed to be in a particular place, and I like to get there early. However, many people I know are consistently late, and it is because they do not ask themselves questions about time. They know they have to be somewhere at one o'clock, for example, but they do not ask themselves when they have to leave home in order to get there on time, or how long it will take them to prepare for the meeting. For time management purposes, ask questions like these of yourself and others:

- What specific time shall we meet?
- When do I have to leave to get there on time?
- When exactly do you need this completed?
- Realistically, how much time will this take to complete?

What

These questions are not as explicit as the others. They often involve concepts, objects, or a myriad of other possibilities. *Who* questions ask for a person and *where* questions ask for a place. But *what* questions are more obtuse and will get longer and more varied answers, for example: "What do you think about this issue?" or "What events proceeded this situation?" or "What can be done to solve this problem?" As with this last question, *what* questions can be problem solving questions.

Much miscommunication is caused by parties not clarifying words, concepts, and problems. A *what* question can set the foundation for meaningful communication and problem solving by helping to avoid this type of misunderstanding. Often problems arise due to semantic differences. Asking a question like "What do you mean by that?" clarifies the meaning of words. On the other hand, a question like "What is the problem?" clarifies concepts. In both cases, a *what* question results in better understanding.

There is also another type of this question that is useful to any good questioner—What if? Just by adding *if* you begin to ask about possibilities and consequences. *What if* questions are always smart ones, because you can never be too prepared for what could or what might occur. *What* covers a lot of bases:

- What is the problem we face?

- What can be done about the low morale of our sales force?

- What does everyone think about this proposal?

- What could we be doing differently?

- What happens if we don't succeed?

Why

This is probably the trickiest question to ask. It is often used in an accusatory manner, such as, "Why are you so insensitive?" or "Why haven't you called me?" or "Why don't you do better at school?" Not to mention the accusatory questions we ask ourselves, like, "Why can't I be like everybody else?" A better use of *why* questions is to refocus your thinking when you get off track; they can help remind you of your overall purpose.

My friend Susan related a story about her family trying to plan a surprise party for her eighty-five-year-old aunt. She and her four brothers and sisters met over dinner, and each one had an idea of how the party should go. One wanted a quiet cocktail party in her home with just the immediate family; another wanted a large gathering in a neighborhood restaurant. One of the brothers suggested that they not have a party at all, but rather all contribute to a special gift. The siblings could not agree until Susan asked, "Why did we want to do this for Aunt Bertha?" That question made everyone stop and think. The real reason was so that the whole family, and several old friends, would have a chance to celebrate with Bertha. They then decided to hold the party in the restaurant, invited seventy people, and had a wonderful time.

If you're having trouble making a decision, ask yourself these questions:

- Why are we doing this?

- Why are we having this problem?

- Why did this problem occur at this time?

- Why is this important?

How

We live in an action-oriented society where everything needs to have been done yesterday. We are not used to slowing down and thinking things out step by step. But sometimes we need to sit down, outline one, two, or three ways to accomplish a goal, and then choose the one that best suits the needs of everyone involved. Ask questions like:

- How can we best meet our main objective?

- How can we develop a foolproof process?

- How can we create the most plausible questions?

- How can we break this down into small achievable steps so that the work does not become overwhelming?

NOT JUST THE FACTS, MA'AM

As I mentioned earlier, there are two kinds of information: facts and feelings. We need both to get a total picture. Almost all of the questions above have to do with seeking out facts. That is what detectives do; they spend most of their time gathering evidence so they can lay out a case fact by fact until the mystery is solved. There is always one element that lies at the heart of the matter, and that is motive. Why does the person do what he does? What is the feeling behind the action (greed, jealousy, fear, revenge, self-defense, hatred, etc.)?

In real life, it is not possible or necessary to analyze every situation. But there are times when we want to find out what is really going on with ourselves or with other people.

That is not always easy to do. It is difficult for many people to talk about their feelings, and it can be just as difficult to ask about them. Psychologists and therapists ask about feelings all the time. But for the rest of us, feelings seem to be off-limits.

We often use the word *think* interchangeably with the word *feel*. Even though we may want to know what someone is feeling, we say, "What do you think about that?"

Part of the problem is that we cannot always come right out and ask, "How do you feel about that?" Feelings are more personal than facts, and some people may not want to share their feelings. Also, we do not always know what we are feeling and we may not be able to express our emotions clearly. So a series of questions may be needed to uncover how someone is really feeling.

Suppose your ten-year-old, who is normally very good at schoolwork, suddenly refuses to do his homework. You can't

very well ask him, "What is going on with you emotionally?"
Instead, the conversation may go something like this:

MOM: Why aren't you doing your homework?
CHILD: I don't want to.
MOM: You've always done your homework before.
    What's different about this assignment?
CHILD: I don't like it.
MOM: What don't you like about it?
CHILD: It's stupid.
MOM: Why is it stupid?
CHILD: The problems don't make sense. They're too
    hard.
MOM: Would it help if we read them together to see if
    we can figure them out?
CHILD: Okay.

Without this conversation, the mother might think that the
child was being stubborn or lazy, when the truth is he doesn't
understand the problems. The same concept can apply to an
employee who is suddenly not performing well or to a spouse
who is inexplicably angry or upset. Although you can't always
change the way someone is feeling, you can usually help by trying to understand the situation from the other person's perspective.

THE FOUR MAIN OBSTACLES TO GETTING THE RIGHT INFORMATION

Why is it so difficult to get the information we need? Sometimes people just don't want to share information with us. Most
of the time, however, people are not being secretive; they are
simply not communicating as well as they could. That's because
four obstacles to getting information are built in to the way we

communicate. These are interrelated and we often experience more than one obstacle at a time. There is only one way to overcome these obstacles, and that is by asking questions.

> IQ As you know, in a deposition in January, I was asked questions about my relationship with Monica Lewinsky. While my answers were legally accurate, I did not volunteer information.
>
> —President Clinton, address to the nation, August 1998

Obstacle #1: People don't volunteer.

Often it's not what we say that causes communication problems, it is what we don't say.

I had guests from out of town one weekend, and we decided it would be fun to go see an off Broadway show in the evening. I looked through the newspaper and found one I thought we might like. I called the theater and asked what time the show started that evening. "Eight o'clock," came the helpful reply. "And how much are the tickets?" I asked. "Twenty dollars," the gentleman replied. "And what time is the performance over?" I inquired. "Ten-fifteen," he answered politely.

My friends and I trooped gamely downtown to the theater. I stepped up to the box office.

"I would like four tickets for tonight," I said.

"Oh, we're sold out for tonight," said the man in the box office. "We've been sold out for weeks."

The one question I had forgotten to ask on the phone was whether they had tickets for that night's performance. If I had only asked that one last question, we would not have traveled all the way to the theater for nothing.

IQ A periscope allows the commander of a submarine only limited vision. The periscope will show you only what you look at; if you don't look at something, you won't see it. And the same is true of questions: one only gets what one asks for. If you don't ask for something, you won't get it.

—Avinoam Sapir, president, Laboratory for
Scientific Interrogation

Most people are not reticent on purpose. Many times, they do not provide information because they do not see its relevance or they do not make the same mental connections that you make. The person in the box office answered each of my questions truthfully. The problem was that he answered only what he was asked; he did not volunteer any other information.

The gentleman did not omit the sold-out information on purpose—he had known for weeks that tickets were not available; from his point of view it was well-known information. And I thought that anyone answering all my other questions would realize that I needed tickets for that performance. Neither one of us was thinking the situation through.

The positive side to this type of situation is that it can teach you questions you should always ask. For example, I missed a plane once because I did not ask the right question and the other person did not volunteer information. I was staying at a large hotel in Dallas. The night before I was to leave, I called down to the desk and asked what time the airport van left in the morning. He told me the van left at 8:15, which should give me plenty of time to make my plane.

What he did not tell me was that a large convention at the hotel had ended that evening, and that a huge group was leaving first thing in the morning. When I got down to the lobby, there was a long checkout line, and a longer line for the van. I had to wait over an hour, and I missed my plane.

Now, whenever I need that kind of information, I always ask, "Do you expect a lot of people to be checking out or needing the van at that time?"

Even if you think you have gotten all the information you need, there is one way to make sure—end the conversation with a final clarifying question. This is an old trick that reporters use. At the end of every interview, even if it has been extensive and lengthy, the reporter will ask, "Is there anything you want to add?" They often get their best quotes in response to this question.

When you need specific information, even if you think you've gotten everything, ask, "Is there anything else I need to know?" That question stimulates thought (remember power #2). It makes the other person go back over the information she has just shared—and maybe come up with one or two facts she has neglected to mention.

IQ I'm a nobody who wanted to be a somebody. I should have been more specific.

—Lily Tomlin, comedienne and actress

Obstacle #2: People speak and think in generalities.

If you have ever participated in sports, you know that a coach would never tell you to "play better" without giving practical suggestions to improve your game. Your coach must be specific, telling you to run faster, keep your knees bent, hold the bat higher. You cannot play better just because you are told to do so. If it were that simple, wouldn't you already be doing it?

In business, the best manager does not tell you to "do a better job." The manager has specific criteria he or she expects you to meet and tells you what those criteria are, all the way from coming in on time to producing quarterly reports. A good teacher tells students exactly what they need to do to pass exams and do well in class. The best coach does not rely on motivational speeches alone to improve a player's performance—he or she lets the player know exactly what areas need work and guides practice sessions accordingly.

Unfortunately, many times we are not that specific about what we expect from others. The problem is that nobody can fully perform a generalized task. So why aren't we more specific? Perhaps it is because *we* know what we mean, and we assume other people know what we mean as well (see obstacle #3). Or we are not exactly sure what it is we want, and we hope that other people will be able to define our wishes for us.

A manager who says, "We have got to improve efficiency around here," may have no idea what steps should be taken to accomplish that goal. He may be hoping that his staff will know what to do even if he does not. A mother who tells her son, "You have got to do better in school," may not know how to help that child with his homework; she hopes that he will find a way to improve on his own.

Generalities tell us nothing. If the generality is negative ("I don't really like it"), we assume the worst. It is counterproductive, because it does not tell us how to improve for the next time. So if you are on the receiving end of a negative generality, you could ask, "What specifically don't you like about it?" or "Can you point out the areas that need improvement?"

If a generality is positive ("It's great"), we are pleased, but we do not know what to do with the information. It is not as valuable as specific praise, which shows that the person has truly recognized your effort. For example, I sent someone a thank-you card last week. She called to tell me that she had received the card and had found the lines of the verse inside particularly heartwarming. That specific praise made me feel good, because it meant she appreciated the fact that I had spent time looking for the right card.

It can be difficult to ask people to be more specific about the praise they are giving, because it can seem as if you are fishing for compliments. It helps if you let people know why you want them to be more specific. For instance, suppose your boss comments on a presentation you gave by saying, "You did a great job." You could then say, "Thanks. Can you tell me what you thought I did well so I can do it again in my next presentation?" Not only will the information help you repeat your excellent performance, it will reinforce those qualities and assets in your boss's mind.

We do not get generalities only at work. People use general words and phrases all the time. A few years ago, I looked at our apartment and decided it was time to paint. It had been many years since the last paint job, and I wanted to spruce the place up. At breakfast the next morning, I asked my husband when we were going to paint our apartment. He responded, "Soon." Good, I thought.

For the next few days, I imagined all the colors I wanted and how they would go with our furniture. After a month, I approached my husband again, filled with ideas and excitement about the project. Again, he told me that we would do it "soon." To this day, I have plenty of ideas and the paint samples on hand, and I am ready to go whenever "soon" arrives.

Soon is a definite red flag. It could mean ten minutes, an hour, or a few weeks. There are many other words that are red flags for generalities, including:

always	about	fewer
more	better	good
improve	increase	never
many	worse	could
might	every	everything
just	less	like
tall	short	people
several	very	all

Some phrases that are red flags as well:

I don't like it   it doesn't suit our needs
we can't afford it   a few miles
let's do it   that's a good idea

Whenever you hear these words or phrases, be sure to ask the person using them to be more specific.

IQ We think in generalities, but we live in detail.

—Alfred North Whitehead, mathematician,
philosopher, cosmologist

I first realized how generalities could derail the information-gathering process when I began presenting sales workshops. I would ask members of the class what they wanted to gain from the course. Almost always I received the answer, "I want to be a better salesperson." But what specifically did that mean to them? It would be impossible for me to succeed unless I knew what they meant by *better*.

Now in my workshops, I ask each person, "What are the key elements that contribute to making someone a better salesperson in your business?" I can then focus my seminar based on their answers. If I do not ask that question, I have to rely on my own judgment about what makes a good salesperson, which may or may not apply to their own sales challenges. The lesson I learned from that experience is that if you want to get specific information, you have to ask specific questions.

An effective technique to get the answers you want is to start by asking general questions and then gradually get more specific. Moving from the general to the specific can be effective for any type of questioning. Police interrogators have found that when they ask a general question, they don't get the information they need. For instance, in *Memory-Enhancing Techniques for Investigative Interviewing,* Ronald P. Fisher and R. Edward Geiselman found that asking a general question like, "Was there anything unusual about the robber's appearance?" usually elicited a simple no. Not only is the question vague, it also implies that a simple yes or no answer will be sufficient. Instead, Fisher and Geiselman suggest that detectives ask, "What was the most distinctive feature about the robber's appearance?" This encourages the witness to concentrate on the robber's appearance, and to paint a vivid mental picture. After the witness has answered this question, detectives can follow it up with the final clarifying question, "Is there anything else we should know?"

So if you are getting vague, unproductive answers to questions you are asking, try making your questions more specific. Think about the purpose of the question before you ask.

IQ The question of purpose can be answered by discovering our intents with respect to answers. The question assumes this form: *What do I want the answer for?* Related general questions include:

- What is it that I want to know or to find out?

- What kind of answer do I want?

- How will that answer work to tell or to show me what I intend it to do?

- What will I do with the answer?

—J. T. Dillon, *Questioning and Teaching*

Obstacle #3: People assume.

Miscommunication is not only the fault of the speaker. As listeners, we have to take responsibility for making sure we understand what people are saying to us. When people speak in generalities, we often fail to question them because subconsciously we have filled in the gaps with our own assumptions. We assume that we are on the same wavelength as the speaker, when in fact, we may be speaking at cross-purposes.

People often say to me, "Call me first thing in the morning." I'm a very early riser. I could call them first thing in *my* morning, but I do not think they would appreciate it. So when people ask me to call them first thing, I ask, "What does 'first thing' mean to you?"

We most often assume things when we are dealing with authority figures: doctors, lawyers, teachers, stockbrokers. The most basic assumption is that these people are experts, therefore they know better than we do. So we do not ask as many questions as we should, and often there are unforeseen consequences.

We assume, for instance, that a lawyer will keep us apprised of everything that is relevant to our case. Some friends of mine made this assumption in a case that involved the bookkeeper they had employed who embezzled a large sum of money from them. When the bookkeeper was arrested, the case became the State of Pennsylvania against the bookkeeper. They were told that the bookkeeper's arraignment would take place on a certain date. Then the date was moved up two days, and my friends did not find out until after the fact. They were not required to be in court, so the lawyer did not think it was important.

It might not have been important to the lawyer, but it was very important to the victims of this crime! My friends assumed they would be notified of any changes; they never realized that they had to ask the lawyer to inform them of any court proceedings that involved this case.

We are often afraid to question our assumptions because we do not want to appear ignorant. But in situations where there is a lot at stake, we have the right to every piece of information we need. In fact, the greater the consequences, the more important it is to stop and ask yourself, "Have I thought this through thoroughly? Am I making any assumptions here?"

> **IQ** Knowing is the enemy of learning. . . . We've all got to be learners. Learners are people who are constantly questioning everything all the time, including, and with most difficulty, their own assumptions about what they know and what they don't know.
>
> —Larry Wilson, founder and vice chairman,
> Pecos River Division, AON Consulting

While I was writing this book, I kept asking myself, "Why do we make so many assumptions?" I realized that we have to make certain assumptions in our everyday lives, or all movement would stop. When we go into a store or office building, we assume it is well built and will not fall down around us. We assume that the water we drink is safe and the food we eat is not contaminated. If we did not make these assumptions, we would spend our lives worrying about everything that could possibly go wrong.

We also make assumptions about ourselves. We all have preconceived notions about what we can or cannot do—especially about what we cannot do. We suppose that the limitations we put on ourselves are facts and not beliefs.

> **IQ** No one can make you feel inferior without your consent.
>
> —Eleanor Roosevelt, former First Lady

In order to get over these negative impulses, you can ask yourself a series of questions. You might say, for instance, "I could never run a marathon." Then the questioning would go like this:

> Q: Why can't I run a marathon?
> A: Because I'm out of shape.
> Q: How can I get in shape?
> A: I can start exercising.
> Q: When do I have time to exercise?
> A: I could take a brisk fifteen-minute walk every morning before work.
> Q: That's possible. Then what?
> A: Then I could work up to longer, faster walks, until I am ready to start running.

If you need inspiration for not making assumptions, look at Lance Armstrong. A world-class bicyclist, he was diagnosed with cancer and told that it was terminal. But he did not assume he would die. Instead he asked himself how he could keep training while undergoing treatment. When most people would have given up all hope, he kept working. And in 1999, three years after he was told he had six months to live, he made a stunning comeback and won the Tour de France.

Questions must be asked and answered in positive terms. You cannot ask yourself a question like, "Why am I so lazy?" or "How come it is so much easier for other people to stay in shape?" Such questions are not based on truth and reality, and they will only lead you down the wrong path. Ask questions that can be answered and acted upon. Then keep asking yourself questions, one at a time, until you have broken down your own assumptive barriers.

Obstacle #4: Words mean different things to different people.

Even the beautiful people have a problem with this one. What follows is a true story that happened at a beauty pageant. Narrowing the field was proving difficult because so many of the women were uncommonly beautiful. Finally, the contest was narrowed down to five young women, and each one was placed in a soundproof booth. Each one, by turn, was asked a question, "Can you describe your ideal date?" The judges wanted to know how each one would describe her ideal companion.

The first four all talked about a young man with a good sense of humor, a candlelit dinner, a gift of flowers, and a good-night kiss on the cheek.

The fifth contestant was asked the same question: "Can you describe your ideal date?" Her answer? "My ideal date would be May first because the flowers are starting to bloom and spring is in the air."

The words of the question were the same, yet they meant something completely different to the fifth finalist. Obviously, the judges were not impressed with her answer—she was not crowned the winner.

That kind of misunderstanding is all too common. Suppose your boss calls a meeting and announces, "There is going to be a major overhaul in this department." The boss means that the walls are going to be painted, new carpeting will be installed, and his office is being enlarged. But you and your colleagues are in a panic—because you take a "major overhaul" to mean that everyone is going to be fired!

It is only human nature to perceive things uniquely. We were all brought up in different environments. That's why IQ tests are no longer considered as reliable as they once were. They are biased toward the dominant culture group. For instance, suppose an analogy question on the test says, "Plate is to place mat as cup is to [blank]." Most of us can easily answer, "Saucer." But if you came from a culture or environment where people didn't use place mats or saucers, how would you answer? The fact that you could not answer the question would have nothing to do with your intelligence, only your background.

When someone speaks to you, you do not see the words they are saying. Your mind creates a picture that represents what the words connote to you. Think about what these words and phrases mean as you read them:

home	fancy restaurant
occupation	large family
vegetable	flower

When I think of a flower, I see a perfect American Beauty red rose on a green stem with two leaves. Roses are my favorite flowers. But that word may not bring the same picture to your mind. In fact, it would be surprising if it did. So you must be sure that the person with whom you are trying to communicate is seeing the same picture you are. Ask questions like these:

- What do you mean by that?

- Do you have something specific in mind?

- Can you give me an example?

Not only do different words have different meanings, but the way we put them together changes their meaning as well. Putting emphasis on one word instead of another can have a drastic effect on what a sentence means to someone else. Most misunderstandings fall into this category, as demonstrated by the following story.

After weeks of enduring terrible pain, Carol Harris made an appointment to see her doctor.

"You have a rare disease," said her doctor. "If you follow my instructions, you should be able to keep it under control. The most important thing is this—you can't eat too many green leafy vegetables."

Carol thanked her doctor, rushed home to her husband, and told him exactly what the doctor had said. That night, after comforting his distraught wife, the husband served a dinner of the finest salads, string beans, peas, and Brussels sprouts.

Carol jumped up from the table and knocked the plate to the floor.

"What's wrong?" her husband asked.

"Are you trying to kill me?" she screamed. "You know the doctor said I can't have too many green leafy vegetables!"

Here was a simple misunderstanding. Carol thought the doctor meant she should limit her intake of green leafy vegetables, and her husband thought the opposite. The next day Carol had to call her doctor and ask the question she should have asked before: "Do you mean I should eat a lot of green leafy vegetables, or not?" As it happened, he meant, "Eat lots of them—they're healthy!" The English language is so complex, it is a wonder we can communicate at all.

Even in the information age, we cannot know everything. We try, but it is not possible. And even when we find answers to some of the mysteries of life, we only generate more questions. For years, scientists struggled with the question, "How can we prolong life?" Now that we have developed technology that can keep people alive even when they are no longer functioning on their own, the question has become, "Should we prolong life?"

We will never be able to get all the information we need. But by getting into the habit of asking for information, you significantly reduce the number of times you say, "Why didn't I ask . . . ?"

To succeed in today's world, we must have all the particulars. We cannot attain power, wealth, or happiness without them. The only way to get those particulars is to ask questions and break down the communication barriers that stand in the way of getting the information you need. When you do that, you have the upper hand in every aspect of your life.

IQ Want to know the secret to being a hot-shot diagnostician? A brilliant analytic mind, you would guess, or maybe a guy with encyclopedic knowledge?

Forget it.

The secret is asking the patient lots of questions; it's as simple as that.

—Dr. Myron R. Schoenfeld, *Strictly Confidential*

5

POWER NUMBER FOUR

Questions Put You in Control

Conquest is easy. Control is not.

—CAPTAIN KIRK, "Mirror, Mirror,"
Star Trek, October 6, 1967

WHAT IS CONTROL?

A close friend recently found out she had a debilitating disease. When she first heard about this in her doctor's office, she felt helpless and confused. Her mind went blank. She felt as if her life was totally out of control.

When she got home, she began asking questions of herself. "What do I know about this disease? What does anybody know about this disease? Are there doctors who specialize in its treatment? Are there societies, associations, or support groups for this disease?" The more questions she asked, the more she felt she was regaining control. Questions gave her a place to start. They took her away from her fear and allowed her to start thinking rationally.

It is not only illness that make us feel out of control. We feel that way when we are angry or frustrated, when we are nervous or fearful, or when we are uninformed or do not know as much as we think we should about a particular subject. We feel out of control when someone is criticizing us or putting us down. And we feel out of control when we find ourselves in difficult situations.

What is this state of control that we so often seek? Despite what most of us think, control does not mean having power over another person. My definition of control is *knowing what you want and getting it effectively while considering the rights of others.*

When we are in control of ourselves, we are able to think more rationally. We are clearer in our own thinking and in communicating our thoughts to others.

When we're in control, we can acknowledge our emotions without being ruled by them. We can govern our emotions in situations where getting emotional can be harmful to us—for instance, if your boss is offering you criticism or if a client gets annoyed at you.

When we are in control, we are better able to get what we desire from others—whether it is getting the right information, coaching someone at work, or getting our children to change their behavior.

HOW DO QUESTIONS PUT YOU IN CONTROL?

The two basic aspects of control concern how you handle your emotional state and how you deal with difficult situations.

Controlling Your Emotional State

Human beings are emotional creatures, but that does not mean you have to be at the mercy of your emotions. You want to be emotional at appropriate times, not when it is going to be harmful to you. Questions help you get out of a right-brain, emotional state and into a left-brain, rational mode of thinking. If you are frustrated with a client who keeps changing her mind, for instance, you do not want to fly off the handle and risk losing her business. Instead you might say, "We are coming up against our deadline. Can we talk again tomorrow after you've clarified what you want?" or "Can we make a final decision that will allow us to complete the project on time?"

Questions force you to slow down your thinking process, which in turn has a calming effect—on you if you are asking self-questions, and on other people if you are asking questions of them. Recently, I was having an extremely busy day. I was trying to reach a client, but I was frustrated by her company's complicated automated answering system. I wanted to get back to the main switchboard to get some information, but I couldn't seem to do it. This should not have been a big deal, but sometimes it's the little things that trigger these out-of-control feelings. Finally, I had to stop and ask myself, "Is this situation really worth getting so upset about?" The answer, of course, was no. But it was not until I took a breath and asked the question that I was able to stop my emotions from getting the better of me.

Later on in that same hectic day, my assistant used a question to help calm me down. I was getting overwhelmed by the number of things I had to accomplish, when he asked, "What must you do today and what can wait until tomorrow or the next day?" Because of his question, I was then able to prioritize my tasks for the day and move some over to the next day. I no longer felt overwhelmed and was able to do my work with no trouble. Because of my assistant's question, I had gained control of my emotions and was able to finish the day's duties without any trouble.

Controlling Difficult Situations

A difficult situation usually arises when you perceive some-one else as having control over you. To many people, *control* is a highly charged word; so many of us feel that others have controlled us at some time or another. It makes us feel power-less. Certainly as children, we are under our parents' control, and as we grow older that feeling often gets transferred onto various authority figures, such as teachers, doctors, lawyers, supervisors, and managers, etc. Women, especially, often feel that they have been controlled by men, first by their fathers and then by their spouses, because the men were the ones who controlled the purse strings (these situations are changing, however, as more women become equal or greater breadwin-ners in the family).

Asking questions puts you on an equal basis with the other person. First, because questions demand answers; if you ask, people will answer. Second, questions get people to think—and, if you ask the right question, to think in your direction. And third, questions give you information, and information is always a source of power. With all these powers behind you, questions can give you the control you need in any situation.

One of the exercises I do in my seminars illustrates this; it is called the "hot potato." These are the rules: Get a partner. Start a conversation by asking a question, any question. Your partner must give you a brief answer, then ask you a question. You give a short answer, then ask your partner a question. For example, a man asks, "How did you travel to this event?" and the woman answers, "I drove to the airport, took a plane, and then took a cab to the hotel." She takes control by changing the direction of the conversation and asks, "What are your three main objec-tives in attending this meeting?" The man responds, after some thought, that he hopes to meet some interesting people, do business, and get to some good restaurants after the meeting. He then asks her how she likes her room. And she asks him what food he likes the most.

You'll notice that the person who asks the question controls the direction of the conversation. By asking the right questions, you can steer any conversation in the direction you want it to go.

One of the best examples of this is during a job interview. In a typical interview the employer asks you a question and you, as the job seeker, are supposed to answer it. The employer asks another question. You answer it, and so on. The interviewer has discovered some things about you, but what have you learned?

If as a job seeker, you came to me for counsel, I would tell you to break this routine and to ask some questions yourself. You have two objectives in a job interview: to find out if the job is right for you and to convince the employer that you are right for the job. Neither of these will be accomplished if you sit back and let the interviewer control the entire situation.

But most of the time, that is exactly what we do. We simply answer the questions we are asked, then we stop talking and wait for the interviewer to ask another question. That leaves the control totally in the interviewer's hands. You can take control by getting into the asking habit. Instead of waiting for the next question, you should be prepared with questions you want to ask the interviewer. Then when you have answered the interviewer's question, ask one of your own.

For instance, you might pose this important question: "What qualities and skills are needed for a person to succeed in this position?" Depending on the response, you could take what was said and match it to your own qualifications. Suppose the interviewer says, "The person who would do the best at this job would be organized, detail-oriented, and work well in a team environment." Then you could tell the interviewer how you demonstrated one or all of those skills in your last job. You would have successfully steered the conversation in the desired direction so that you could talk about how qualified you were for this job. Think how much more in control you would feel!

WHY DO WE WANT TO BE IN CONTROL?

It's part of our human nature to want to be in control of our circumstances. We feel that we face better odds if we are in command and not at someone else's mercy. That is why many people are afraid to fly—because they have to leave all the decisions up to someone else, someone they do not know and may not even see. It is also why drivers are nervous about being passengers. I know that I experience a certain amount of anxiety when my husband is driving, and he feels the same way about me. It is not that I do not trust him . . . it's just that, like the old commercial used to say, "I'd rather do it myself."

The issue of control is a complicated topic that includes many gray areas. We want to be in control, but we do not want to be controlling. We want to be independent and spontaneous, but we do not want to be reckless. We want to take control during difficult situations, but relinquish it when necessary. As with other things in life, the goal is balance—to keep a level of control that is not destructive to ourselves or to others, but that we can depend on for strength and support.

We shift control back and forth in social situations all the time. If you are at a party or social event and someone asks you a question, you answer, then you ask a question. For instance, if a party guest asks, "What do you do for a living?" you answer, and then you ask, "And what about you?" We do this naturally, without thinking.

But when we get into certain business situations, we often give up control. If we feel the other person is in a superior position, or has more authority, we give answers and forget about asking. If you get into the asking habit, however, you can exercise control in any situation.

You do not need to be in control all the time or in every situation. If you go to a party or social event, you are there to meet people and to have fun. You do not need to be dominant in that situation. But if you are at a business conference, you may want to take control of some conversations in order to get specific information you need. If you are trying to persuade someone, which could mean making a sale, you want to be in control. If you want to change someone's behavior, you want to be in control.

I learned how easy it is to be in control several years ago when I was on a board planning a fund-raiser for our organization. Everyone on the board was enthusiastic about planning this event, and we decided it would be a wonderful idea to hold it on the cruise ship the *Queen Elizabeth 2*. We got so excited—we could all just picture the thrill and glamour of the evening. Then the chairman of the board, Helen Galland, got up to speak. She had been the CEO of Bonwit Teller Corporation. She is a petite, warm, friendly woman. She simply stood and asked a question. "If we spend the money to rent this luxury liner, and the evening is not a success, it will bankrupt our entire budget," she said. "Is the glamour and excitement worth the risk?"

Of course we knew it was not. Her one question controlled the direction in which we were going; it got us refocused onto a much more practical plan. She didn't have to lecture us or try to manipulate us in any way. She just asked a question that got us thinking.

A journalist is always struggling with the issue of control. A successful and effective journalist is in a tricky position; he must ask the right questions, and control the conversation, without offending the interviewee. The journalist is dependent on the other person for the information he needs to write his story. If he offends the other person in any way, he or she may stop talking to him. The journalist must lead the interviewee down the right road, but not push too hard. People will let you lead the way if you do it with grace and sincerity.

Salespeople must walk the same fine line. As a salesperson, you must ask the right questions to get the information you need, but if you push too hard you can lose the sale. Customers can be controlling too, and must be treated delicately. Otherwise you may lose the sale. If you have a customer who talks and talks but never really says anything of relevance, or who changes the subject, trying to evade the issue, you need to keep her on track. Her chatter could be masking her anxiety about your product. When she ends a sentence or takes a breath, ask a question related to what she is talking about. Ask it in a strong, authoritative way, such as, "What is the main obstacle standing in the way of our reaching an agreement?" Then ask, "If you were in my shoes, what would you do to convince you that what I offer is valuable and beneficial?" This way you can keep control, and at the same time gather the information you need to answer her objections.

CONTROL MEANS BEING ASSERTIVE, NOT AGGRESSIVE

Being in control does not mean you need to manipulate every situation to your end no matter who you have to step on to get there. The control I am talking about is subtler. It is a way of accomplishing your goals in a specific situation, without being forceful or pushy. It is being assertive, not aggressive.

According to *Webster's New Universal Unabridged Dictionary, aggressive* means "characterized by or having a tendency toward unprovoked offensives, attacks or invasions; moving militantly or menacingly forward." This means going after what you want without considering the consequences to others. That is *not* what I mean by being in control.

In the same dictionary, the word *assert* means "to state with assurance and confidence; to state strongly or positively." In other words, it means going after what you want while you keep the consequences to others in mind. When you are assertive you are in what I call the "C mode": calm, centered, charming, composed, collected, and coolheaded.

Being in control means knowing what you want, being prepared, and making conscious decisions about how to steer a conversation—all without hurting the other person or making him feel negative emotions.

DIFFUSING DEFENSIVENESS

It should never be your goal as a questioner to manipulate another person. You are not trying to establish conflict with the other person; your aim is to build a relationship. You do not want to create jagged edges; you want to smooth them out.

Being in control does not mean telling other people what to do or making bold statements and commands like, "Do this! Do that!" It does not mean asking strident and accusatory questions like, "Why don't you do this? Why haven't you done that?"

Any highly emotional situation makes us feel uncomfortable and out of control. We try to get that control back, and if we do not know how to do it, we rely on commands and accusations. However, in order to be in control of a communication, you need to be in the C mode—calm, cool, and centered—and asking a question (a smart question, not an accusation) can give you the time you need to take a deep breath and regain your composure.

What happens when we are on the receiving end of an accusation? We make excuses. We get defensive. Any type of criticism can trigger a defensive reaction. Anything we perceive as criticism can set us off. Once, as I left a client's office after a meeting, my client stopped to speak to the office receptionist. In a very calm, polite manner she said, "Please be sure the mail is on my desk by three o'clock." The receptionist, apparently thinking she was being criticized, snapped, "I always get the mail to you as soon as I get it. I can't help it if it does not get here on time!" This particular statement, whether a criticism or not, caused both people harm. The receptionist was hurt and angry about the hidden accusation that she was not performing her duties. This caused her to react in a way that could be interpreted as irrational and unprofessional. My client unwittingly caused tension between herself and the receptionist, hurting their professional relationship, which could ultimately lead to more disruptions in the office. My client would have done well to have thought out her statement beforehand and considered whether it could be seen as a criticism and cause the receptionist to lose control.

Human beings waste a lot of time being defensive. When someone attacks us, to any degree, we go into a "fight or flight" mode—we either return the hostility or try to come up with an excuse. But if you ask a question, you can diffuse the hostility, find out where it is coming from, and then offer a reasonable solution. For instance, you might ask, "Can you explain to me why this upset you so much?"

When you ask such a question, the other person is encouraged to stop yelling, think, and give a more rational answer. Learning to ask a question, even in the midst of a volatile situation, can help you become less defensive and more proactive. One of the best ways you can diffuse hostility, fear, or anger is to steer the conversation out of its emotional context and into a more rational direction. Sharon Livingston, a market researcher married to a psychologist, says that her husband knows just how to calm her down when she is agitated. He will ask her questions about her car. Sharon loves her car, and it gives her something concrete to focus on until she can get her emotions back under control.

There are many circumstances in which you can use questions to diffuse an emotional situation. For example, if your boss begins to lay into you for a mistake you have made, you do not want to get angry or defensive. Try the technique Sharon Livingston suggested. Get your boss out of the emotional, right-brain, scolding mode and into a more logical, left-brain frame of mind. Get him or her thinking about the problem. When your boss chastises you for making the error, do not load on the excuses. Instead, try saying, "I am sorry I made this mistake. What can you suggest to help me, so I can avoid making the same mistake again?" People love it when you ask for their help. Not only will this get the person thinking in terms of finding a solution, it will build his or her ego as well.

You can use this same technique with a parent or spouse. Many people feel that their parents try to control them, a feeling that starts in childhood and does not always get resolved in adulthood. When someone makes an abusive or manipulative comment to you, resist the temptation to answer with a counterattack, debate, or defensive attitude. Instead, try to clarify why they are so angry or hurtful. For instance, you might say, "I think I must have misunderstood you. Could you repeat that for me, please?" It is one thing to make a hurtful remark in the heat of anger. It is another to repeat it. Or you could say, "I know you would not have said that unless you had a good reason. Can you tell me what that was?"

Another tactic is to be sympathetic to the person who is exhibiting the controlling behavior. For instance, if your spouse starts complaining, "What's the matter with you? Don't you know how to clean up around this place? Why do I always have to come home to a dirty house?" you might answer with, "I know you too well to believe that you are so upset about a few toys out of place. You must have had an awful day at work. Do you want to tell me about it?"

CAN'T I TALK MY WAY INTO CONTROL?

Your boss probably thinks he is gaining control, even if only on a subconscious level, by lecturing you. But is he really? Does talking always put you in control? Think about a time when you had to give a presentation in front of a group. You were probably nervous before you started. Your heart was beating fast and there were definitely butterflies in your stomach. You calmed down as you went along, however, and things were going swimmingly, until someone raised his hand to ask a question. Then your heart started beating hard against your chest as if looking for a way out, and those darn butterflies started doing back flips. Why? Because you were no longer in control. You had no idea what the question was going to be or if you would be able to answer it.

Did you know that the president, or any public official, devotes more time preparing for a press conference than he does for a regular speech? This is because these people know they are at the mercy of the press, reporters who are armed with an artillery of questions. When the reporters start to shoot their bullets, the speaker knows he will have trouble keeping control. Participants in my PowerSpeak workshops always say that they are most nervous during question-and-answer sessions. Members of the audience are free to ask any question they want, and the speaker must answer, even if the answer is "I don't know."

By asking a question about a specific topic or idea, you steer the conversation in that direction. As soon as you ask your question following a presentation, everyone's attention shifts onto you and onto your need for information. The speaker's focus shifts, and the audience's focus shifts along with it.

Taking control of a conversation does not mean expressing your opinions and lecturing about your ideas; it means shifting the focus and leading the discussion in a particular direction.

It is a common misconception that the person doing all the

talking is the person who has control. We see this not only in politics and business, but also in our personal lives. Imagine that you are at a dinner party thrown by your best friend. Practically everyone you know is there. People are mingling and catching up on good times, and you run across someone you haven't seen in years. Suddenly you remember why: He is a nonstop talker who does not let anyone get a word in edgewise.

He probably feels that he is in control of the conversation. But is he? Do you actually listen to him? Don't you usually tune him out and just nod politely, all the time thinking, "How do I get away from this crashing bore?"

If no one is listening, whom is he controlling? A conversation implies interaction between two or more parties; it is a dialogue. Person A talks and person B listens. Based on what was said, person B responds. Then person A speaks again. With a nonstop talker like your old friend, there is only a monologue. It is like the old riddle: If a tree falls in a forest and no one is there to hear it, does it make a sound? If a person is talking and no one is listening, is he really in control?

In fact, you gain control by encouraging someone else to do the talking. Police investigators have found that while on the surface it would seem that the interviewer should take the obvious role of leading an eyewitness through an interview, it is really the eyewitness who is better qualified to take the lead. That is because the witness is the one with all the information. If she perceives that the investigator is doing all the work, she will wait until she is asked before volunteering any information. An investigation is seldom successful when an eyewitness plays such a passive role.

> **IQ** On the surface, it may appear as if the Interviewer is giving up control . . . by encouraging the Eyewitness to do most of the talking. In fact, the Interviewer always retains control. He can terminate the interview or shift the topic of discussion as he chooses. Nevertheless, to maximize the amount of information generated, the Interviewer should lead the Eyewitness to *believe* that she is directing the flow of information.
>
> — Ronald P. Fisher and R. Edward Geiselman, *Memory-Enhancing Techniques for Investigative Interviewing*

DO YOU TAKE CONTROL OR GIVE IT AWAY?

Some people feel that they must always be the one in charge. They are *control freaks* and must have control in every situation. Other people, *control meeks*, constantly relinquish their control; they are more comfortable allowing others to be the dominant personalities.

Control freaks must have their hand in everything. They try to make everything go their way, from the home to the workplace. They are like puppeteers who try to write the play, set the stage, and pull the strings of everyone around them. They feel grounded and secure only when they are running the entire production.

What should you do if you have to deal with a control freak? It's usually best to give him or her a reasonable amount of control in appropriate situations and conversations. For example, if you are starting a new job and your boss is taking you under her wing, it is okay for her to have control. If you threaten her need for control, you may lose yourself a worthy ally, not to mention your job. But if she tries to control situations she cannot or should not control—in your private life, for instance—it is your job to let her know and regain some control for yourself. Give control freaks some leeway, but do not let them completely take over. Ask questions, in a softened tone of voice, that get the control freak to explain his or her motives: "Can you clarify your reason for wanting me to do this?"

One of my early editors was a strong, domineering woman, and I had trouble standing up to her. She expected me to be available to her at all times. When I found out I had to go out of town for a week near a book deadline, I knew I had to call and tell her. For several days, I practiced what I was going to say. Predictably, when I told her, she said, "What do you mean you're going out of town? You have to do this and this and this. . . ." I stopped her and said, "Wait a minute. You never cared before where I was going or what I was doing. Why are you giving me a hard time now?" For the first time, she stopped in her tracks. She had to think of an answer, and she could not come up with one. She even apologized.

Control freaks tend to be impatient. Their own questions are usually direct. When my editor called my office, she never even identified herself. She simply said, "Is she there?" Questions to control freaks should be direct as well. If they see your questions as a subtle attempt to get control, they will become extremely defensive. Keep your questions brief and to the point. Stay away from questions that are couched in terms of feelings. "How do you feel about this?" is not a smart question to ask a control freak. Instead, ask questions that get you the information you need—"When do you need this?" or "What's your overall purpose?" or "How can we do this better?"

The polar opposite of control freaks are people who are too shy or too fearful to want to have control—the control meek. They allow themselves to be dominated by others. They let everyone else make decisions for them and will silently go along in whatever direction others have set for them. These are the people who never speak up in meetings or in group settings. Even in one-on-one conversations, it is difficult to get them to make a choice or voice an opinion.

However, you can use nonthreatening questions to get the control meek out of his or her shell. This will establish a rapport with the shy speaker. Do not go in gung ho and too controlling; it will be too much for this type of person. Once you have gotten him or her to be more active, you can step up your questioning. In a meeting or group setting, you can say, "This meeting is a chance for everyone to give suggestions. I know you have got some good ideas, Charles. Would you share them with us?"

If you recognize yourself as being a control meek, asking questions can be an effective way to help you gain confidence as well as control. Trust your natural curiosity. Ask some simple *what* and *how* questions. Start out slowly—do not try to jump too far ahead of yourself. The key is to get just outside of your comfort zone and stay there for a while. Once you feel comfortable there, take another small step, and another, and another—until you have conquered your fear. Questions are the great equalizer. By becoming a questioner, you level the playing field and gain a greater advantage.

ASKING EFFECTIVE QUESTIONS

Questions are the ideal way to gain control, but not all questions are as effective as others. Some of the least effective are questions that put the other person on the defensive ("Why didn't you bring the right document?") and questions that include derogatory remarks about the other person ("How could you be so stupid?"). Those kinds of questions are not only hurtful, they are also ineffective when you are trying to gain control.

Here are some examples of ineffective questions:

1. **Excuse-provoking questions.** These questions turn people off. Instead of encouraging someone to change or improve his or her behavior, you're giving him or her an out—an opportunity to provide you with excuses. So

instead of asking, "Why do you keep coming in late?" you might say, "This is the third time this month you've been late. How can we prevent this from happening again?" Other excuse-provoking questions include:

- Why didn't you finish this on time?

- Why didn't you tell me?

- How could you forget my birthday?

2. **Demeaning questions**. Some people think that they can gain control by making the other person feel inferior. They use questions as a weapon ("What's the matter with you? Why can't you ever do anything right?"). But those questions will never produce a positive result; they will simply reinforce any negative feelings that already exist. Other examples of demeaning questions include:

- What were you thinking?

- What are you—out of it?

- How could you do such a thing?

   It is difficult to maintain a meaningful dialogue when your questions are accusatory. Then both you and the person you have asked are forced to deal with excuses and explanations, when you should be trying to solve the problem. Once emotions and excuses enter the equation, it is difficult, if not impossible, to get back on a logical track.

Effective questions, on the other hand, help the other person get on your wavelength. You want other people's thinking to be parallel to yours. You want to tap into the power of questions to stimulate thought. If you pay attention to the questions you ask, and you ask them sincerely, you will get people to think, to solve problems, to create better ways of doing things, and to give you information and insight.

Here are some examples of effective questions:

1. **Problem-solving questions.** These stimulate thought; they help people bypass the excuses and explanations to get into action-oriented thinking. Some examples of problem-solving questions include:

   - How can we do this better?

   - Who has the know-how and resources to get the job done?

   - What did we do wrong?

   - What did we do right?

   - What would happen if we . . . ?

   - Does anyone have any ideas?

2. **Questions to get information.** These are specific, focused questions with a purpose behind them. This type of question is direct and straightforward and moves people into fact-oriented thinking. Some examples of informational questions include:

   - What do you think about . . . ?

   - What are the benefits of this product over the competition?

   - Tell me, why *shouldn't* I buy this product?

   - How will this help me?

   - How is this different from . . . ?

   - Who is involved?

A QUESTION OF DELIVERY

What is the best way to deliver these effective questions? To make these effective questions even more effective, deliver them in a calm, straightforward manner. Ask one question at a time. For example, "Is there anyone else, besides yourself, who can help me?" Allow for a response before asking the next question.

The quality of a response is affected not only by the content of the question, but also by its manner of delivery, especially its pace and timing. We sometimes tend to ask one closed-ended question after another, in a rapid, staccato style. However, that style of asking usually elicits responses of poor quality. People become resistant to answering and feel that you are interrogating them.

To use questions effectively, slow your pace of asking; allow one or two beats to go by between the end of a response and your next question. Do not let your eye contact waiver and don't be afraid of silence. Silence tells the other person that you expect her to continue; therefore, she will dig deeper into her thought process to answer the question.

PREPARATION IS THE KEY

The most effective way to gain control in any situation is to be prepared—to gain as much knowledge as you can ahead of time so that your questions will get you the answers you need.

Recently, Sheila, a friend of mine, was having a problem with her boss. The boss put Sheila on a shift she didn't like, and Sheila wanted to confront him about it. She asked me how to approach her boss. My advice? Prepare her questions beforehand. And decide on her purpose for asking. Did she want to understand why her shift was changed? Did she want her boss to change his mind? I advised her to think about questions she could first ask her boss to gain a better understanding of why her shift was moved—for example, "Can you tell me the factors that went into this decision?" Then, once she understood the reasons, she could go back and ask, "What would have to happen in order for me to get my old shift back?"

You do not always have to accomplish your goal in one conversation. You can often stay in control by defining your purpose and asking questions. Then, after you have had time to think about the answers you receive, you can return with a second purpose and more questions.

> **IQ** The most important factor in any situation—whether you're considering buying a car or going to a job interview—is to be prepared. Know as much as possible in advance. Then sit down and think through your questions. What is it that you want to know? If they say X, what are you going to do? If they say Y instead of X, how will that change the situation? That's how I prepare for a witness. I keep refining my questions until I make sure the witness can only give the answer that I want.
>
> —David Golomb, president,
> New York Trial Lawyers' Association

That is the method Emily Prince used when she had a problem at work. She was a midlevel executive at a company, with a nice corner office. She went into work one day to find that the office manager was moving her things out of her office. She was so startled, she did not know what to do. She called me and recounted the story, and I could tell how upset she was by the tone of her voice. I told her to go speak to the office manager, and ask if he could wait ten minutes before making any changes, as she had to speak to a client. The office manager agreed.

Emily called me back again, and we went over some of the questions she could ask the manager. Her purpose was to find out why he was moving her out of her office. When she questioned the manager in a calm, coolheaded manner, he informed her that a hot new executive was starting work the next day, and he was putting him in her office because it was the largest one on the floor. Instead of getting angry, Emily asked several more questions about the new executive and how he would be functioning in the department. Because of Emily's questions, the office manager realized that the new executive needed an assistant right near his office—and Emily's space did not allow for that. He managed to find another office down the hall that suited everyone better.

IS CONTROL EVER BAD?

Just as there is cholesterol that is good for your health and cholesterol that is bad for your health, there is control that is positive and control that is negative. Control that makes people feel angry, intimidated, and put down is not productive in any organization or relationship. Using questions to gain positive control, on the other hand, gets people to solve problems, become involved, defuse their anger, and think in a specific direction. And that kind of control is healthy for mind, body, and spirit.

IQ "Would you tell me, please, which way I go from here?"

"That depends a good deal on where you want to get to," said the Cat.

"I don't much care where . . ." said Alice.

"Then it doesn't matter which way you go," said the Cat.

—Lewis Carroll,
Alice's Adventures in Wonderland

6

Questions Get People to Open Up

He was better at asking questions than at answering them, with the result that by the time we were in New Jersey, he already knew everything he wanted to about me.

—MICHAEL KORDA, *Another Life*

EMOTIONAL QUESTIONS, REVEALING ANSWERS

Every year, on the night of the Academy Awards, Barbara Walters hosts a television special during which she interviews three of the year's top newsmakers. This program always garners high ratings. Audiences tune in faithfully to get a glimpse into the personal stories and inner workings of some of our most famous citizens. And then, of course, there is the crying. It has become almost a tradition that one or two, or even all three, of the interviewees will be moved to tears.

110

How is it that Barbara Walters is able to get so many different people not just to answer her questions, but to be so candid in front of millions of people? It is mostly because Ms. Walters is an expert in the art of the interview. It is also because of the fifth power of questions, which is that questions get people to open up.

This power deals with the emotional aspects of questions. A well-thought-out question, by its very nature, can force us to go beyond what we know and into the realm of what we feel. Questions take us beneath the surface of our lives and help us examine, analyze, and understand ourselves and others with whom we live and work.

IQ Some questions are asked for information; other times, they're asked to find out something about the person to whom you put the question—to understand the attitude or the character or the biases of the person to whom you're talking.

—Anthony Lewis, columnist, *New York Times*

New York Times columnist Anthony Lewis gives an example (an extreme one, he admits) of a question designed to evoke an emotional response. Lewis had read an article, by a British journalist, that was favorable toward Argentinean dictator General Pinochet during his British court case. "We had an exchange of correspondence, and then he wrote me with, I thought, amazing candor, that he thought Pinochet was a great man, and that it was very bad to drag him through the courts this way. I wrote back and complimented him on his candor, but I said, 'Would you be willing to say that to the wife or son or daughter of someone who was tortured to death on Pinochet's orders?' That question was designed to both embarrass the recipient of the question and also to elicit a response that would tell me more about him."

Some people are more naturally willing and able to share their underlying feelings than others are. They are warm, giving people who do not take much prodding to expose their more vulnerable side. Others are more shy by nature, and more difficult to get to know. But even the most reticent person will respond to the right question.

Recently, a colleague complained that she was having problems communicating with her untalkative teenage son. Every day when her son came home, she asked, "How was school today?" Every day, she got the same answer. "Fine." I suggested that perhaps the question was too general. Did she expect her son to tell her everything that had happened throughout the day? Where was he to begin? Maybe it was not that he didn't want to talk to her, but that he just didn't know what answer she was looking for.

I recommended she ask her son, "What was the most annoying thing that happened to you at school today?" That way, he had something concrete on which to focus. I also suggested alternating the question frequently so that she wasn't asking the same thing each day, for instance, "What was the funniest thing that happened to you at school today?" or, in these unfortunately dangerous times, "What was the scariest thing that happened to you at school today?"

I also asked her to think about what she was doing when she asked her son about school. It turns out that she was usually working at the computer or she was in the middle of fixing dinner. She never actually stopped what she was doing to ask about his day at school. Although my friend did not intend it this way, the message was: "I am asking about your school day because I am supposed to be interested, but I am not interested enough to interrupt my chores and listen to your answer."

Now, when her son comes home from school, my colleague stops what she is doing (even if it is just for five minutes), looks her son in the eye, and asks him a specific question about school or any other topic relevant to his day.

My colleague tells me that her relationship with her son has improved dramatically. And his answers to her questions have opened up many different areas for discussion.

THE "LET'S TALK ABOUT ME" FACTOR

Why does this power work? For one simple reason: Most people love to talk. Most of all, they love to talk about themselves, and they love to talk about the things that interest them. There are several reasons for this:

- *It's the topic we know most about.* You do not have to do a lot of research or have a degree in anything to talk about yourself. And no one else is a greater authority on the subject.

- *We need to unburden ourselves.* It's been proven over and over again that it is much healthier, psychologically, to let out what is bothering us—rather than keeping it all inside—especially when things are not going well. We have a need to share our problem and, hopefully, get sympathy, support, and/or advice from the people we care about.

- *We want to convey a particular message.* There are certain topics we feel very strongly about and some that affect us emotionally. These subjects can be political, ethical, moral, or religious. As humans, we feel the need not only to share these views with others, but also to try to convince them to feel the same way we do.

- *Silence makes us uncomfortable.* Unless we are extremely comfortable and in a familiar environment (at home with the family or with close friends, for instance), there usually comes a period of awkward silence. To fill

that gap, we start talking, often about the subject we
love most, ourselves.

There are many situations where we want to get people to
open up. First, there are social occasions. Imagine that you are
invited to a party and you do not know anyone there. Most of
us feel awkward and shy in those circumstances. Some people
feel they need several cocktails before they can begin to talk to
people and have a good time. But if you have got the questioning habit, you don't need a social lubricant like alcohol! A question is your very best tool. All you have to do is go up to an
individual or a group of people and start asking them questions
about themselves: "What kind of work do you do?" or "What's
the best movie you've seen lately?" or "What's the most interesting party you've ever been to?" or "What's the most embarrassing experience you have ever had at a party?" or "Have you
ever gone to a party where you didn't know anyone? What
would you do?" or "Why do you think so many people don't
like parties?" Since people love to talk about themselves and
their thoughts, they will begin to open up immediately.

You can use this skill anywhere, not just in social situations.
And not just face-to-face. We do more and more business over
the telephone these days. Many clients are asking for training in
teleconferencing, which of course involves many participants
speaking and listening over the phone lines. Because teleconferencing programs are quite sophisticated, one must know the
name of each person participating. I do a lot of teleconferencing
in my business, and I often talk to several doctors at once. So in
order to get everyone involved, I might say, "Doctor Ames, I
know this is an area on which you have written extensively.
What additional insight could you bring to us?" Using the doctors' names and referring to their expertise will draw them out.

If you ever attend a business meeting or conference, you have
a perfect opportunity to network and make contacts. You will

accomplish a lot more at this type of event if you stop trying to sell yourself and start getting people to open up to you. If you show yourself as someone who is interested in who they are and what they do, they will be more interested in you.

As a questioner, the easiest way to get people to open up is to ask them about themselves. Imagine that you are a reporter assigned to do a story on someone. You get the story by asking questions. But you have to be careful of what and how you ask. You do not get people to open up by being an interrogator ("Are you married? How many children do you have? How old are they? Do they go to public school?"). You do not want to make the other person feel as if he or she is being pumped for information.

It is not so much the who, what, when, and where you are looking for, it's the how and the why. How did they get from one emotional or physical place to another? Why did they make the decision they made? You want to discover the most fascinating things about the person in order to make your story interesting. Ask questions like: "How did your education prepare you for your present position?" or "Why did you get involved in politics in the first place?" or "How did you come to this decision?" or "Who was the person that influenced you the most in your career?" or "What obstacles have you had to overcome?" or "Can you tell me something unique about yourself that no one else would know?" You must put on your questioning detective's hat and listen for clues from the other person.

You must also get clues from their voice and body language. If a person has been speaking slowly and quietly and suddenly answers one of your questions in a louder, more animated tone, you have likely hit on a good topic. If he or she leans forward, uncrosses his or her arms or legs, or starts making bolder gestures, these are all signs of opening up, and you might want to continue with your current line of questioning.

PURSUING THE RELUCTANT TALKER

It doesn't take much to get most people to start talking. But you probably know someone like John, a man I met at a friend's house recently. Throughout the evening, John was very quiet, almost taciturn. He did not contribute much to the rather lively conversation—the most we got from him was an occasional insertion of factual information. From this, I gathered that John was smart but shy. At one point, John and I found ourselves alone in the den. At first, of course, we experienced that old standby, awkward silence.

I asked him a few questions about what he liked and did not like about living in New York City and got the staccato answers. Then I asked him what he did that made him happiest. "Well," he said, "that's easy. I play chess."

"Oh," I replied, "I saw a wonderful movie a few years ago called *Searching for Bobby Fischer*, about a child chess prodigy. Did you play as a youngster?"

You can guess what happened next. The floodgates opened as John began happily telling me all about his childhood exploits as a chess player. When the others came back into the den, they were surprised to see us deep in conversation. The end result was that not only did John open up about his love of chess, but for the rest of the evening he was much more able to participate in the general discussion.

LOOK FOR AREAS OF COMFORT AND CONFIDENCE

Chess is John's comfort zone. It is where he feels most confident and knowledgeable. Even just talking about chess puts John in that zone. If you want to get someone to open up, use questions to discover their areas of comfort and confidence. It may take several tries, but once it happens, it enables the reluctant talker to feel comfortable with you and extend the boundaries of his zone.

However, you cannot change someone's nature. Just because John opened up at this particular party does not mean he is now and forever a more open person. He might be on his way, but he might also revert to his old self in another social situation.

And the truth is that men and women do not open up equally. Men are usually more reticent speakers. Psychologist Beth Althofer says that men "tend to be more concrete, although they would call it analytical or objective. Women tend to be more intuitive, more concerned with expressing their feelings."

In an article in the *New York Times*, Deborah Tannen tells the story of a man and woman who meet at the end of the day. He asks her how her day was, and she tells him, including "what she did, whom she met, what they said and what that made her think and feel." When the woman asks the man the same question, he replies, "Same old rat race."

The problem is exacerbated when, at a party that evening, the man regales a group of people with a story about something that happened at work. The woman is crestfallen that the man would tell his friends what happened, but not her. According to Tannen, the woman sees this as a failure of intimacy. The man, however, sees no reason to entertain someone he is so close to with a "story performance."

"This creates a paradox," says Tannen. "Many women were drawn to the men they fell in love with because the men told captivating stories. After marriage, the women expect that the closer they get, the more the men will open up and tell. Instead, to their deep disappointment, after marriage the men clam up."

Men may be more reticent to talk, but it is still possible to get them to open up. Suppose you were married to John, the chess-lover I met at the party. Or you were John's boss, and you wanted John to keep the lines of communication open. You won't get him to open up by confronting him directly with questions about his behavior ("Why didn't you tell me how you felt?"). First, you have to get John into his comfort zone. That does not mean you talk about chess every time—there are other subjects John feels confident about as well. Once you discover those subjects, you can start from a place in which John feels secure, and then begin to ask questions in the areas that concern you.

WHY DON'T WE OPEN UP MORE?

We want people to open up for two main reasons. The first is to get new information from them. That information could be technical or emotional. For instance, if your deliveries are not coming in on time, you need technical information; it could be because the trucks do not leave early enough or because the loaders are too slow. On the other hand, the problem could have an emotional base, such as if the dispatcher is angry at you for something you said about his work methods.

The second reason we want people to open up is to solve problems, both left-brain problems (intellectual and work-related) and right-brain problems (emotional and relationship-oriented). A work-related problem might be how to assign shifts fairly to a group of new workers who all request the same hours; an emotional problem might be finding out why your child, who loves sports, has suddenly dropped off the soccer team.

You will never get to the root of a problem if someone does not open up and tell you what the problem is from his or her perspective. Imagine that you have an employee who always comes in late. You may try discipline or warnings or even docking her pay to make her start coming in on time. If you ask a question like, "Why are you always late?" you are not going to be successful, and you risk putting her on the defensive and shutting off all communication. If you ask the question in this way, you stand a better chance of getting an answer: "From my experience, I've discovered that when people are late, often there is a good reason. You must have a good reason, too. Is there some way I can help you solve this problem?" This type of question can get her to open up and tell you the real reason she is consistently late. You may find out that her child has disabilities and must take a special school bus that has recently changed its pick-up to a later time. Or it might be that she hates her job. The first instance is probably solvable; the second may not be. Either way, it is important that you know the real reason. Once you find out what the problem is, you may be able to come up with a mutually beneficial solution.

Why is it that some people are so hesitant about being open? There are several possible reasons:

- *We don't have a clear idea of what the problem is.* The example above is fairly concrete. There is a tangible reason for the mother's tardiness. But not all are that clear. Suppose this employee did not have that excuse, but instead was feeling a general lethargy and was finding it hard to get out of the house. She might have trouble expressing these feelings, since she is not really clear about them herself.

- *We have been hurt in the past.* Perhaps the person trusted someone, expressed his or her true feelings, and was hurt as a result. It will be difficult to get through to such a person unless you can show through your body language, your concentrated listening, and your careful questions that you will not repeat the past experience.

  Evelyn and Janine were cubicle neighbors at work who were on the verge of becoming good friends. Evelyn shared confidences with Janine, but began to notice that Janine never told her anything other than superficial stories about people she knew. After a few weeks, Evelyn noticed that something was bothering Janine, and she decided to investigate.

At first, Janine would not tell her what was wrong. Then Evelyn asked, "Janine, is there a specific reason you don't want to tell me what's wrong?" Janine then told Evelyn that a few years earlier, Janine had been up for a promotion in a different job. She told a coworker that she wasn't sure she had the skills for the job, even though she wanted to try for it. The co-worker told their boss this confidence, and Janine did not get promoted. Ever since, Janine had been reluctant to open up to anyone with whom she worked.

Evelyn then told her, "I can understand how you feel. And if you don't want to share certain things with me, that's fine. I do want you to know that I would never betray a confidence, so if you want to tell me what's going on, I'll be glad to listen. Is that all right with you?"

Although Janine did not open up to Evelyn immediately, she did begin to trust her more and more until she was finally able to believe that Evelyn would not betray her.

- *We feel there is a penalty in telling the truth.* There are times when we are unwilling or unable to face the consequences of telling the truth. It is difficult to admit that we've done something wrong or made a mistake, especially if we know we are going to be punished in some form or other.

- *We are afraid of being judged.* We may fear that our ideas, or even worse, our emotions, will be analyzed and come up short—that people will think us stupid or uninteresting or just plain wrong. For instance, Mary Gonzales is a hard worker who has a terrific idea for solving the problem of late mail deliveries. However, two years ago she had made a suggestion about a computer upgrade that would have required a fairly large investment, yet would have solved a lot of the company's database problems. Her idea was dismissed with, "That would never work." She was judged before anyone even considered the validity of her suggestion. Oddly enough, several months later, the company installed the very program she had suggested. Naturally, she will never share her solutions again. It's a shame, too—all those good ideas going to waste, including the one she has about solving the late mail deliveries, just because of premature judgment.

- *We feel our ideas are not appreciated.* Women, especially, often tell me that they are reluctant to share their ideas at work. They have seen too many instances when their ideas were scooped up by someone else in the department, who then took credit for them. Or they tell me that when they do voice their ideas, no one pays attention. When that happens over and over again, it is difficult to convince the person that she will be taken seriously.

There are times when it is extremely important to get people to open up, to go beyond their fears, anxieties, and reluctance, because this is the only way to get the information you need. It is necessary to get information from your spouse, from your children, from your children's teachers, from your boss or your coworkers. If you are doing all the talking, you are not going to get what you want or need.

QUESTIONS SHOW THAT YOU CARE

IQ Last year, after airplane production at the Boeing Company became so fouled up that the aerospace giant was forced to halt assembly . . . for several weeks, the company's top executives began holding . . . monthly teleconferences for reporters and Wall Street analysts.

Month after month, as [top executives] were peppered with questions, Alan R. Mulally, the head of the new space and military-contracting businesses . . . sat by in silence. No one ever asked him a question.

"It was kind of like, 'Doesn't anybody care?' " Mr. Mulally recalled in a recent interview.

—Laurence Zuckerman, "Boeing's Man in the Line of Fire,"
New York Times, November 8, 1998

Whether we admit it freely or not, we all like to be asked questions about ourselves, our interests, our opinions, our careers, our areas of expertise. Why? Because it makes us feel interesting and valued. And the more interesting and valued we feel, the more we are willing to open up. This is true in business and in our personal lives as well.

I have several single, successful women friends. They are all talented, high-powered women and are particular about the men they date. A few years ago, one friend told me that the thing she looks for on a first date is how many and what kind of questions the man asks. She went on to say, "If he isn't asking about me and what my interests are, I can tell he doesn't really care. If he had any interest in getting to know me, he'd ask about me."

I asked my other single friends about this and they all agreed—if a man doesn't demonstrate interest, he doesn't deserve a second date.

The same concept applies in business. In a poll of one hundred buyers from the National Association of Purchasing Managers, the second most important factor listed in making a buying decision was the salesperson's empathy. Buyers look for salespeople who are sincerely interested in them and in their business. They do not want to feel they are just another stop on the sales rep's route. They want to know that the rep understands and appreciates their unique goals and challenges. They want to deal with salespeople who take the time to ask questions that help them understand the buyer's position.

That is one of the reasons most of us do not respond well to telemarketers. They start off by asking what we know is an insincere and scripted question: "How are you today, Ms. Leeds?" I am reasonably certain that I could answer, "I am not very well at all; in fact, I think I am having a heart attack," and they would go on to say, "That's good. Ms. Leeds, I'm calling from XYZ Long Distance Services. . . ." We feel we are nothing but a phone number and a commission to these people, which is usually the case. They don't really care about our needs or values, nor do they want to know anything about us.

IQ   By asking sincere questions and patiently waiting for a response before moving on to the next question, you again show concern for the customer. If you skip through the questions and don't wait for a sound answer, you demonstrate insincerity. It shows you don't really care about the answers—you're just asking questions for effect. This will have an adverse effect on the customer—it will anger him because you're wasting his time and you're trying to con him by acting as if you care about him.

—Robert Shook, author of
It Takes a Prophet to Make a Profit

There is an old saying, "People don't care how much you know until they know how much you care." You show people you care by focusing on ways to make them feel important. Often, just giving someone your undivided attention will make him or her feel important. Let others know that you have heard what they are saying; repeat important points back to them. Concentrate on discovering what concerns them most at this moment, and then let them know you understand those concerns and that you will do your best to help alleviate them.

That means, of course, really listening to the answers you get. It doesn't help to get someone to open up if you are not listening. A few years ago, I started seeing a therapist. I went to her for six months, although I always had the feeling that she wasn't really listening to me. Finally, I was telling her about a situation and I mentioned my sister by name. "Who's that?" she said. Six months of therapy and she didn't know who my sister was! I could tell by that one question that she did not care enough to listen to me and I never went back to her again.

One of the ways that you let people know you are listening is by building on previous questions and answers. In other words, explore a subject thoroughly. If you ask, "Where do you live?" make your next question related to the answer you get, like, "Have you lived anywhere else?" or "If you could live anyplace in the world, where would that be?" Do not follow your first question by asking, "How many children do you have?" unless children have come up in the person's answer.

To get an idea of how this works, watch television interviews. Some interviewers, like Larry King and Barbara Walters, are very good at listening to answers and building one question on another. Other interviewers seem to have a list of planned questions and go down their list no matter what the interviewee says.

PUT YOUR BODY INTO IT

You get people to open up not only by what you say and what you ask, but also by your physical demeanor. Your words may get people to trust you partway, but your body language and tone of voice will really convince them.

Suppose you ask your spouse the question, "Did anything special happen at work today?" while you are sitting at the kitchen table reading the newspaper and eating peanuts. To your spouse, the question may seem perfunctory and insincere.

Suppose instead that your spouse comes into the kitchen while you are reading and eating. You put down the paper, stop chewing, make eye contact with your spouse, and ask the question. I guarantee this time you will get a meaningful answer.

Eye contact is an important element of getting people to open up. When you ask someone a question, look him directly in the eye. Let him know that you are interested and available to listen. When he is talking, be aware of how your body is responding. People can tell when you are not really listening by the way you're tapping your foot, looking at the ceiling, or fiddling with your hair. If you want to show interest, lean your body in toward the other person. Keep your limbs open and relaxed. You do not have to keep your eyes locked on his, but make sure you regain eye contact every few seconds.

Your voice can also pull people in or push them away. If you yell a question at someone from another room, or toss it over your shoulder while doing something else, you will not get the response you want. If you are on the telephone, it is even more important that your voice be warm and inviting. And do not forget to pause after you ask a question. Give the other person a chance to collect his or her thoughts before you rush on to another question or, even worse, answer the question yourself.

How many times have you asked a question and then answered it yourself without giving the other person a chance to respond? This is something that I do—and something I am working on changing. I am an expressive, talkative person, and I don't even realize that I am not waiting for an answer. But I will often say something like this to my husband: "Let's go to a movie tonight. Here's one you'd like to see, wouldn't you? We could have an early dinner, see the movie, and be home by ten." I never even give him a chance to voice his opinion.

But I am changing my pattern of communicating by changing how I ask my questions and by waiting for people to answer. I make fewer assumptions. And my husband now sees me in a different light, more caring and open to his suggestions and point of view. It is allowing me, after many, many years of marriage, to reexplore my relationship with my husband. It's exciting, and all it took was a new way of using questions.

OPENING UP TECHNIQUES

Several techniques can be helpful when you're asking questions in order to get people to open up, including these four:

1. **Develop a good rapport.** Make sure that you treat the other person as an individual, not a category like "customer," "client," or "employee." Don't just ask questions like, "How are you today?" to be polite. People are fascinating and everyone has a story to tell. You'll be amazed at how getting to know people, even if only for a few minutes, can add interest to your day and your life.

2. **Start with broad, open questions.** Give the interviewee plenty of room to reveal himself. Do not interrupt his narrative. As the interview or conversation continues, you can begin to ask sharper, more direct questions. For instance, if you are a manager looking to hire a new employee, you might start out with a question like,

"Why would you like to work for this company?" Once you have encouraged the candidate to talk openly and freely, you might ask a more pointed question, such as, "What specific talents and skills do you have that would be helpful in this job?"

3. **Save the most difficult questions for late in the conversation.** If someone is afraid of the consequences of telling the truth, he or she will probably be hesitant about opening up and telling the entire story. If you need to get detailed information as well as emotional data, go for the detailed information first. Expert police investigators, for instance, start off by asking eyewitnesses to describe their activities before the crime, what happened as the crime began, and the assailant's appearance—anything that involves remembering details—before they go on to ask about the moment when the gun was fired. If they ask the question about the gun too soon, the eyewitness is likely to be so overcome with emotion he won't be able to remember any details at all.

4. **Use nonverbal signals to indicate interest.** As the other person is talking, nod your head slightly or lean forward in a nonthreatening manner. Make frequent eye contact with him and keep your gestures flowing and open. Avoid leaning too far away from him, keeping your arms or legs in a closed, crossed position, or tapping your fingers or toes nervously. If you appear uncomfortable, the other person will be uncomfortable as well, and less likely to open up.

TRUTH, LIES, AND OPENING UP

> **IQ** A person has to be awfully intelligent to be a good liar. If you want to know if someone is telling the truth, ask fairly simple questions. First, you just listen to him. Then after he's finished talking, you ask very broad questions. The simpler you appear to the individual, the better off you are. If you're too sophisticated, he may not give you candid answers, he may just answer yes or no so as not to give himself away.
>
> You want to get details. Ask the person how he got from point A to point B. Then you let him go on, you let him roam the turf, so to speak. Fifteen minutes later you go back and say, "Oh, by the way, would you tell me that again? How did you get from point A to point B?"
>
> —Jim Murphy, licensed private investigator
> and president, Society of Former FBI Agents

Sometimes we need to get to the truth. We need to know if a child is on drugs or is doing something else we do not sanction. We want to know if an employee is stealing or if a spouse is cheating. Not all cases are that dramatic, but it can be helpful to know that there are ways of determining whether or not someone is telling the truth.

Mamie Murray of Atlantic Forensic Investigations and Consultants notes that people have been asking questions and trying to detect deception since the beginning of time. Ancient techniques involved having the suspect spit out a mouthful of dry rice or putting hot coals inside the suspect's mouth. The idea was that if you could not spit the rice out easily, or if the coals blistered the inside of your mouth, you were being deceptive. The principle was that a nervous person would have a dry mouth, whereas the innocent would have ample saliva to pass such a test.

Murray contends that the best way to tell if someone is lying is to pay close attention to the person's language choices. In fact, she says, most people do not lie, they omit. You must listen not only for what is said, but also for what is not said. For instance, a woman confronts her husband, whom she suspects of being unfaithful:

"Have you been fooling around on me?"

"I can't believe you're asking me that question! I am hurt that you don't trust me. You know me better than that. I love you and I would never hurt you."

At no time did the husband deny having an affair. But he never directly answered the question, either. So, in his mind, perhaps, he was not lying. But if I were his wife, I would be highly suspicious. The wife then has a choice: She can further explore the issue—she might say, "You haven't answered my question" and insist on an answer. Or she can try to live with the uncertainty.

Listen to the words people do choose. For instance, suppose your daughter borrows your cardigan sweater and loses it. If you confront her directly with, "Did you lose my sweater?" you will back her into a corner and she will have no choice but to deny it, especially if she knows you will be really angry. It's natural to avoid telling the truth if you know there is a negative consequence attached to it.

However, it's awkward for people to lie. So if you ask, "What happened to my sweater?" your daughter may answer by saying, "I don't know. I saw it in your room, and then it was gone." She is avoiding the direct details of everything that happened between the time she saw the sweater and the time "it was gone." That will give you a hint that she had something to do with its disappearance. But it may be difficult for her to admit that outright. You can help her by suggesting a reason for her behavior. You might say, "I wouldn't blame you if you wanted to try it on with your new outfit. It is probably just the same color pink, don't you think? Is that why you borrowed it?" Give her a plausible out while getting her to admit her lie.

Some people will try asking the questioner a question to buy time or prepare an answer. Some examples:

- Could you repeat the question?

- Why would I do something like that?

- Shouldn't we discuss this at another time?

- Could you be more specific?

- What's your point?

Although in most cases, it's important to ask clarifying questions, this kind of stalling tactic can be another indication that the person is not being totally truthful.

Getting people to open up has many rewards. You can find out what's really bothering a person, determine hidden intentions, uncover lies and omissions, and discover what motivates him or her. With that knowledge, and the questioning habit, you can build better relationships at work and at home, get the information you need, and help others around you feel that they are cared for and valued.

> **IQ** Merf . . . had a quality of perfect sympathy. She also had a gift for interrogation, for getting everyone's life story—with the result that any number of people walked out of our house a little taller, as if they were about to become the subjects of biographies. Naturally, they came back.
>
> — Jay McInerny, "Naked on the Grass,"
> the *New Yorker,* January 18, 1999

7

POWER NUMBER SIX

Questions Lead to Quality Listening

The most desperate need of men today is not a new vaccine for any disease, or a new religion, or a new "way of life." Man does not need to go to the moon or other solar systems. He does not require bigger and better bombs and missiles. . . . His real need, his most terrible need, is for someone to listen to him, not as a "patient," but as a human soul.

—TAYLOR CALDWELL, *Listener*

THE QUESTIONING DETECTIVE LISTENS

Why do we ask questions?

The best explanation is the simplest: to get an answer. But unlike the chicken riddle that ends across the road, getting an answer is only the beginning of our journey. It is what we do

131

with the answer that counts. And we cannot do anything at all with the answer unless we know how to listen.

Most people consider themselves good listeners. We should be; we do enough of it. A recent survey conducted by the U.S. Department of Labor states that of the total time we spend in communication, 22 percent is spent in reading and writing, 23 percent is spent speaking, and 55 percent in listening.

Despite what we may think, however, most of us are not good listeners. Take the quiz at the end of this chapter to find out how you rate. Remember that there are only two ways to get information—by observing, which requires reading and watching, and by questioning, which requires listening. If, as the Department of Labor survey shows, we spend twice as much time listening as reading, you can imagine how much information is missed because of poor questioning and listening habits!

If you are not listening well, you are missing out on the power of questions. A question is useless if you do not listen carefully to the response. When you combine the listening and questioning, they are synergistic. When you ask better questions, you get more focused, meaningful answers, and the more likely you are to listen well. The more focused your listening, the better you will be at determining your next question, which will get you a better answer . . . and so on.

Successful people do very little talking; they spend most of their time asking questions and listening so that they can gather enough information to make decisions and solve problems. They know that it is not possible to get that information if they are doing all the talking. They also know that a question with thought and purpose behind it gives them a vested interest in the response; the more they have at stake in the answers, the more likely they will be to listen to what is said.

Imagine once again that you are a detective, trying to solve a crime or determine someone's motives for taking a particular action. Would you confront a suspect and start rattling off theories until you came upon one that made sense? Of course not.

You could go on forever without hitting on the one true answer. So how does a detective uncover a suspect's true motive? By asking questions, getting the suspect to divulge his innermost secrets, and listening carefully for any hidden clues the suspect may subconsciously reveal.

The same concept applies to any type of communication. If you are in a discussion with someone—a spouse, a child, an employee, a coworker, a customer—and you start spouting off reasons you *think* he or she might have acted in a certain way, you could go on forever without hitting on the truth. If you are truly interested in getting information and solving problems, you will ask questions, stop talking, and listen.

HOW DO WE LISTEN? WITH FOUR ORGANS

Detectives use many different tools when they are looking for clues. You, too, have several essential listening tools, or organs, to listen with.

The first and most obvious listening organ is our ears. Unfortunately, we often take this tool for granted. I once scheduled an important business meeting with my British publisher at a popular New York restaurant. We had both heard a lot about the food and the service, but no one had warned us about the atmosphere. The tables were crowded so closely together we could not help but eavesdrop on other people's conversations. Waiters were reciting daily specials as silverware banged against dishes and music was piped in over loudspeakers. The restaurant would have been fine for a social conversation, where it is okay to miss a few details, but not for a business meeting. The publisher and I finally gave up on our meeting, finished our meal, and rescheduled for another day.

Now whenever I schedule a business lunch or dinner, I call to ask the restaurant not only if they will have a table available, but how noisy the restaurant is likely to be at the time I wish to eat.

The second listening organ is our eyes. When we are face-to-face, the eyes (the speaker's and the listener's) are vitally important. When you are listening, you must focus your attention, and your gaze, on the speaker. This does two things. First, it lets the other person know that you are listening. Second, it helps you to listen—it is difficult to look someone in the eye while he is speaking and not listen to him.

When your eyes wander, so does your mind. You do not need to stare steadily at the other person, but you should make contact every few seconds. When you are listening and interacting with another person, your eyes are an essential aid—or a vicious betrayer. Lack of eye contact is the first clue that someone is not listening to what you have to say. That is why you often hear a frustrated parent demanding of her child, "Look at me when I'm speaking to you!"

The eyes are involved in another aspect of listening as well. We pick up all sorts of clues from people when they are speaking, although not all of these are verbal. Effective listening also involves effective looking. Some clues come from the speaker's body language. Look to see if the person who is speaking is leaning back in his chair with crossed arms and tense muscles. If so, he is probably holding something in. If, on the other hand, he is leaning forward with open arms and a relaxed position, he is probably more comfortable with the subject or with the listener, and is likely to be more forthcoming.

The third listening organ is our mind. We think much faster than we speak. So while we are listening, our minds are racing ahead. This can be distracting if what we are thinking is not related to what is being said, but it can also give us time to ask ourselves questions while we are listening: "Do I understand what is being said? Do I understand its relevance to me? Is there any action I need to take because of what is being said? Do I understand not only what is being said, but what is going on beneath the words?"

That last question, above, touches on the heart's role. **The**

fourth organ of effective listening is our heart. If you listen only halfheartedly, you will not really *hear* what is being said. This is something that psychiatrists, therapists, and spiritual counselors deal with all the time. Many people are afraid to deal with issues that make them uncomfortable, so they talk around them. It is up to the counselor to sort out what is really going on. Rabbi Matthew D. Gewirtz of Congregation Rodeph Sholom in New York City finds this a common problem, especially when dealing with children.

"They speak to me about something that they are going through," says Rabbi Gewirtz, "like, 'I think you should talk to Peter because his grandfather died and I think he is really sad.' Often times, they are right. But most of the time, what they are really asking me is, 'It scares me that Peter's grandfather died. Can you help me?' There's a deep question in there, and then I have to ask them: 'Do you feel scared that Peter's grandfather died? It makes us all think about mortality, doesn't it?' What I am really saying is, 'You are scared that you are going to die. You are scared that your grandfather is going to die.' Rarely will a child come up to me and say, 'I am scared,' or 'Can it happen to my family?' so I have to ask the question instead."

Because he is listening with all four organs, the rabbi knows that the child's questions about Peter are also about himself and his family. This ability to listen to what is being said beneath the words is what enables us to understand each other on an intuitive level. It is also what has thus far stopped science from inventing true artificial intelligence. In the twenty-first century, it is likely that technology will advance so far that computers will be able to listen and respond to what we say. This technology will no doubt be useful, but it will never replace the one advantage humans will always have over computers—the ability to listen with our ears, eyes, mind, and heart.

IQ A good listener is not only popular everywhere, but after a while he knows something.

—Wilson Mizner, playwright

LISTENING WITH PURPOSE

Whichever organ, or combination of organs, we use for listening, we all have the ability to be good listeners. So why are some people better at it than others? And why are we all better listeners at some times more than at others? There are several reason for this. The first is that we are all *I-centered*. The more a topic concerns us, the more relevant and meaningful it is to us, the better we will listen. If a friend talked to me about the U.S. Open tennis championships, I would listen carefully because I love the game. If the same friend started talking about football playoffs, however, I would certainly tune her out.

It is not only our preferences that make a difference; the situation itself often dictates how well we listen. For instance, imagine that you are a beginning skier, about to take your first run down anything other than the bunny hill. You hear a faint rumbling in the background. As you look up at the snowcapped mountain, it begins sliding toward you. Suddenly, your ski instructor says, "I am the resident expert on avalanches around here, and there is only one way to survive." How will you listen to his instructions? Very carefully!

You do not have to be in a life-threatening situation to listen well, but often you do need a definite purpose or a motivating reason for listening. Otherwise, you may not pay attention. Some of those motivating reasons include:

- To gather information
- To clarify and verify information

- To make a decision or form an opinion
- To help someone else make a decision or solve a problem
- To obtain feedback or a response from someone
- To find out whether you have been understood by someone else
- To gain insight into someone's attitude or emotional state
- To lend support as a friend or advisor

The more time we spend in formulating the question, the more meaningful the answer is to us and the harder we will listen. Focusing on a questioning approach slows you down, causes you to be more thoughtful, and magically improves your listening.

Sometimes it is helpful to ask the other person how he or she would like you to listen. I realized this recently when I returned from a visit with my granddaughter and called a friend to tell her all about it. I was very excited to relate all the precious things my grandchild had done while I was visiting, but I never got the chance. As soon as I said the word *grandchild*, my friend went off on her own stories about her grandchildren and never let me get a word in. It is not that I was not happy to hear her stories, it is just that she, like most of us, was being so I-centered she did not think about my need for her to listen.

The more important the topic is, the more important it is that you know what is expected of you as a listener. This is especially important when someone comes to you to complain or is upset or angry. You can then ask these three questions:

1. Do you want me just to listen?
2. Do you want me to ask questions and interact with you?
3. Do you want me to give you advice?

Asking these questions forces the other person to think about what she wants you to do. It also helps you fulfill her needs from her perspective.

We all get into patterns of listening, both good and bad, just as we get into patterns of speech. Learning to be a better listener can help you change your patterns so that you not only get the information you need, you also become more responsive to the needs of others.

WHY DON'T WE LISTEN BETTER?

> **IQ** Man's inability to communicate is a result of his failure to listen effectively, skillfully, and with understanding to another person.
>
> —Carl Rogers, psychologist

One of the most unfortunate facts of today's world is that most failed relationships, both business and personal, are due to a general lack of listening skills. Many people entering couples therapy complain first and foremost, "My mate doesn't listen to me." When that happens, therapy often revolves around getting people involved in exercises, such as Imago Therapy developed by noted psychologist Harville Hendrix. Couples are asked to stop whatever they are doing, face their partners, and carefully listen to and then paraphrase what each has to say.

Many people discover that they haven't really been listening to their spouses for years. They have stopped listening in part because they think they know the other person so well, they know what he or she is going to say. But when they stop and really listen, they begin to realize how much they have been missing.

Listening can be a problem at work as well. A recent survey by Select Appointments North America, quoted in the September 1999 issue of *Training and Development*, found that 80 percent of responding executives rated listening as the most important skill in the workplace and 28 percent rated listening as the skill most lacking in the workforce.

So why aren't we better listeners? One of the main reasons is that there are few rewards for listening well. Most behavioral scientists will tell you that if an action is not rewarded (or it is ignored, as in the case of listening), it is not repeated. There are rewards for speaking well, selling well, negotiating deals, playing sports well, and being academically smart. But there are not many obvious rewards for listening. We do not often applaud someone and say, "Wow, he is a *great* listener!" There are no plaques inscribed, First Place for Listening, nor any competitions to see who can listen most in any given quarter.

The rewards that you do get, such as gaining information and making another person feel better, are quiet and thoughtful, not showy or active. No one becomes a star or a hero for listening well. People are rewarded for activities that are high-energy and easily measurable and observable, which does not describe listening at all.

Here are several other reasons we are not better listeners:

- *Listening takes work.* It takes focus and concentration to listen to what someone else is saying, especially if the subject matter is not of immediate interest. In *Compassion*, Roger A. Lewin states that listening is an activity of "enormous complexity and requires the commitment of extensive resources."

- *We are not trained to listen.* As we go through school, we are taught the communication skills of reading and writing, but we are rarely taught listening skills. Several years ago, many companies began to realize that their employees were not communicating well, and they began offering courses in listening. However, most of these tried to teach listening as a stand-alone skill; they did not address the relationship between asking better questions and improving listening skills. These courses, though well intentioned, had little effect on improving workplace communications.

- *We have short attention spans.* Years ago, before movies, television, and the Internet, people got much of their news and entertainment from the radio, a medium that required concentrated listening. Today, we have MTV, VH1, Headline News, remote controls, and ten-second sound bites. We tend to take in everything in short, easily assimilated chunks. Very little in our lives seems to require concentrated listening; therefore, we don't get a lot of practice in listening to anything for longer than a minute or two.

- *We do not have time.* Effective listening takes time. The person who is speaking needs time to express her thoughts, and the person who's listening needs time to process what has been said. But we are often overloaded.

Not long ago, my friend Emily's daughter got into trouble at school for cheating on a test. The daughter tried to tell Emily about the incident three different times. Each time, Emily, a single parent working long hours to make ends meet, put her off. The first time, she said, "Not now, honey, I have to run to the store." The second time, she told her daughter, "We'll talk later; I have to make dinner and then take Johnny to basketball practice." And the third time she said, "Can we talk about this in the morning? I'm exhausted." When the principal called to talk with Emily about her daughter's behavior, Emily was shocked. "My daughter didn't even tell me about it!" she told the principal. "Well," he said, "she was upset, but she confided in me that you are so busy you never have time to listen." Emily realized that her priorities were not in order, and that she was not setting aside time simply to talk with and listen to her children. Now when her children come to her, she asks, "Is this something that needs my full attention?" If they say yes, Emily stops what she is doing and sits down to listen.

- *We feel an urgency to express ourselves.* We are certain that if we explain ourselves convincingly, we will get the other person to see things our way. And the best way to do that is to talk, isn't it? No, it is not, and a freelance copywriter I know found this out the hard way.

  Jack was being interviewed for a job as a copywriter for a new Internet site. He was excited by the opportunity to get involved on the ground floor of a start-up company. Because he was so nervous, he spent the whole meeting talking about himself. He talked about all the work he had done in the past and how he saw his career going in the future. He never asked about the new venture, what the interviewers were looking for in a copywriter, or how they saw their company's future.

  "I should have been asking them questions about what they needed from me, and listening to find out how I could help solve their problems," says Jack. "I missed a great opportunity because I was too busy selling myself."

THE CONSEQUENCES OF NOT LISTENING

Jack's missed opportunity is a typical consequence of not listening to what someone else has to say. Jack cut off his listening possibilities before they had even begun. A more common occurrence is that we only half-listen to what people are telling us, usually because we are too busy thinking of the next question or formulating objections or counterexamples.

As a result, we miss all kinds of information. And we make mistakes, sometimes costly mistakes. One salesperson who sells coupon advertising to local merchants recently made such a mistake. Rita closed a deal with a merchant who sells prepaid phone cards. The merchant told her that the ad was to read "200 minutes for $24.00" and "1,000 minutes for $120.00." But Rita was not listening carefully, and thousands of ads were sent out reading, "2,000 minutes for $24.00" and "10,000 minutes for $120.00." Needless to say, that phone card merchant is no longer a client of Rita's.

Rita's mistake occurred because she didn't listen carefully and she did not evaluate the answer. She did not ask herself if what she thought she heard made sense. Logic would tell her that two thousand minutes was too much time for twenty-four dollars, but because she was in a hurry, she didn't ask.

Rita eventually straightened out her mistake by reprinting the ad and apologizing, but she could not erase her error completely. The merchant spread the word about her inaccuracy and she began to lose business. As Rita learned, poor listening can lead to far-reaching mistakes.

Tamar Howson, senior vice president and director of business development for SmithKline Beecham, says, "Without careful listening, incorrect information can be shared and/or misinterpreted, which can lead to a chain of decisions and actions that have a negative outcome." It is like the old game of telephone, where one person whispers a sentence in another person's ear. As the information gets passed down the line, one person after another mishears and misinterprets, so that by the time the message gets to the last person, it barely resembles the original information.

Because it is so easy to mishear and misinterpret information, it is vitally important to ask questions before making any important decision or taking any major actions, questions like: "Is the information on which I am making this decision accurate? What is the source of the information? Is this a source I can trust? What resources can I use to check the accuracy of the information? What will be the consequences if I act on mistaken information?"

We miss more than information when we do not listen well. We can also miss out on understanding the people with whom we are trying to communicate. As a result of not listening, we might miss an answer, or part of it, and pass up the opportunity to discover the speaker's state of mind. Listening also gives us the information we need to form opinions about a person's character and decide whether or not we can believe everything we are hearing.

> The very limited development of our capacity for listening is responsible for much suffering and misery in life . . . . [The] cultivation of this capacity can contribute to . . . the forming of moral character, encouraging communicative relationships, awakening a compassionate sensibility and the understanding it bears with it . . . [and] reversing processes of alienation that . . . turn more and more into an instrument of nihilism, raging self-destructively.
>
> —David Michael Levin, *The Listening Self*

When we do not listen, we suffer personally, as well. First we suffer when we do not listen to how we sound to others. Some people are so full of themselves they don't hear or see themselves as others hear or see them. They think they are so smart, so funny, or so interesting that everyone else will be more than happy to listen to them. In truth, these people are usually crashing bores. As Susan RoAne writes in *What Do I Say Next?* "If the voice we hear most often in conversation is our own, it's time to reassess."

Each of us also has an inner voice that speaks to us, and we suffer when we do not pay it proper attention. This is the voice that tells us when something is not quite right; it is often a voice that asks us questions that we ignore at our peril. As I have mentioned, I run in a park near my house every morning. Sometimes I run very early in the morning when there are not many people around. I have learned over the years that I must listen to the voice in my head that warns me away from potentially dangerous situations. If I am asking myself, "Should I run down this path? Does it look safe? Is it too deserted?" I need to answer these questions before I go on. If I do not, I am liable to get myself in trouble.

There are other times when that voice inside is not warning of danger, but is instead trying to convince us of our lack of self-worth. It tells us that we cannot achieve our goals, that we are not good enough, that we will never succeed. Take every opportunity to question this voice. Listen selectively and sort out the truth from expressions of insecurity. Ask yourself, "Why should I believe these negative thoughts? Are these facts or feelings? Is it fear that is stopping me from reaching my goals? If so, what one small step can I take today that will begin to move me toward my goal and silence the voice of FEAR: False Evidence Appearing Real?"

THE BENEFITS OF QUALITY LISTENING

Great ideas, it has been said, come into the world as gently as doves. Perhaps, then, if we listen attentively, we shall hear amid the uproar of empires and nations a faint flutter of wings, the gentle stirring of life and hope.

—Albert Camus, philosopher

Learning to listen well does take time and effort, but the benefits of quality listening far outweigh any hardships. Now that we have seen what consequences not listening well can produce, let's look at some of the advantages.

One of the greatest advantages of quality listening is that it makes us more empathetic. Empathy, or identifying with the feelings, thoughts, and attitudes of another, is one of the most important ways we have of communicating and forming relationships. Everyone seeks to be understood by other people, because understanding brings appreciation. Psychologists have long known that the desire to be appreciated is a fundamental principle of human nature, and listening is one of the highest forms of appreciation you can show another person. Only when we can put ourselves in someone else's shoes can we begin to understand that person's point of view.

And that is what listening is really all about—trying to see a problem or situation the way the speaker sees it. Ask yourself questions about the person who is speaking: "What is this person feeling? Is he or she afraid, hurt, angry or upset? Do I understand not only what this person is saying, but what he or she really means to say?"

It is through the process of questioning and listening that empathy emerges. In *Question-Reply Argumentation,* Douglas N. Walton asserts that through this process, each person (the questioner and the listener) becomes "more fully aware, not only of the other's position [empathy], but also of his or her own position [knowing oneself]. . . . Even though reasonable dialogue may have a contestive or disputative aspect, at the same time it can be seen as a process of communication and collaborative interaction. In a nutshell, that is the beauty and the value of good dialogue."

> **IQ** Dialogue is a process of successful relationship building ... by performing the seemingly simple act of responding empathetically to others and in turn being heard by them, we transcend the constricting confines of the self. The act of reaching beyond the self to relate to others in dialogue is a profound human yearning. If it were less commonplace, we would realize what a miracle it is.
>
> —Daniel Yankelovich, *The Magic of Dialogue*

The art and skill of collaborative interaction—questioning and listening—can have a profound and positive effect on your personal and professional success. When you stop, ask questions, and practice quality listening, you will gain many advantages:

1. **Quality listening makes people feel special and cared about.** Remember, questions show that you care, and careful listening adds to that impression. It shows that you respect what others have to say and are willing to take the time to hear, and at least consider, their opinions. It makes your children feel loved, your coworkers and staff feel appreciated, and your clients feel important.

   Quality listening makes the other person feel *valued*. When Emily, the single mother introduced earlier, started setting aside time to really listen to her children, several things happened. Her daughter's behavior changed markedly; there was no more trouble at school. Emily's daughter had been acting out, trying to get her mother's attention. She also suffered from low self-esteem, because she felt that if she had something worthwhile to say, her mother would be listening to her. When Emily began listening and gave her the attention she craved, her daughter felt that she was a loved and valued member of the family.

2. **Quality listening can alert you to problems or opportunities you did not know existed.** The first step in problem solving is knowing which problem to solve. Asking thoughtful questions and listening to the responses will open your eyes to what is really going on. And opportunities lurk in the most unexpected places. My staff and colleagues often laugh at me because I always come back from a plane trip with someone's phone number or business card. I am known as a great networker because I ask questions and then listen. Most of the time, because I listen carefully, I find that there is some connection that can be made.

3. **Quality listening makes you seem more intelligent.** Good listeners are often perceived as being smart because when you listen well you ask smarter questions.

4. **Quality listening reduces mistakes.** Have you ever walked away from a conversation and suddenly realized there were several points you did not clearly understand? Or worse, you think you understand what is being asked of you, only to find out later you got it all wrong? These kinds of errors are time-consuming and costly. If you had been listening carefully to begin with, you could have asked clarifying questions to make sure you understood what you were being asked to do.

HOW TO START LISTENING BETTER

Listening is one of the most difficult skills to teach in my questioning workshops. Participants take the quiz you will find at the end of this chapter to determine their present listening ability. I tell them to answer honestly; to answer the questions not as they think they should be answered, but in the way that best describes their current listening habits.

Once they have compiled their answers, I ask them to close their eyes so everyone will answer honestly. Then I ask those who scored as "excellent" listeners to raise their hands. No one ever does. Only 5 to 10 percent categorize themselves as good listeners and the remainder are divided among fair and poor, with a surprising number in the poor category.

That is the bad news. The good news is that listening is a skill, and since, by definition, a skill can be learned, there are a number of things you can do to improve your listening skills:

1. Listen for intent (feeling). When people speak, they include information from both the right brain (feeling) and the left brain (fact). To fully understand the person who is speaking, we should be "listening between the lines," using all four organs—our ears, eyes, mind, and heart—to really hear what someone is saying.

When we are speaking, we use a technique called *vocal variety* to help make ourselves understood. This means that we emphasize certain words and phrases over others. When you are listening, it is your job to pay attention to this vocal variety and weigh and evaluate what is being said—not everything has equal importance. When someone is speaking, listen for nuances like the stress placed on certain words and the emotional intonation of the voice. If you doubt how significant such details of delivery can be, consider the sentence below. It has five different meanings, depending on which words are stressed.

Imagine that you are trying to persuade a group of women to contribute a thousand dollars to a charity in which you are involved. One woman says, "*I* don't think, at this point, we would be interested in contributing a thousand dollars to this charity." This means you have not yet convinced this one individual. That does not mean others in the group are not interested.

If you hear, "I don't think, *at this point*, we would be interested in contributing a thousand dollars to this charity," it may not be the right time to be asking. You might have to wait for the group's next fiscal year or until it is in a better budgetary position to help you out.

"I don't think, at this point, *we* would be interested in contributing a thousand dollars to this charity," suggests that, although this group is not interested, there may be others who would be willing to make the contribution. This should prompt you to probe further and find out who else she might have in mind.

If you hear, "I don't think, at this point, we would be interested in contributing a thousand dollars to *this* charity," it is a tip-off that your prospective contributor has an objection to the particular charity, not to contributing in general, and you need to find out why.

Finally, if the prospect says, "I don't think, at this point, we would be interested in contributing *a thousand dollars* to this charity," it might mean that another amount would be acceptable. Now is the time to suggest an alternative amount, even if it's less than you had originally envisioned.

A person's tone of voice can be another clue to how he or she is really feeling. A simple question like, "How are you today?" can elicit a variety of answers, but it's often how the question is answered, and not what is said, that will give you clues as to the real answer. What is the speaker's tone of voice? Is he animated or excited? Or does he sound tired, bored, or frustrated? When Rabbi Gewirtz hears young children tell him about their friends' problems, he has to listen to the tone behind their stories to determine if they are simply relaying facts or if they are scared, worried, or anxious.

2. Listen for content (facts). This is listening with the left brain—making sure that you understand what is being said, that you have the information you need, and that you are not making false assumptions. One technique to improve your skill at listening for facts is to listen as if you will have to explain what is being said to someone else. Another is to summarize or paraphrase what is being said every once in a while to be sure you have gotten the important points.

For instance, after a person has made an important point, you could say, "Let me be sure I have got this right. You are saying that you think this is a good idea, but you are not sure that everyone else on the team would agree?" Rephrase their comments to guarantee you're on the same wavelength.

Lastly, judge the content of what people are saying, not the way they are saying it. People may not use the *right* words, in your opinion, but that does not mean you should discount what they're saying.

3. Listen for who is speaking. We tend to listen more carefully to people we think are important. However, it is easy to appear authoritative; that does not necessarily make it so.

If you go to a surgeon for a medical opinion, he is likely to recommend surgery. If you ask around for financial advice, your broker will tell you to buy stocks and bonds, your insurance agent will tell you to buy insurance, and a mutual funds specialist will tell you to buy mutual funds. You would not listen to what a paranoid schizophrenic has to say about refinancing the second mortgage on your home. Nor would you listen to an eight-year-old boy who is trying to sell you a car. Part of quality listening is determining just who is worth listening to.

When you are listening, try asking yourself these questions:

- Is this person qualified to speak on this subject?

- What underlying motives might this person have?

• Does this person have any prejudices or beliefs that will compromise his objectivity?

THE LISTENING QUIZ

Here is the listening quiz I promised. As I said earlier, when I give this quiz to my workshop participants, I tell them they must answer as they really are, not as they would like to be or think they should be. When you take this quiz, answer truthfully. Only then will you be able to assess how well you practice *quality listening*.

Answer yes or no to the following questions:

_____ 1. I give conscious specific thought to my listening strategy each time I engage in a dialogue.

_____ 2. People often tell me I am daydreaming and not listening to them.

_____ 3. I get impatient and jump ahead, finishing other people's sentences.

_____ 4. I make clear eye contact when I am listening.

_____ 5. I am an expert at creating the illusion of listening when I am not.

_____ 6. People often compliment me on being a concerned, empathetic listener.

_____ 7. When I am unable to give my full attention, I let the other person know.

_____ 8. I often hear people say, "You are not listening to me!"

_____ 9. I listen better one-on-one than when I am part of a group.

_____ 10. At appropriate times in a conversation, I ask for clarification.

_____ 11. I generally make a concentrated effort to pay attention when someone is speaking to me.

_____ 12. I am a master at tuning in and out of a conversation and never missing a thing.

_____ 13. When I first meet people, I always remember their names.

_____ 14. I tend to listen harder when I know I will be tested on the material.

_____ 15. Through my body language, I make a concerted effort to demonstrate my interest.

_____ 16. When someone says something I disagree with or want to add to, I get hung up on that point and stop paying attention.

_____ 17. I am one of those people who does not take notes, because I believe I will remember what was said.

_____ 18. I have made some major mistakes and caused misunderstandings by not listening.

_____ 19. I am willing to change my opinions and strategies after hearing someone else's thoughts.

_____ 20. My listening skills have not improved in the last five years.

The quality listening answers are:

1. I give conscious specific thought to my listening strategy each time I engage in a dialogue. YES. When you think about how you are going to listen, what you will be listening for, and how you are going to focus your attention on the other person, you are doing yourself a great service.

When you give conscious thought to listening better, you will listen better.

2. People often tell me I am daydreaming and not listening to them. NO. If you are hearing this comment often, it means you need practice listening. Focus your attention on the person who is speaking. Review the section in this chapter about the benefits of quality listening, and make it a high priority in your personal and professional life.

3. I get impatient and jump ahead, finishing other people's sentences. NO. Even if you think you can tell what someone is going to say, you do not know for certain. You must listen to everything and maintain focus on the other person, not on what you predict she is going to say.

4. I make clear eye contact when I am listening. YES. Making clear and direct eye contact helps you maintain focus and lets people know that you are listening.

5. I am an expert at creating the illusion of listening when I am not. NO. Some people are very good at the "illusion of listening," or so they think. Most of the time, however, a person can tell if you are not listening. Then you run the risk not only of missing information, but of hurting that person's feelings.

6. People often compliment me on being a concerned, empathetic listener. YES. People respect and appreciate a good listener. Be proud if someone compliments you on being a good listener. It is not easy to do, but there are many rewards.

7. When I am unable to give my full attention, I let the other person know. YES. If you cannot focus on the other person, it is not worth trying. It is better to suggest another time for the two of you to talk—it makes it easier on both parties.

8. I often hear people say, "You are not listening to me!"
NO. You may be habitually I-centered. If that is so, try giving someone else the floor once in a while. Listen carefully to yourself when you do speak, and ask yourself if what you are saying is more important than what you might be learning.

9. I listen better one-on-one than when I am part of a group. NO. When you are part of a group, you should still be listening as if you were going to need to use that information at a later time. It is a bad habit to tune out if you think that other people in the group will listen for you.

10. At appropriate times in a conversation, I ask for clarification. YES. This is the main way questions will help you with your quality listening. It not only helps you get the right information, it lets the other person know you're paying attention.

11. I generally make a concentrated effort to pay attention when someone is speaking to me. YES. Making the effort is most of the work. When you make the effort and really listen, you will be well rewarded.

12. I'm a master at tuning in and out of a conversation and never missing a thing. NO. You may think you're not missing anything, but how can you be sure, if you are not really listening? Once you tune out, you will never get another chance to listen to what you missed.

13. When I first meet people, I always remember their names. YES. Sometimes we are too busy making our own first impression to listen to a person's name. Frequently, too, we are busy assessing the person's appearance and demeanor and we forget how much people value their names and how important it is to remember them.

14. I tend to listen harder when I know I will be tested on the material. NO. It is a facet of human nature to pay more attention when we know we will be tested. This is because if we pass the test, we are rewarded. It helps to remember that listening always pays rewards—in the form of respect, information, and opportunities.

15. Through my body language, I make a concerted effort to demonstrate my interest. YES. It is important to let people know you are listening to them. It makes them feel special and important, which improves your chances that they will talk to you again.

16. When someone says something I disagree with or want to add to, I get hung up on that point and stop paying attention. NO. It is easy to do this. Everyone does this occasionally—some people more than others. If we get stuck on one point, we miss the other, possibly more important points. If you do hear something you want to comment on, make a mental note of it and continue to listen, then come back to it.

17. I am one of those people who does not take notes, because I believe I will remember what was said. NO. No one can remember everything. You will probably remember the information at the beginning and end of the conversation, but what about the middle? That is often the most important.

18. I have made some major mistakes and caused misunderstandings by not listening. NO. I think we have all done this. But the first step you can take is to realize that you can avoid major mistakes and misunderstandings by listening better. The second step, of course, is to practice quality listening.

19. I am willing to change my opinions and strategies

after hearing someone else's thoughts. YES. If you are really listening and open-minded you will change your thoughts and feelings occasionally. Take note of how often, if ever, you do this. We all say we are open to change, but are we? Going through life simply reinforcing your existing opinions seems quite boring to me.

20. My listening skills have not improved in the last five years. NO. Most people when confronted with this question are amazed. They realize with much concern that although they have improved in many areas, listening is not one of them.

If you answered eighteen to twenty statements correctly, you have excellent listening habits.

If you answered fourteen to seventeen statements correctly, you have good listening habits.

If you answered eleven to thirteen statements correctly, you have fair listening habits.

If you answered ten or fewer statements correctly, you have poor listening habits.

No matter what your score, everyone has the ability to listen well. Here is one final secret to determine whether or not you are a good listener. During every conversation, ask yourself this question, "Am I learning anything?" If not, you are talking too much and listening too little.

8

Questions Get People to Persuade Themselves

Every experience in life, whether humble or grand, teaches a lesson. The question is not if the lesson is taught, but rather if it is learned.

—Carly Fiorina, CEO, Hewlett-Packard,
"Making the Best of a Mess,"
New York Times, September 29, 1999

THE SECRET OF PERSUASION

Early in my career as a speaker and workshop leader, I was approached by a man named Joe Billings, an executive in a major brokerage firm. He wanted me to design and implement a training program for some of his managers. I spent time with him, asked him many questions to find out just what kind of program he needed, and told him I would mail him my agree-

157

ment letter within a few days. We agreed to meet in his office in two weeks, at which time he would sign the agreement and we would go over the preliminary outline for the program.

When I arrived at his office, I could see my agreement letter, unsigned, off to the side on his desk. Mr. Billings asked me to sit down, and then explained that he was no longer interested in doing the program. I was devastated. I really wanted this job. My first thought was to try to convince Mr. Billings that he was wrong. Instead, I asked him one question.

"Mr. Billings," I said, "you were so interested in doing the program when we first spoke. What was it that made you so excited about it two weeks ago?"

As Mr. Billings started to go over his list of reasons, he realized they were still valid. His enthusiasm began to build. He kept on talking about how much this training program would do to improve his team's performance and production. I did not have to say another word. Within five minutes he said, "Let's do it!" and reached over and signed the agreement.

What happened to get Mr. Billings to change his mind? Nothing I could have told him at that meeting would have convinced him to hire me. But when I asked him that one question, he was forced to review—in his own words and from his own perspective—the benefits of my program. He sold himself on the fact that training his managers was a good idea.

The secret to persuasion is to encourage a person to come up with his or her own answers to questions or solutions to problems. You can do that by asking questions that lead the person in the direction you want him or her to go.

We are all salespeople in one way or another. We are constantly selling our ideas to others. We want to persuade people to do a certain thing, to think in a particular way, or to go in a specific direction. Even when we might have the best intentions, however, it is difficult to get people to do what you want them to do. The best way to persuade is by getting people to persuade themselves.

I wanted Mr. Billings to think about the reasons he had wanted to hire me in the first place. If I had listed the reasons myself—"But, Mr. Billings, you said that your managers needed training"—I would have sounded defensive. And if I had worded my question differently, I would have sent him in the opposite direction. Asking the more obvious question—"Mr. Billings, you were so interested in doing the program when we first spoke. *What made you change your mind?*"—would have led him into reinforcing his own doubts and negative thoughts. By framing the question in positive language, I framed the answer in positive language as well.

WE BELIEVE OURSELVES

The reason I was able to get Mr. Billings to change his mind is the reason that this seventh power of questions works. People believe what *they* say, not what *you* say. We humans are stubborn. We like to think that we are right and that we know what is best for us. Most of us are naturally resistant to someone else trying to tell us what to do.

Our logical, left-brain thoughts might be telling us the other person "has a point," while our emotional right brain thinks we know better. Often this conflict leads to confusion and indecision. The right brain says yes and the left brain says no, or vice versa.

For several months, Janice tried to convince her husband, Frank, that they needed a new car. Frank wanted to make repairs on the old car; he liked the idea of owning a new car but did not want to spend the money. Janice researched new cars on the Internet, made lists of features she thought Frank would like in a new car, and brought up the subject almost every night. But Frank would not budge.

Finally, one night Janice asked Frank, "What would have to happen to make you decide to get a new car?"

Frank answered that the cost of repairs would have to build up to such a large amount that buying a new car would be more economical. So Janice went back through their checkbook, added up all the money they had spent on repairs in the last year, and presented the figure to Frank. He had not realized how many bills they had actually accumulated. When he saw the figures, he agreed that a new car was in order.

Janice did not convince Frank to buy the car. Her question let her know what it would take for Frank to convince himself that a new car made economical sense. When Frank saw the evidence Janice collected, he sold himself on the idea.

THE PROBLEM WITH LECTURES

Janice could have talked until she was blue in the face and never have persuaded Frank to buy the car. In fact, the more she insisted, the more he resisted. Frank wasn't about to buy a car just because Janice thought it was a good idea.

No one likes to be told what to do. When I was a young girl, my room was always a mess. My mother was always trying to get me to straighten it up, telling me, "Go clean your room!" I resisted her at every opportunity. I was determined to have my room the way I wanted it. Whether I actually liked living in a messy room was another subject altogether. I never stopped to think about the benefits of having a clean room. It was more important to me, at that rebellious stage we all go through, to get my own way. And my mother, like most other parents, did not realize the power of getting me to realize the benefits for myself. Instead, she resorted to lecturing.

Despite the fact that parents, teachers, and other authority figures habitually lecture people, it is not a technique with long-lasting results. I often ask my seminar participants how they feel when someone is lecturing them. I get responses like: childish, angry, ashamed, and frustrated. Their responses are never positive; participants have never told me that a lecture made them change their minds or their behavior.

We lecture because it is the easy way out. We get to vent our emotions and we do not have to take anyone else's views into account. But what makes it easy also makes it ineffective. The person you are lecturing is not being engaged or encouraged to think. In all likelihood, he is not even listening.

Telling is easy; asking is tougher. Asking requires deliberate thought and action. Asking questions forces you to slow down your own thoughts as you listen to the other person's answers. The other person has to stop and think in order to answer your question, and that is exactly what you want. Getting someone else to think—along the lines that you are thinking—is what persuasion is all about.

But you can change your life, and the lives of others, by using questions to get them to persuade themselves. You can build better relationships, exert more authority and control, and appear more thoughtful and intelligent—all by asking the right question at the right time.

THE SELF-DISCOVERY PROCESS

The first step in solving any problem is admitting that there *is* a problem. If you know anything about addiction and recovery programs, you know that a person with this kind of problem cannot be helped unless he wants to help himself. The fact is that a person with *any* kind of problem cannot be helped unless he or she wants that help. We each have to discover for ourselves why this is a problem that needs to be solved; otherwise we might come up with a temporary fix that will not stop the problem from cropping up again later.

As the old saying goes, catch a man a fish and you feed him for a day; teach him how to fish and you feed him for a lifetime. This means that if you give someone a solution, you have solved one problem; if you get someone to discover a solution independently, he will learn and remember. What is the best way to get people to discover their own answers? By asking the right questions.

IQ ———————————————————————————————
Questions differentiate a superior doctor from an average one, in that an average doctor will ask a question and not listen to the answer. A superior doctor will ask questions and listen to the answers. An exceptional doctor will create an environment where the patient asks their own questions and answers them.

—Jon Strauss, M.D.

Therapists and counselors have known for many years that when you come up with your own answers and when you say something in your own voice, you will take ownership of that idea.

Therapist Beth Althofer explains it this way: "I would much rather ask a leading question than make an interpretation to a patient, no matter how brilliant I think that interpretation is. Most often these questions will be designed to help the patient make important connections for herself. It's healthier if she makes them, because it strengthens the patient's abilities, and it also helps her to claim ownership of the insight.

"Take, for example, a patient who is ranting and raving about how unfair her boss is being to her. As a therapist, I know that she is repeating a battle with her father that she could never win. I don't tell her that. Instead I ask her, 'Do you think there's something in this fight with your boss that might connect to some old rankling injustices?' I don't even mention her father; she'll do that herself and feel better for coming to it on her own."

People remember best those things they discover, realize, learn, and experience themselves. If you want someone to change behavior, to digest and remember something, he has to think of it himself. The only way to get someone to accept an idea is to ask him a question and let him give the answer back to you.

COACHING WITH QUESTIONS

There are many situations, besides therapy, where the questioning approach can lead people to discover things for themselves. In some situations, both personal and professional, you might do well to take on the role of a coach. A coach's job is to encourage and educate. One of the most effective methods of coaching is to use feedback as your principal tool: you ask questions, and the person you're coaching feeds back information to you.

Coaching can be defined in many ways. It can be as informal as cheering from the sidelines or as formal as instructing in a workshop, but the principle remains the same. It is this feedback principle I used not long ago in a workshop I was conducting. Two participants, sitting in the back of the room, were chatting away during the first part of the morning. When we took a break, I approached the two people and said, "Excuse me, but I noticed that you two are having a conversation back here while I'm teaching."

My background as a high school teacher tempted me to follow that statement with another one—"Please stop talking. It is distracting me and disturbing everyone else!" That same high school background taught me that this lecturing tone would only cause the talkers to get defensive. So I chose instead to use a questioning approach. I asked, "How do you think your talking affects the other people in the seminar?" They both answered that they were sure it was annoying and distracting to everyone else. They promised to stop talking, and they did.

Here is another example. Ellen is a freelance writer who was having a problem with a client. This client, Donald, would set a time at which he would call Ellen to discuss their project, and then he would miss the appointment. After this happened twice, Ellen confronted Donald and told him that this was a problem, because she had arranged her schedule around their phone appointments. He apologized and said it would not happen again.

They arranged another appointment, and he again did not call. When Ellen called to see what had happened, Donald said, "Oh, I got busy. I didn't think you'd mind if I called later." Apparently, their previous conversation had gone in one ear and out the other.

The next time this happened, Ellen used the questioning approach:

ELLEN: Donald, we need to talk about missing these phone appointments. What do you think happens when you say you're going to call and then you don't?

DONALD: You probably get upset.

ELLEN: Is there anything else you think happens?

DONALD: You might have missed something important while waiting for my call, or perhaps you could have scheduled your day differently if you knew I wasn't going to call.

ELLEN: Yes, that is true. Is there anything we can do so that this doesn't happen anymore?

DONALD: I'm sure I can let you know early in the day if I have to change our appointment.

ELLEN: What time do you usually know how your day is going?

DONALD: Oh, I know by ten or ten-thirty. I could call you by ten-thirty and let you know if I have to cancel our appointment or change it to another time.

ELLEN: That's great.

Donald did change his behavior, and he called Ellen by 10:30 A.M. whenever he had to postpone their phone appointments.

This time, because Donald had come to his own conclusions, he was able to discover the consequences of his own actions, and to come up with a solution he was willing to follow.

PERSUASION IN SELLING

In the situation above, Ellen was actually selling Donald on the idea of giving her advance notice of changes in his schedule. Coaching, persuading, selling—these are all members of the same family. In all of these situations, the goal is to get the other person to see things from your perspective.

Selling has gotten a bad reputation over the years because of the old pitchman. A pitchman would try to convince customers that his products had benefits that didn't really exist. That is not what the art of persuasion is about. If there are no benefits for a customer, there should be no sale. What an honest salesperson tries to do is to get the customer to see the existing benefits for himself.

What is your main goal in making a sale? To get the other to person to buy? Yes and no. You want to sell your customer your product, but ultimately you want to create a relationship with your customer. Every sale that is made involves a relationship. No matter how brief the time spent on a sale, a bond is formed between the buyer and seller. The things we buy become more important to us when there is a real human being, and a real human relationship, behind them.

More important, most business is done on a repeat basis or through referrals. If you satisfactorily sell your customer a product she is happy with, she will either come back and buy from you again or she will refer someone to you. If you are lucky, she will do both.

Building a relationship with a customer means becoming aware of her needs, then matching up those needs with the benefits of your product or service. How do you do this? By asking questions to discover the explicit wants, needs, and desires of your customers.

The most effective way to make these discoveries is to start with broad, open-ended questions. In the pharmaceuticals industry, for example, you might ask about a particular issue that is relevant to the customer. If you were selling a drug for treating diabetes, you might ask, "Doctor, what are some of the issues you're facing with your patients who have diabetes?"

You want to find out if the doctor is experiencing any problems that you might be able to help him solve. Your next questions would then get more specific, and move from open-ended to more closed-ended questions. The next question might be: "That's interesting, doctor. What problems does that cause for you and for your patients?"

You might follow that with a question that would tell you more about how the problem affects the doctor: "Doctor, what are the ramifications of that problem for your practice?" You keep pointing until you hear clearly defined needs.

Then you ask questions that encourage the doctor to state the benefits he would like to see in a product, for example, "Doctor, what factors do you consider most important when choosing a specific drug to prescribe for your patients with diabetes?" When the doctor gives you the information, you can then state, "From what I understand, it sounds as though you need a product that is going to help reduce side effects for your patients, which will also reduce the number of times patients call your office. If I can go ahead and explain how my product will meet those needs, would you be open and willing in prescribing it?"

With those kinds of questions, you can get the customer to see the benefits for himself. Once he has stated the benefits, you will have a much easier time showing him how your product can help solve his problems.

This approach has been proven successful time and time again. The most successful salesperson who ever worked for Equitable Life Insurance sold more insurance than any other employee for more than twenty-five years. His approach was short and simple. Larry would sit down with prospective clients in their living room, lean in close to them, look them in the eyes, and say, "Tell me, why do you need life insurance?" They would tell him, and within no time, they had sold themselves a policy.

PERSUASION IN CHILD-REARING

We all lecture our children. "Be home by ten o'clock! Eat your spinach! Leave your brother alone!" Or, like my mother, "Clean your room!"

What is the reaction to this lecturing? Most children grumble and make excuses and try to get out of doing what they have been told to do. After a lot of bickering, someone gives up. Either the child gives up and cleans the room, or the mother gives up and cleans the room herself.

Everyone, and especially children, either consciously or subconsciously rebels against authority. Child-rearing guru Rudolf Dreikurs writes in *Children: The Challenge,* "If our attention is centered upon the needs of the situation rather than upon 'making him mind me,' we may discover ways to stimulate the child to respond." Dreikurs tells parents to let go of *demanding* and grab on to *winning* cooperation. This eliminates the power struggle that so many parents deal with in raising their children. Once the power struggle is gone, persuasion can work.

Persuasion through questioning with children is the same as it is with adults. The child needs to buy into the reasons behind your demands. You want your child to see the benefits of cleaning her room, not because you say so, but because she sees the benefits herself. If your child is staying out beyond his curfew, try asking, "What do you think happens when you stay out too late?"

Getting people to persuade themselves is not an easy process. Done poorly, it can seem condescending or manipulative. It takes practice. But it is worth the effort, because this is the most effective way to influence a permanent change in thought and behavior.

9

SELL, LEAD, THINK
===

Use Questions to Transform Your Organization

If you want people to think, you must get them to exercise their brains, not merely follow orders.

THE THINKING ORGANIZATION

One of today's most popular business misnomers is the notion of the *learning organization*. Widely popularized in the bestseller *The Fifth Discipline* and other writings by the management guru Peter Senge, the idea of the learning organization has captivated millions of businesspeople around the world because people want to feel they are continuously learning. Yet so far, few companies have devised practical ways to transform their corporate cultures to accommodate the new demand for continual learning, and even fewer have successfully managed such a transformation. The mission is a commendable one: to create an entity that is constantly absorbing information and

169

ideas and then finding ways to use them to improve the creativity, productivity, and strategic thinking of its people. The idea of the learning organization remains a pie in the sky for too many companies because they have no practical ways of accomplishing this mission.

My work as a business consultant, teaching companies about the power of questions, offers a more productive and practical alternative to the learning organization: the *thinking organization*. Too many businesses, and businesspeople, get caught up in automatic, rote patterns of behavior. They fail to think through the reasons, the implications, and the purposes behind their actions. As a result, when change occurs—as it inevitably does—companies and their employees are caught flat-footed, unready to respond except with the old solutions that are, almost by definition, inadequate for the new circumstances.

A company where asking questions is consciously, intentionally, and repeatedly encouraged—just as meeting sales targets and reaching profit goals are—is a company where thinking takes place. In such a company:

- Employees on the front lines, in sales and service, learn about the marketplace from the questions they ask customers.

- Middle managers constantly examine how the company's processes are succeeding or failing based on the questions they ask their staffers.

- Top managers keep tabs on the overall strategic health of the organization by the questions they ask employees at every level.

The result is a *virtuous cycle* of continuous feedback that raises the company's consciousness to new and ever-more-effective heights. This is what I mean when I talk about a thinking organization.

As you will see in this chapter, the power of questions can have a transforming effect on any organization. Questions can stimulate intellectual growth, turning a stagnant organization that is slowly losing ground to its competitors into a thinking organization that recognizes and understands trends and changes in time to take full advantage of them. Questions can dramatically improve the productivity of salespeople, jump-starting the sales growth that is so vital to the long-term survival and growth of any organization. And questions can increase the effectiveness of leaders at any level of an organization, enabling them to train, motivate, guide, and inspire employees to greater heights of achievement.

QUESTIONS AS A CATALYST FOR CHANGE

Several years ago I was approached by a partner in a mid-sized investment banking firm. He faced a problem that is a familiar one in today's business world. His company was made up of bright, talented people who knew their field and were dedicated and hard-working. However, the results they were achieving did not seem to measure up to their potential. Sales growth was lackluster, profits were stagnant, the staff in customer service spent much of their time fielding complaints, and employee morale was poor. It was a pattern of disappointing performance that might have been barely acceptable a generation ago but could only spell long-term disaster in today's intensely competitive climate.

The causes of the malaise were not obvious—if they were, they would have been fixed long ago. So we examined the various departments of the company and discussed the kinds of problems each was experiencing. We focused first on sales because sales is where business growth begins and where improvements can have the most immediate impact. As we studied the company, a pattern became clear. The employees had fallen into the dangerous habit of automatically using methods and procedures that had once been effective, but had now become outmoded—not dramatically so, but just enough to erode the company's competitive edge. As an organization, they had lost the instinctive urge to learn and to grow. The result: a sense of inertia and drift that pervaded the firm.

"Can the power of questions make a difference?" the partner asked me. We decided to find out.

Together with the management team, we developed a year-long plan for changing the corporate culture of the organization from one based on *telling* to one based on *asking*. The program was launched with a presentation by the partners in which they rallied his team behind the following challenge:

"As individuals get into patterns of communication, so do organizations. To break down the barriers within our organization, to outsell our competition, and to please our clients and customers, we must abandon our instinct to *tell*. We must ask better questions—questions that challenge our beliefs and make us think."

What followed was an intensive, year-long educational effort aimed at a reshaping of their corporate culture, using the power of questions as the organizing concept. We started with the company's management team, hoping that the leadership could set an example for the rest by using their newfound questioning skills. Ultimately, we included every employee in the firm, from the receptionists and customer service representatives to the all-important sales team. We used workshops, role-playing exercises, training sessions, and individual coaching. Our goal: to make everyone see *questions* as their primary communications tool.

Change came slowly at first. Management experts agree that a corporate culture is so intangible, so unconscious, and yet so pervasive that changing it is perhaps the most difficult challenge any company can face. Most of the employees were reluctant to change their communication style; after all, they had achieved a measure of success using their old approach, why should they change it now? Others, understandably, were skeptical; some viewed the power of questions as just another quick fix.

THE SALES TEAM LED THE WAY

The breakthrough came in the sales department. We had trained the sales managers in the use of questions especially carefully, having previously seen what the power of questions can do in the sales arena. We soon found that a few of the salespeople, those who had felt frustrated by their lack of success using traditional selling techniques, were willing to experiment with the power of questions. They began to use the techniques of what I call *Dialogue Selling*, a question-based sales methodology I will explain in detail later in this chapter. The results were immediate; in fact, their sales and commissions began to increase the very first week.

As you might imagine, word spread—first among the others in sales, then among the other departments. Little by little, the staff began to buy into the idea that asking questions can make a profound difference in our effectiveness as businesspeople—not only in selling, but in managing, building, and growing a company.

Nine months into our experiment, I received a phone call from my client. "Dorothy," he said with an audible smile in his voice, "I'm going to fax over the latest sales figures and other reports from my management team. I think you'll find them interesting."

I was astonished—and delighted. In the current quarter, company sales had increased by no less than 56 percent. The head of the customer service department reported that the backlog of complaints had been cleared up and replaced mainly with thank-you notes. And the human resources department reported a 37 percent decrease in employee turnover, saving the company millions in hiring and training costs.

I am happy to report this firm's improved performance continues to this day. Is the entire turnaround attributable to the power of questions? Perhaps not; maybe all we did with our training programs was establish some positive momentum for change, setting free the skills and energies that the talented staff had been eager to put to use. But I am convinced that refocusing the company's communication style around *asking* rather than *telling* was the catalyst for all the change that followed.

A QUESTION OF VALUES

It is easy for businesspeople to see the importance of creating a thinking organization. This is a difficult challenge, however. One reason is that the dominant mentality of today's corporate culture is one of telling, not asking. In most businesses, managers tell their employees to perform better, without asking questions that could help identify roadblocks to success and clarify misunderstandings as to the goals and objectives of the process. Team leaders run meetings with fixed agendas and little time for questions or open-ended discussion, thus stifling creativity. Salespeople tell customers why their product or service is best, without asking questions to determine the needs, interests, and concerns of the customers. And service staff tell clients what the company can and cannot do for them, without asking the clients what they want.

Am I exaggerating? No. My assessment is based on both what I've observed in most companies and what employees and managers report.

Furthermore, when business leaders praise the idea of open communication, it is often little more than lip service. Think of the last meeting you attended that was conducted under the auspices of a divisional vice president or other high-ranked business leader. How much real questioning of the leader's pronouncements took place? If tough questions were asked, how were they greeted—with openness, receptivity, and honesty, or with veiled or obvious hostility? In most businesses today, the latter response is all too common.

> **IQ** Leaders must rely on others within the business to raise questions that may indicate an impending adaptive challenge . . . . Thus, as a rule of thumb, when authority figures feel the reflexive urge to glare at or otherwise silence someone, they should resist . . . . One has to get accustomed to getting on the balcony, delaying the impulse, and asking, What *really* is this guy talking about? Is there something we're missing?
>
> —Ronald A. Heifetz and Donald L. Laurie, "The Work of Leadership," *Harvard Business Review,* January 1997

From a personal standpoint, this attitude is understandable. The business leader is privy to information those beneath him or her cannot share. He or she may enjoy a breadth of perspective that the rank-and-file employees do not have, which enables the leader to understand the necessity for decisions that might seem to others arbitrary, unfair, or shortsighted. Under such circumstances, the leader may resent having to answer questions that feel hostile or uninformed; the temptation is enormous to pull rank and shut off communication.

In the end, however, the followers, the leader, and the organization all suffer when a telling mentality wins out. The followers never receive the information that might enable them to understand their roles and fulfill them better; the leader loses the chance to gain valuable insights into the mind-set of his or her employees, anything that might be affecting their ability to carry out the mission. Consequently, the organization suffers from the resulting misunderstandings, resentments, and loss of morale that are inevitable.

Years ago, I worked in an advertising agency whose work included creating product catalogs for department stores. It was a time-consuming, detail-oriented job. One day the manager, Jerry, called an urgent staff meeting to address a nagging problem. Numerous small but embarrassing errors were persistently creeping into the catalogs—misspelled words, incorrect prices, mismatches between products and their descriptive copy, and the like.

Wisely, Jerry started the meeting with questions: "What's the reason for the errors in the catalogs we produce? What can we do to eliminate or at least minimize them?" No sooner was the question out of Jerry's mouth than the art director raised his hand and declared, "A big part of the problem is the time pressure we are under. We've had to hire a lot of temporary workers to help with the catalogs, and there's no time to train them properly. That leads to mistakes."

Jerry's response was an unfortunate one. He immediately told the art director, and everyone else in the room, "No, that's not it. You're absolutely wrong." The result? Jerry had effectively squelched the possibility that people in the company would ever again bother to ask smart questions or answer them with honesty and insight.

It is not enough to ask smart questions. You also must be prepared to listen to the answers. Lodewijk J. R. de Vink, chairman, president, and CEO of Warner-Lambert, puts it well: "Effective listening is the foundation from which to ask questions. Without it, questions may become merely hollow statements."

As Jerry's story illustrates, it takes time to build a questioning culture, but it can topple in an instant. Developing such a culture and sustaining it takes hard work, but the benefits are well worth it.

SIMPLE STEPS TOWARD A QUESTIONING CULTURE

Changing from a telling to a questioning mind-set must begin at the top. If employees do not see their managers and top executives using an open style of communication, including the power of questions, they will never adopt such a style themselves. Moreover, a company that wants to encourage questioning must also reward it. This can be done in a host of ways, some subtle, some obvious.

1. **Model the questioning culture.** Start with yourself. Whatever your role in your organization—whether you are a leader, a follower, or, like most people, a little of both—begin consciously to respond with positive body language and speech to the questions you are asked on the job. It is not easy to do this, especially when your first emotional reaction is anxiety, uncertainty, or anger. Slow down. Smile, repeat the question, and perhaps buy time with a friendly comment like, "Good question! Let me try to come up with a helpful answer." The more you model such positive responses to questioning, the more other people will feel encouraged to behave in the same way.

2. **Build questioning into every business activity.** Whether it is a formal or informal meeting, a sales call, a phone conference with a client, a presentation by human resources or management, or an announcement of good or bad news, allow time in your agenda for questions and encourage people to ask them.

3. **Create multiple platforms for asking and answering questions.** If your company or department newsletter does not have a question-and-answer page, create one— and encourage hard-hitting rather than softball ques-

tions. Why not offer two tickets to a show or a dinner out as a reward for each month's best question? Mount a question box by the watercooler, and post responses on the bulletin board nearby. For larger businesses it may be a good idea to create a company-wide telephone hot line or e-mail address for employee questions—the sensitive kind of worker may feel uncomfortable about asking in an open forum or in front of a supervisor. Consider appointing a corporate ombudsman to answer questions and troubleshoot when ordinary channels do not work. Have the CEO and others in top management hold periodic press conferences at which employees are encouraged to ask anything they wish. And, of course, use your company's web site to supplement all these forums.

I have seen the power of questions help to revitalize organizations of all kinds—including my own consulting businesses, Organizational Technologies and Theater for Learning. We have consciously created and implemented a company-wide system of questioning. It includes such features as a series of simple strategic questions to ask new clients, which helps us both to qualify them for our services and to identify their needs, concerns, and interests. It also includes the company-wide habit, by now deeply ingrained, of questioning one another to clarify anything we do not fully grasp. This system has saved us enormous amounts of time, energy, and money.

Here is a simple example. We recently needed to conduct a series of information-gathering interviews in which we would speak with a long list of businesspeople—some were current clients, and others were people we knew only indirectly. We devised a set of questions to ask and turned the management of the project over to a staffer—a bright and capable young woman who, fortunately, had been fully steeped in our question-based business culture. Before getting started, she asked me a host of intelligent questions, including the crucial one I had simply overlooked, "Do you want me to handle all these interviews the same way?" As soon as she asked me this, I recognized the magnitude of the public relations disaster her question had averted. While many of the businesspeople on the list would be happy to be interviewed by my young staffer, a few were longtime clients and friends who would have felt puzzled and perhaps even insulted to be approached by anyone other than the company president—me.

In a busy office, it is all too easy to issue instructions you think are clear and complete, but often they are not. Only a business culture that truly encourages questions can save you from your own mistakes.

As a general principle of business, then, the power of questions is essential to running any company. It is also crucial to many of the most important specific functions of your organization, starting with the most important function of all—selling.

> Confucius is reported to have said that if he were made ruler of the world the first thing he would do would be to fix the meaning of words, because action follows definition.
>
> —George A. Steiner, *A Step-by-Step Guide to Strategic Planning*

SELL BETTER—CHANGE YOUR DEFINITION

In business nothing happens until the sale is made. There is no such thing as a healthy business with anemic sales; and, almost any business problem can be alleviated by a healthy increase in sales.

Yet one of the most powerful tools for selling, the power of questions, is sadly neglected in sales training and management.

We tend to buy into the mythology of the salesperson with a suitcase and a smile, selling purely on the basis of personality, charm, and instincts. The assumption is that selling is a talent that cannot be taught, developed, or improved.

I have found that this assumption is false. I have worked with salespeople from some of the biggest and most successful businesses in the world as well as from small, entrepreneurial companies that are eager to grow. In the process, I have discovered that specific communication techniques characterize the most effective salespeople—techniques that can be analyzed, explained, taught, practiced, and improved. It is not necessary to guess what makes a great salesperson: we know. And the power of questions plays an important role.

Here's my definition of a sale:

A sale is a series of questions designed to uncover needs and wants, build relationships, and foster commitment.

As you can see from this definition, I consider questioning central to the art of selling. And people who embrace this definition will forever think and act differently in regard to selling. Yet, like other businesspeople, most salespeople have absorbed the dominant telling culture. This impairs their performance in measurable ways. To put it bluntly, the biggest problem with most salespeople is that they talk too much—they *tell* rather than *ask* their clients and customers. As a result, they turn people off, fail to gather essential information, and miss opportunities to build relationships, win allies, and make deals. The sales they do make come about through the sheer quality of their products and services, and their success rate is only a fraction of what it could be.

Later, when these salespeople graduate to the role of sales managers, they perpetuate the problem, understandably so, because they revert to the familiar habit of telling rather than asking. The organizations that employ them may end up spending millions on reengineering and other supposed panaceas in an often fruitless search for renewed profit. The real solution is often, simply, to sell more . . . which requires a fresh look at how salespeople talk with customers.

IQ Research has shown that successful salespeople ask up to 58 percent more questions than do unsuccessful ones.

—Peter McKennirey, sales training consultant

Changing from the customary telling mode to an asking mode can make any salesperson more effective. This works in a host of ways. Asking questions of a customer or prospects allows the salesperson to:

- Qualify the prospect by determining whether or not he has the need and the desire for your company's product or service.

- Learn about changes in the marketplace, including customer perceptions of your company and your competition.

- Easily uncover and respond to objections that may prevent a sale.

- Move more quickly and powerfully to close a potential deal.

Furthermore, a sales dialogue based on asking rather than telling holds out the potential of building a stronger personal connection between the salesperson and the customer. By asking questions, you learn about the customer's interests, needs, problems, desires, hopes, and fears—feelings to which you can respond with products and services of value. The simple act of the customer's responding to your questions creates a potential bond between the customer and you that, in time, can lead to a long-term, mutually beneficial business relationship.

Using an example from the financial services industry, Robert L. Shook, supersalesman and author of *It Takes a Prophet to Make a Profit*, describes the process this way:

A stockbroker connects with a client through questions that show he's not just interested in racking up a sale but really has an interest in the client. He will ask questions such as, "What are your investment objectives? Are you more interested in income or growth? What is the value of your current portfolio? When do you plan to retire? What kind of lifestyle you would like to have when you retire? What do you estimate you'll need in today's dollars to retire?" By asking questions like these and listening intently to the answers, you show your customer that you care. These questions also force the prospect to give you very personal answers. By answering them, he is committing himself to buying. Why? Because why else would a person tell you such personal information?

QUESTIONS CAN TRANSFORM YOUR SALESPEOPLE

It might seem strange that more professionals in the highly competitive world of selling have not already seized upon this simple secret and put it to work for them. But a significant obstacle for many salespeople in improving their questioning skills is a simple misperception of their current sales technique.

In my work as a sales training consultant, members of my team and I have tagged along on over a thousand actual sales calls. Many were recorded on audio- or videotape for later analysis. We wanted to learn exactly how this relatively successful and highly professional sales force was currently communicating with its customers. We discovered that salespeople who thought they were asking a lot of questions usually were not. When we played back the tapes and asked them to count the number of questions they had asked, they were often shocked by the results. Instead of asking eight or ten or twelve questions in the course of the conversation, as they recalled doing, they had really asked only one or two . . . then started telling instead. And once they started, they never stopped!

The same is true of salespeople at most companies. Most of them have a telling mentality, not an asking one. It is not easy to change. And the first obstacle is to understand and recognize the problem.

SELLING AND THE SEVEN POWERS

How can the seven powers of questions transform you into a more persuasive salesperson?

Power #1: Questions demand answers. One of the most basic yet thorny challenges faced by salespeople today is the difficulty of creating dialogue with customers and prospects. Everyone feels busier than ever; most people seem to be eager to end the sales call even before it gets started. If the salesperson uses her valuable time with the customer to deliver the latest canned sales pitch, the result will be glazed eyes and a quick end to the conversation.

Instead, ask questions. Simply by responding, the customer gives you a chance to react, to ask another question, to advance the dialogue. Result: involvement, a sense of connection, and psychological movement in the direction of a sale.

Note, however, that not just *any* question will work equally well. The better your question, the better the answer. It is important to have in mind a clear purpose for your question and ask it with sincerity and impact.

Power #2: Questions stimulate thinking. As important as you are, few sales calls begin with the customer focused on you and the product or service you offer. Most clients are distracted and harried by a dozen other responsibilities; you and your company are probably low on the agenda.

Asking questions is a way to break through this curtain of distraction. By asking questions about the customer's interests, problems, desires, and needs as they relate to the product or service you sell, you can open doors in your customer's mind.

Dale Moss, director of sales worldwide for British Airways, says it vividly: "Asking questions is a most intelligent method of learning for both the person asking the questions and the person being asked. It focuses on *thoughtful consideration*, which I'm certain spawns wonderfully creative and helpful thoughts." Thus, asking questions is a great way to establish a positive, thoughtful tone for the sales dialogue.

Power #3: Questions give us valuable information. By asking questions, you can learn about what is happening in the marketplace for your product or service: how customer needs, attitudes, and opinions are changing; how new competitors or new strategies from old competitors may be affecting your company's position; how trends in the economy and the society at large may influence your business's future. The information you gather simply as a salesperson imbued with the asking mentality may be more useful than the reams of data generated at high cost by elaborate market research studies.

Power #4: Questions put you in control. Every sales call has a definite goal, whether it is to close a deal, to strengthen a relationship, to resolve a complaint, or to increase a commitment. Asking questions is a powerful way to steer the dialogue, subtly and without manipulation, toward whatever your goal may be.

The person who asks the questions controls the sale.

—Sales adage

Power #5: Questions get people to open up. People love to talk about themselves. By asking questions, you show that you care—and not just about making a sale or earning a commission, but about providing your customers with a product or service that truly meets their needs and improves their lives.

By contrast, the person who talks all the time and never asks a question appears uncaring, uninterested, and self-involved—not the sort of person with whom we like to talk. Nor is this the kind of person from whom we want to buy.

Power #6: Questions lead to quality listening. As we have seen, most people need to do a better job of absorbing information, ideas, and feelings from those around them. Failure to listen with true attention is the cause of many misunderstandings, mistakes, and arguments. It is also the cause of much ineffective selling. Asking questions makes it possible to focus. If you go into every selling dialogue with a series of questions whose answers matter to you, and then you concentrate on really hearing, digesting, and interpreting the responses you receive, the amount you learn will grow exponentially—and so will your positive connections with your customers.

Power #7: Questions get people to persuade themselves. Decades' worth of overexposure to advertising—on TV and radio, in newspapers and magazines, on billboards, on the Internet, and now even in movies—has elevated the instinctive sales resistance of most people to all-time highs. No one wants to be talked into anything, and we all tend to stiffen when we sense that someone is trying to do that.

It is far more effective to get prospects and customers to *sell themselves* on the virtues of your product or service. The power of questions can help, as in this example:

Ted, a client of mine, recently converted his office communications system to a state-of-the-art and expensive new e-mail and voice mail system. As so often happens when a complex new technology is introduced, everyone in the office said they hated it. But when he asked them, "Would you like to go back to the old system?" they immediately responded, "No way!" So Ted followed up with another question, "Why not?" In answering him, they listed all the advantages of the new system— advantages they had overlooked while wrestling with the difficulties of the changeover from the old system, but which his question stimulated them to consider.

This is a perfect example of how asking questions can encourage people to persuade themselves. If Ted had tried to argue with his staff—to *talk* them into liking the new system— they would have argued back, and soon their resistance would have stiffened into permanent opposition. Asking questions had the opposite effect.

Always

Be

Conversing,

Clarifying,

Connecting, gaining

Commitment, and . . .

Closing!

I am convinced that salespeople need to ask more questions— in fact, they need to build their approach to selling around the power of questions. I refer to this strategy as *Dialogue Selling*. I have taught this strategy to sales staffs at some of the world's most successful companies, and I believe it is the wave of the future in selling. So do many of the clients with whom I've worked. A vice president of sales at AT&T, Bob Focazio, sums it up best: "If you increase your questions by only ten percent, you'll increase your sales and productivity by twenty percent." That's a good bargain in anyone's book.

Let's take a closer look at how the power of questions can help you through several phases of the selling process.

QUALIFY WITH QUALITY, CLOSE WITH QUANTITY

The first, and perhaps most essential, way of using questions in the selling process is in qualifying sales prospects. It is a truism of selling, but one that is so important it is worth repeating: Prospects who are qualified are always easier to close. The more you know about what your prospective customers need and want, and the more closely you can relate those needs and wants to the product or service you offer, the better your chances of selling. Asking questions is the best, and often the only, way to learn what the client really needs and wants.

I am drawing a distinction between *needs* and *wants*. It may be possible to assume, perhaps accurately, what the customer needs. If you are a car dealer, you can assume, when Karen walks through your showroom door, that she *needs* wheels to get around, to transport her family, and to carry the occasional bag of groceries or suitcase. But you can never know what Karen *wants* in a car without asking her! And it is her wants that will determine whether Karen buys an S.U.V., a tiny two-door model that gets great gas mileage, or a luxury sports car with all the trimmings.

Whenever you meet a new customer or prospect, become a detective. Make it your business to learn all you can about his or her background, values, interests, biases, experiences, worries, dreams, fears, and goals. Learn to pick up on clues of every sort: dress, language, demeanor. And, above all, ask questions—lots of questions. This applies to selling both products and services, big or small. The more you can get the prospect to talk, the better your chances of qualifying him or her accurately, and the better the odds of a sale. In fact, many sales experts say that qualified prospects are at least 50 percent easier to close.

In qualifying, we do need to ask a few closed-ended questions, but the greater emphasis should be on open-ended questions—getting your client to talk. Closed-ended questions should be used minimally during the sale. The reason so many salespeople use them is because they are the simplest kind of question. In fact, open-ended questions can get you the information you need and much more. The *real* purpose of probing in selling is not only to get information, but to get your clients to think. Here is an example of how one open-ended question can replace several closed-ended questions and still give you all the information you need. The typical auto dealer who has just met Karen might use such closed-ended questions as, "Do you drive a domestic or imported car right now? How many children do you have? Do you drive mainly in the city or on the highway? Would you like a two-door or a four-door? What color are you looking for?" But we want you to be better than typical. This open-ended question gets you that information and more: "What do you need and want in a car?"

Traditional open-ended questions are a great tool that every salesperson should use. But even more powerful is a special kind of open-ended question I call the *Super Probe*: "Can you describe for me how your buying habits have changed in the last two years?"

What makes this question so powerful? Super Probes are open-ended questions that are *directive* rather than *general*. They tend to produce thoughtful, careful, detailed responses. Notice how the specific wording of the question above guides the prospect to explain quite *precisely* not only how he makes purchasing decisions but also how his habits have changed over a specifically defined period of time—the last two years. The answer will paint for the sales rep a very clear portrait of the prospect's buying profile and how it is evolving, vital information that can be of enormous help in guiding the client toward your product or service.

In crafting Super Probes for use in your own selling dialogues, do not use the traditional question words *who, what, where, when, why, and how*. Instead, use words like *explore, describe, investigate, analyze, illustrate, illuminate, decode, inspect, unearth,* and *translate* to get your client to *explain* himself. Alternatively, use phrases like *walk me through, unravel the mystery, shed light upon,* and *hunt down.* Or, to ask your customer to explain the similarities and differences between things, use comparison words like *compare, contrast, weigh, correlate, differentiate,* and *distinguish.*

Here are two Super Probes the car dealer might use with Karen: "Tell me what you like and don't like about the car you're driving now and how that will impact what you're going to buy," or "Compare the car you're driving now with the car of your dreams, and describe the differences to me."

Notice that many Super Probes are not questions in the traditional sense—they do not end in question marks, for example. As we have seen, *implied* questions may be just as powerful as *explicit* questions, if not more so.

The beauty of the Super Probe is that it challenges the client or customer in a stimulating, interesting way. If you engage your customer intellectually and emotionally, you will get him or her to spend more time with you. These questions force your client to think, and, because they are more interesting, they provoke more honest and meaningful answers. Finally, they help you stand out from other salespeople who ask more routine questions, encouraging your client to see you in a different light—as more intelligent, thoughtful, and caring.

Suggestion: If your job includes selling, set aside time to develop five Super Probes that are appropriate for you to use with your clients, customers, and prospects. Then try them out on the job next week. I'll bet your selling dialogues will be more interesting and fruitful than ever before.

AN OBJECTION IS AN UNANSWERED QUESTION

As every salesperson knows, even when you are armed with a thorough knowledge of your customer and her needs, the road to a sale is rarely free of potholes.

One of the continual challenges faced by salespeople is resistance from the customer who, for reasons good or bad, is unwilling to follow where you want to lead him or her—toward a sale. The power of questions can help here, too. The secret is a simple one: Treat objections as unanswered questions. Act as if the customer has asked you a question rather than given you a statement of rejection. Restate it in question form if you like. Then respond to the question posed, as in these examples:

PROSPECTIVE CLIENT: Your product really isn't any different from anything else on the market.

SALESPERSON: It seems you are asking what really makes our product unique. Is that correct? Then let me explain. . . .

PROSPECTIVE CLIENT: Your product is too expensive.

SALESPERSON: I guess you're wondering why our product is worth a slightly higher price than the competition's. Am I right? The reason is . . .

PROSPECTIVE CLIENT: Your product is too complicated to use.

SALESPERSON: Perhaps you want to know what training is available to help you easily use all the outstanding product features. Would that address your concern? Here's what we provide. . . .

Get the idea? Notice how reframing the objection in the form of a question accomplishes several objectives: It eliminates the emotional component—the sense of personal rejection that might tempt you to respond defensively or angrily. It places you in the position of helpfully answering a legitimate question rather than rebutting an unfair accusation. And it shifts the focus from the negative (the objection) to the positive (your response to the question). This way the exchange moves the selling dialogue forward, toward a sale, rather than stalling it in a tug-of-war between opposed points of view.

Part of the Dialogue Selling program is the 6-Step Objection Handling Process. Here's how it works:

1. **Be an active listener.** Let the prospect know that you hear and understand his or her concerns, and thank him or her for expressing them.

2. **Ask the prospect to explain her concerns.** Use probing questions to unearth as many details as needed to make sure you fully understand the concern being raised. And use self-questions: Ask yourself, "Do I fully understand the problem?" Do not proceed until you do.

3. **Isolate the objection.** Find out whether the issue you have unearthed is the only or main concern. You want to discover any hidden concerns, any unanswered questions, that may prevent the prospect from buying.

4. **Set up ground rules.** Ask the prospect if he or she will agree to go ahead if her question is answered.

5. **Answer the question with benefits.** Respond to the question by showing how some feature of your product or service will meet one or more of your prospect's needs or wants. The more fully you can tie your product or service into the prospect's needs, the fewer objections you will hear. One of the great benefits of questions in selling is that it sets up your benefit presentation. By ferreting out not only the objectives, but the real needs and wants, you can be sure your presentation falls on eager ears, rather than disinterested ones.

6. **Confirm the answer.** Make sure you have answered the question with no misunderstandings. Ask, "Have I answered your question fully?"

This last step is perhaps the most often neglected question of all. We have become so accustomed to the culture of *telling* that it is easy to forget the importance of *asking* to make sure our message has been received. Get into the habit of asking confirming questions, and remind yourself of their importance constantly.

Once you have completed all six steps of this process, you can move on to a good closing question. Take advantage of the forward momentum achieved in responding to the objection by pushing toward a sale. Use a closing question to give your prospect the opportunity to buy.

> **IQ** My most effective questions were when anyone disagreed with me. I would simply say, "Obviously you have a reason for saying that. Would you mind sharing it with me?" It's a nice way to say, "Hey, I'm not disagreeing — but tell me more." I've made all my salespeople learn to use that question.
>
> —Tom Hopkins, master sales trainer and author of *How to Master the Art of Selling*

USING QUESTIONS TO CLOSE THE DEAL

Of course, every aspect of Dialogue Selling that we have discussed so far leads to the same ultimate objective: making a sale. Here is where the greatest benefit of asking questions comes into play. *Salespeople who ask more closing questions close more deals.* Get into the habit of asking every prospect at least five closing questions. If you do, you will find that the number of sales you make will rise steadily.

Building your closing routine around questions has an additional benefit. Many salespeople find that this method of closing reduces the sense of anxiety they formerly had about the moment of truth. In fact, moving to the close can even become *fun* for the salesperson who uses questioning as the primary tool.

My research shows that most salespeople ask too many closed-ended questions in the sale. But when it comes time for the close, they become tentative. Even the valiant falter. The best place for closed-ended questions are . . . at the close! I once hired a young woman, an aspiring artist, to try her hand at selling for my organization. Kathy had no experience in sales, but she was personable, smart, and eager to learn—so much so, in fact, that she absorbed my sales techniques and followed them to the letter. Among my other lessons, she took to heart my admonition to use at least five closing questions during every sales call. Actually, she developed her own system for keeping score of her closing questions: Each time she asked one, she would draw a little circle on the page in her notepad. Invariably, she reported, by the time she'd drawn the fifth circle, a sale would have been made!

Perhaps I trained Kathy *too* well. In her first six months, Kathy chalked up more sales than anyone I had ever employed. But then she came to me and, a bit apologetically, declared, "You know, I'm having so much fun selling—and I've gotten so good at it—that I've decided to apply my new skills to my artistic career." Kathy left my company and started using the power of questions to sell her artwork. Today she has a thriving studio, and she's still using an array of powerful closing questions to garner high prices for her paintings.

As a salesperson, you must be the judge as to how and when to move toward the close. Many factors affect this important issue of timing: the nature of your relationship with the customer, the tone of the dialogue, the urgency of the customer's needs, financial considerations, and so on.

You may feel uncertain as to whether the prospect is ready to make a purchase. If so, you can gauge his readiness by using test closing questions. These are designed to measure whether or not the prospect understands and accepts the ideas you have shared with him, how his thoughts and feelings may or may not have changed as a result of the dialogue, and whether factors you don't yet know about may be affecting his readiness to take action. Here are some sample test closing questions to try:

- Of all we have talked about today, what has been the most helpful to you?

- Would you share your thoughts with me about the things we have discussed?

- Of what we have discussed today, what has made the most sense to you?

The answers to questions like these will tell you whether there are fresh objections to be dealt with or whether the prospect is ready to be moved toward a closing question.

You will want to have a variety of closing questions in your sales arsenal. Remember, the most effective salespeople use several closing questions at various stages of the selling dialogue, so to avoid sounding monotonous or stale, you should prepare a number of alternative questions to use. Here are a few to try:

- Is it a deal?

- How much more of our product will you be using?

- Will you recommend our product to your committee for final approval?

- Can we agree on a contract now?

Of course, for most salespeople, one successful sales call is not enough. Follow-up is a crucial part of the long-term selling process. Use the power of questions to build an effective, ever-growing *sales relationship* with your customers.

PROBING THE MIND OF THE MARKET

I can still recall the worry and frustration in the voice of the sales director. He had called me in to help retrain his salespeople. The problem? Lack of sales growth, of course. But there was a more specific cause we had already pinpointed: failure of the sales force to recognize changes in the marketplace. "I want my salespeople to *understand* their clients' businesses," the sales director exclaimed. "How can they sell effectively otherwise?"

It is an all-too-common complaint. The single greatest obstacle to success for most companies is a lack of accurate knowledge about the marketplace. Think of any of the great business blunders of recent decades, from the launch of New Coke to the handheld Apple Newton to the collossal box-office bomb *Waterworld*. Somewhere near the heart of each of these fiascos was a fundamental misunderstanding of what customers want. On a smaller scale, similar missteps happen every day—largely a result of the failure of salespeople to *ask questions*.

To avoid such problems, market research was invented, and high-priced consulting firms were formed to provide it. Today, market research is a billion-dollar industry employing thousands of people whose sole job is to look inside the minds of customers and interpret what they find for the benefit of businesses.

Market researchers have developed a host of specific tools for carrying out this job, including written questionnaires, telephone surveys, focus groups, and one-on-one interviews. They have developed quasi-scientific methods for testing new products and services, including test marketing in limited geographic

areas and testing offers via direct-mail and Internet advertising.
They are masters of statistical and psychological analysis.

When all of these tools are deployed with skill, intelligence,
and common sense, the results can be valuable. They can also
be misleading and downright disastrous. Almost every modern
marketing fiasco you can think of, back to the Edsel, was sup-
ported by three-ring binders full of research data that suppos-
edly guaranteed success. Market research is also extremely
expensive and comes with no guarantees.

Make no mistake, I am not opposed to market research. But
before your company spends big bucks on outside consultants,
or establishes its own in-house research capability, make sure
that you are taking full advantage of what can be learned about
the marketplace simply by asking questions. After all, your sales
force is out there every day, speaking with those who make up
your prime marketplace—your clients and customers, your sales
prospects, and your potential customers who currently buy
from the competition. Are your salespeople using that opportunity to gather information about trends, issues, changes, concerns, needs, and opportunities that exist in the marketplace?
And is there a system in place for collecting the information they
gather, distilling it, and sharing it with others in the company?
If not, why not?

The power of questions that you have learned to employ
throughout this book applies in spades to the market intelligence function. And if you do decide to supplement the efforts
of your own staff by hiring specialists to conduct particular market research programs, make sure that those you hire have true
expertise in the art of asking questions. Many market researchers
do not, as indicated by the fact that they generally fail to probe
deeply enough, beginning with a failure to engage with their
clients at a deep enough level of insight and understanding.

A client told me a story about an experience her company
had in hiring a market research firm to poll teenagers about a
new product under development. The consultants met with the

client firm and duly designed a survey to elicit reactions and feelings about the new product. But they never thought to ask their client the simple question, "*Which* teenagers are you interested in?" Fortunately, my client saw the survey questionnaire before the work was done, and she caught the mistake; the researchers had planned a costly survey to include both boys and girls, although the clients were interested in reaching females only!

Develop your own market research capabilities by tapping the power of questions, especially using your own salespeople as the front line in the marketplace. It is a far more cost-effective way of connecting with your customers than via long-distance polling. As Tamar Howson, senior vice president and director of business development for SmithKline Beecham, suggests, "asking questions of your customers and prospects allows you to gather valuable market research into company perceptions, strengths and weaknesses, competitive advantages and disadvantages, usually for free or at relatively low cost."

IQ What do I get from asking questions? The ability to quickly learn what others have learned already, so as not to reinvent the wheel. Smart questioning also shows me the roadblocks ahead and helps me identify the road map to my future. In the end, I often get *more* information than I need to make a sound decision.

—Douglas W. Melton, president,
All Professional Integrated Solutions

The only thing that can stop you from gaining valuable insights through your own questions is the danger of complacency. Experienced salespeople, like businesspeople in every functional area, find it easy to stop learning and to take for granted that the lessons they learned in the past will remain applicable forever. Dale Moss of British Airways puts it well:

"The big trap for all successful salespeople is that, after a period of time, they think they know their clients completely. The questions stop, and the dissonance begins . . . small at first, profound in the end. How can you have accurate data without 'refreshing the files?' The best tool is still the artful use of smart questions."

If you are a salesperson, remind yourself constantly to look for fresh information about your customers by asking questions. If you are a sales manager, make asking questions a key part of the process by which you train, evaluate, and reward your salespeople. Increased sales and profits will follow.

EVERYONE IS A SALESPERSON

As you have seen, the power of questions can have a huge impact in the area of selling. In many of the organizations I have served as a consultant, the sales impact of questions has been enough in and of itself to convert the entire organization to the benefits of an asking culture.

Furthermore, the techniques for using questions in selling are widely applicable to other areas of business. After all, every businessperson sometimes functions as a salesperson, whether literally or figuratively. You are a salesperson whenever you represent your organization in public, whenever you have to persuade one person or many to adapt your point of view, whenever you seek to lead a group toward a goal of your choosing. So everyone in business should master the concept of Dialogue Selling; it is a powerful tool that belongs in everyone's kit.

THE LEADERSHIP POWER OF QUESTIONS

The power of questions extends to every aspect of organizational leadership. Here are some key questions you can use to guarantee your organization is on a solid leadership track: Do our top leaders articulate a clear vision of the future? Are we continuously developing our leadership pool? Do we have strong, cohesive teams? Are we able to manage change effectively and with full organizational support?

Human beings—their needs, interests, strengths, and weaknesses—are at the core of every business function, and effective communication between and among people is crucial to making those functions operate efficiently. Therefore, the power of questions as a tool for communicating affects every business function; and anyone who hopes to lead any type of organization successfully had better master the art of asking.

> Better managers tend to ask better questions.
>
> —Lodewijk J. R. de Vink, president, chairman,
> and CEO of Warner-Lambert

There are many distinct business functions in which the powers of questions play a crucial role. They include the hiring process; training, coaching, and mentoring; conducting meetings; and creative problem-solving. A sure way to transform your organization is to make questioning skills part of your hiring process and training strategy. To give them full validation, include questions as a separate category in your performance reviews, forms, and interviews. You cannot expect your people to focus on questions unless the organization values them, rewards them, and gives them visibility.

HIRE PEOPLE WHO ASK QUESTIONS: FORCE THEM TO THINK

I have talked about the importance of transforming the traditional *telling* culture of most businesses into an *asking* culture. One of the best ways to create an asking culture is to start by hiring people who know how to ask smart questions. And the best way to hire smart askers is to ask smart questions during the hiring process.

Of course, the traditional job interview is built around a question-and-answer dialogue; in that sense, it is one of the few business functions in which the power of questions already gets its due. But I am speaking here about more than your own use of smart questioning techniques when interviewing job candidates. I am recommending that your interviews consciously focus, in part, on the candidate's ability to use questions effectively on the job.

Having a set of questions that probe deep into the candidate's questioning abilities and thinking skills will result in your finding more qualified candidates. Ask the candidate to describe how he or she handles work problems, and listen carefully to how the candidate handles your question. Does he or she *ask* you what type of work problem you want him or her to focus on? Has he or she *clarified* any ambiguities before she begins her description? Does he or she define the problem by *asking* what it is? Does he or she *ask* others for their ideas about a solution? Does he or she *question* the old ways of solving the problem? Does he or she *ask* whether there are deeper underlying issues that could be causing the problems? These are all-important factors in how a candidate solves problems. If the candidate's problem-solving efforts begin with probing questions, he or she is probably an effective asker; if not, the candidate may be prone to leaping into action based on nothing more than assumptions, which may or may not be accurate. That way lies disaster.

To elicit the most detailed, specific, and revealing responses to your interview questions, use the questioning techniques we have discussed in this book. Open-ended questions will generally provoke more interesting responses than closed-ended ones. Super Probes can work well in the job interview; rather than starting questions with the traditional *who, what, when, where,* and *why,* try using *describe, explain,* and similar words, like this:

- Tell me about an important presentation you recently made, and explain how you prepared for it.

- Walk me through a typical day on your last job, and explore some of the problems you might face.

- Can you compare for me the best and the worst bosses you've worked for, describing their similarities and differences?

Also take note of the questions the candidate asks *you* during the interview. Look for candidates who ask questions that clarify, probe, and provoke thought. The more curious the candidate is, the better for your company. Curiosity may have killed the cat, but it will boost an employee's productivity.

INFLUENCING BEHAVIOR: TRAINING AND MENTORING

Businesspeople sometimes think of training as discrete functions handled by specialized staff members—outside consultants, perhaps, or the people in the human resources department. In reality, however, training, coaching, and mentoring—three variations on the theme of teaching—are basic tasks of every manager. Whenever you comment on the work of a subordinate, lead a meeting in which some new procedure or policy is explained, or sit down with a staff member to discuss her career track and offer some advice about her future, you are acting as a trainer, coach, or mentor. A thinking organization, by definition, is one in which knowledge is shared rapidly, efficiently, and intelligently among employees. Therefore, a mastery of the basic techniques of training is important for every manager.

Questions Are the Catalyst

As it happens, much of my business career has been devoted to the training function, so I have given quite a bit of thought to the role of questions in training. The fact is that questions are crucial to every stage of the training process. A question is the catalyst that sparks thinking, motivation, and application. Consider, for example, the first stage, often referred to as the needs analysis. This is simply the step in which you as the trainer determine what needs to be taught. It may be a formal stage, involving employee surveys, interviews, and meetings; it may be very informal, involving no more than a question or two during a routine staff get-together. In any case, the initial needs analysis requires the use of specific, thought-provoking questions. I have seen all too many companies waste millions of dollars on training that was ill-conceived or poorly executed simply because of a failure to ask smart questions beforehand.

Thus, rather than asking in a general way, "What kind of training do you need in using the new project-tracking forms?" you should ask such specific questions as, "Which parts of the forms are familiar to you? What parts are new to you? Can you list any words used on the forms whose meaning isn't clear? Where would you go to gather the information needed to complete the forms? Can you explain the system for routing and checking the forms after you have completed them?" and so on. The answers to questions like these will tell you how to prepare a working session with your staff that will be truly informative and useful.

Interviewing only one or two people during the needs analysis may also be a costly mistake. In many cases, employees at several levels and in several areas of the company must be interviewed to determine what training is needed: the people to be trained, their managers, the others in the company with whom they interact, and perhaps the end users—customers or clients. For example, suppose your company has adopted a new telephone and software system for handling customer service inquiries. You are involved in planning a day-long session to get everyone in the customer service department up to speed on using the new system. In planning what to cover during that session and how to cover it, don't speak only to a few customer service staffers. Also speak to the telephone operators who will route the calls, the sales reps and retail managers who will be referring customers to the customer service department, and even a selection of typical customers who have had occasion to use the old system. You will learn a lot from these interviews, and you will be prepared to develop a training program that will head off problems you would otherwise never have anticipated.

Of course, maintain an asking mentality during the actual training sessions as well. Using questions to drive, direct, and focus the discussion keeps trainees involved and learning, while a straight lecture is boring and uninvolving. For most managers, this skill doesn't come automatically, it takes deliberate planning. When you are preparing any kind of training, coaching, or teaching meeting, your preparation should include developing a list of specific, mainly open-ended questions with which to keep the discussion free-flowing and lively. And, as always, it is crucial to really *listen* to the answers. You may find the session moving in a direction you didn't anticipate; a problem you never dreamed of may turn out to be of vital importance, while other areas you assumed were problematic may not be. Remain open to these possibilities, and respond to the needs of those you are training. After all, if your teaching has not worked for *them*, it has not worked at all.

Specific questions, remember, get people to think: "How would you compare the first time we launched a product to how we are doing it today?" or "How would you contrast our competitors' advertising and marketing strategy to ours?" or "If you had to prioritize the steps in preparing a meeting, what would your list look like?"

Finally, asking questions when the training session is over is equally important. Leave enough time at the end of the meeting to ask questions such as: "What did you learn today?" or "Can you summarize for the group the most important points we have covered?" or "Can you give me three specific examples of how you can use what you have learned?" These questions will serve as an evaluation of your training, from which you will learn exactly how effective you have really been as a trainer. These questions also reinforce the training. It is okay for the trainer to summarize the lessons at the end of the session, but when the trainees summarize the lessons themselves, they are much more likely to retain and use those lessons on the job.

Even more important than the individual growth and change as a result of training is the impact on the organization. At the conclusion of training, the following questions will keep you focused on the main purpose of training—to improve the organization: How specifically will this training benefit the organization? How will we measure the results? How will we determine if this training was worth our investment?

THE ART OF MENTORING

A word about mentoring, which can be described as a kind of one-on-one career coaching process. I am pleased to see that more and more companies are recognizing the value of mentoring as a tool for developing leadership talent. Many are creating formal or informal mentoring programs, in which executives are paired up with younger managers to provide ongoing guidance, advice, and help. It's an extraordinarily useful technique when it is done properly.

The mentoring process, I have found, is often modeled on the therapist/patient relationship. That is, the mentee seeks out the mentor when a career, work, or management problem is too difficult to solve alone. The mentoring session that follows generally consists of the mentee describing the problem to the mentor, who dispenses advice and guidance according to his best lights. It is not unlike the therapeutic relationship between a client and a therapist or counselor.

The problem is that few mentors have a deep understanding of how an effective therapeutic relationship is developed. Mentors are usually busy, often high-level executives whose instinctive tendency is to jump quickly into problem-solving mode: "I had the same problem ten years ago, and here's what you have to do. . . ."

Thus, they tend to give advice without adequately drawing out the mentee. The advice may or may not be appropriate for the underlying problem. Even if it is appropriate, it may not be fully understood or accepted by the mentee because it feels imposed from on high rather than developed jointly and collaboratively.

If you find yourself in a formal or informal mentoring role, try to avoid snap answers. Start with questions instead—preferably open-ended questions or Super Probes—designed to elicit a thorough, detailed exploration of the problem and its causes:

- Can you walk me through the problem—how it started and how it got to this point?

- Outline for me what you have done to deal with the problem so far? How has that worked?

- Have you ever seen or dealt with a similar problem? What happened in that case?

- Prioritize the main obstacles you seem to be facing.

- Which options have you considered? What are the advantages and disadvantages of each?

- Describe how your thoughts and feelings would change if you were on the opposite side in this problem. Does that suggest any steps you might consider?

The resulting discussion will often lead the mentee to solve his or her own problem, and the solution will be one he or she will own—having helped to create it independently.

Furthermore, in the process you will learn a lot about your mentee's reasoning skills, his or her mental thoroughness and maturity. This knowledge can be used both for his or her good and for the good of the organization, in helping to identify the next appropriate step on the mentee's career ladder. It will also help your organization develop thinking, focused executives and staff.

LEARN TO LOVE MEETINGS

Meetings seem to be the bane of contemporary business. Ask any group of businesspeople, "Would you like your organization to hold *more* meetings or *fewer?*" and the answers you will get will be highly one-sided. The common refrain is, "Why can't we eliminate some of these meetings and leave more time for our *real* work?"

Of course, meetings are unavoidable. Any business department that consists of more than two people must occasionally bring all the members of the team together, if for no other reason than to establish a feeling of community. It's impossible to create a coherent sense of the organizational mission without occasionally getting "the whole system in the room." Most people understand this, and so they accept the necessity for meetings—albeit grudgingly.

However, most business meetings can and should be far more productive, interesting, creative, and brief than they are. In fact, learning how to run a truly useful meeting is one of the most important tools for any leader. One of the great values of meetings is that they show, as usual, that the power of questions can help.

1. **Build meetings around answering questions rather than imparting information.** It is rarely necessary to have a meeting simply to make announcements or relate news. Memos, e-mail, the telephone, the company newsletter, and the bulletin board are better venues for one-way communication. If all you want to do is to tell people something, do not waste their time with a meeting.

2. **Use questions to involve everyone in planning the meeting.** When a meeting is truly necessary, get the "buy-in" of those who will participate by having them develop the agenda. Before the meeting, circulate a memo naming the topic for the meeting and asking, "What are the questions you feel we should answer in this meeting?" and, "What questions do you have about the topic of this meeting?" These questions will start the meeting off well by stimulating prior thought, encouraging participation, and sending the message, "We care what you think." Of course, for this to work, you must genuinely pay attention to the responses! If you don't, the *next* time you ask those questions, you'll get no responses at all.

3. **During the meeting, ask more than you tell.** Nothing is more off-putting than a meeting in which one person, usually the manager or presenter, does all the talking, while the audience does all the listening. If you have ever conducted such a meeting, you have probably found that half the attendees never heard or absorbed some of the crucial information presented. "Don't you remember? I talked about that in our last meeting!" It is frustrating, but understandable; most people's eyes glaze over at a barrage of one-way communication. Thus, using questions to drive discussion in a meeting is more than just smart management; it is the *only* way to ensure the attention of your attendees. The American Management Association is one of the nation's leading developers of effective and engaging meetings. I have found its list of great questions for guiding and stimulating meetings extremely helpful. Here is a slightly adapted version of that list for your use in your next meeting:

- To call attention to a problem or a situation: "Why do you think John found it difficult to accept this change?"

- To get information: "What is the difference between staff and line?"

- To uncover causes or relationships: "How does quality control affect this problem?"

- To develop new ideas: "How else can we increase motivation in this department?"

- To test ideas: "Suppose we did it this way, what would happen?"

- To keep discussion to the point: "Can we go back to the problem of Trish's absenteeism?"

- To summarize or end a discussion: "What is the major point that's been made here?"

- To direct attention to another phase of the subject: "What about Ben? What was his responsibility for the mix-up?"

- To bring out opinions and attitudes: "How would you feel if you were confronted by this sudden change?"

- To achieve a conclusion or agreement: "Can we say this represents our own thinking?"

- To bring out reactions to a point made by another person: "How do the rest of you feel about Rachel's point?"

- To suggest an action, idea, or decision: "What do you think the results would be if Barbara told her boss he's made a mistake?"

- To advance a discussion logically: "What is the next step to make certain this proposal will be carried out?"

- To broaden a discussion: "What other factors are important besides the ones we have mentioned?"

- To help explore all sides of a problem: "What are other possible opinions and options in this dispute?"

4. **At the end of the meeting, ask postanalysis questions.** This is perhaps the most often overlooked function of questions related to meetings. If you want to avoid such all-too-common reactions as, "What was the point of that meeting?" do not end the meeting until you have asked one or more questions designed to test the effectiveness of the meeting. Here are some examples to try:

- Did we answer the questions we set out to answer?

- Have any new questions arisen as a result of this meeting? If so, what are we going to do about them?

- What is everyone going to do as a result of this meeting?

- Did everyone get to have their say without interruptions and as fairly as possible?

- In what ways was this meeting valuable to you? In what ways wasn't it?

- Is there anything else we need to discuss about this issue?

- What are the questions we need to ask and answer before we take the next step?

If you make use of all these techniques, you and your staff members may not look forward to your next meeting, but the sense of dread surrounding meetings will surely be greatly diminished!

If you want to learn how an employee thinks, how he handles stress, how much he plans and prepares, how well he speaks, how he deals with difficult people, ask him to run a meeting. You will learn a great deal about his poise, maturity, self-confidence, and leadership skills by watching him handle the issues and challenges as they arise, and so will he.

ON-THE-JOB CREATIVITY AND THE POWER OF QUESTIONS

Creativity is a much-sought but elusive business goal. How do we stimulate creativity? Where do great ideas come from? What makes some people continually creative—the Edisons, Einsteins, and da Vincis—while others rarely reach those heights? These are mysteries no one has solved.

Nonetheless, there are specific techniques that businesspeople can use to provoke greater creativity and to channel it in productive directions. The best-known and most successful is probably brainstorming, an open-ended way of exploring a topic, issue, or problem in a group forum that is designed to generate a large number of ideas—some irrelevant or foolish, some original and clever.

1. **Note that brainstorming and creative thinking are more likely to flourish in an organization that encourages an asking culture.** Employees who know that they will not be criticized or made fun of for asking "dumb" questions are more likely to participate enthusiastically in brainstorming exercises, offering the kinds of "silly" ideas that may not represent solutions in themselves but may stimulate other ideas that prove to be invaluable. You won't evoke a sense of freewheeling creativity in an uptight, telling-based organization just by standing at a white board and asking people to brainstorm. It is important to create a foundation for *everyday creativity* by encouraging questions constantly—not just on brainstorming day.

2. **When you do schedule a designated brainstorming session, use the power of questions to stimulate the flow of creativity.** In my experience, it is best to make these questions as specific as possible in order to generate ideas that are both concrete and relevant to the topic at hand. For example, suppose you've gathered your team to brainstorm ways of improving your company's customer service function. It could be either a freestanding brainstorming exercise or a brief, ten-minute session within a larger problem-solving meeting; the process would be similar in either case. Here are some possible start-up questions to use during the session. Note how they are designed to become increasingly specific and focused:

- How can we improve our customer service?

- How can we become number one in customer service?

- What is the competition doing in the area of customer service that we haven't yet tried?

- What is being done in customer service in industries other than our own?

- What are the most common complaints we're hearing from our customers? What are the most common requests?

- What is the most we can do for our customers? What can we do to surprise, please, and delight our customers?

- If we were customers of our own company, what would we expect and what would we want?

If you are leading the brainstorming session, prepare a list of ten to twenty such questions to prime the pump as needed throughout the discussion. The more specific the questions, the better the results. And, as always, *really listen* to the answers. Be prepared to follow the conversation down unexpected byways, even if they appear irrelevant at first. Then jump in with the question, "How does this relate to the problem of customer service?" A surprising, and fruitful, connection may leap out.

> **IQ** I like to use three kinds of questions when I work on strategic planning with companies. One kind is *fact-finding* questions, about where you are and what's happened already. A second kind is *feeling-finding* questions, which let you check in with your emotional self—measuring fear, distress, euphoria, and other reactions that affect how you handle decisions. And the third kind is *future-finding* questions, such as "What would this company look like if it were perfect? And how can we get from here to there?"
>
> —Larry Wilson, founder and vice chairman, Pecos River Division, AON Consulting

3. **When evaluating the ideas that have emerged from brainstorming—a secondary phase of the brainstorming process—use the power of questions again.** Ask questions like the following:

- What do we like about this idea? What is good about it? Why?

- What *isn't* good about this idea? What path will this plan take us down? Is that where we want to be?

- Can this idea be changed in some interesting way? Can we make it bigger or smaller? speed it up or slow it down? expand it over a wider area or focus it more narrowly? Can we apply it elsewhere?

- How does this idea meet our goal—or fail to meet it?

The last question, of course, is the most important. It pulls the brainstorming session back toward the all-important central goal—the objective that gives meaning to the creative process.

Leading a brainstorming session takes listening skills and tact. It is important to develop a sense for when the participants need to be encouraged to open up and spin out ideas more freely and when they need to be drawn back more narrowly toward the goal. In most brainstorming discussions, these two movements—centrifugal and centripetal—will need to alternate rhythmically. Managing the process is more art than science, a skill that only practice can perfect. The power of questions can help.

IQ Questions are very important in framing projects. They are part and parcel of the logical construction of an exploratory new venture.

—James L. Fergason, pioneer in liquid crystal technology and member of Inventors Hall of Fame

BRAINSTORM WITH YOURSELF

In this chapter, I have spoken mainly about the power of questions as a communication tool *between* people: about using questions to lead, persuade, teach, and influence others. But it is also important to use the power of questions *within* yourself—to use self-questioning as a stimulus for continuous learning and growth, especially in the context of your work and career.

The ways in which self-questioning can be used are almost limitless. In preparing this book, I asked a number of successful businesspeople to describe how they use self-questioning to improve their own sense of focus and direction. Some of their answers have already been highlighted. Here are more wise words to provoke your own brainstorming.

Tamar Howson of SmithKline Beecham suggests the use of self-questions as a way of evaluating where you are in your career. Is your current job the right one for you? Is it time to consider a change? These are issues almost everyone will face several times during a career. Here are some specific self-questions Howson recommends for those grappling with this issue:

- In evaluating your current job: "Am I being challenged and stimulated? Am I contributing? Am I having fun?"

- In considering a new job: "Why should I make a change? Will I be successful at a new job? Is this opportunity right for me? What are the risks? And what are the potential rewards?"

Ronda Dean, vice president of Parke-Davis Women's Healthcare, uses self-questions on the job every day as a way of constantly monitoring and evaluating her own work. She finds self-questioning an invaluable tool for identifying what she should be doing next to make herself and her organization more effective and successful. Here are some of Dean's favorite self-questions:

- What do I know and what *don't* I know? What do I need to find out?

- Who do I need to talk to? What do I need to ask?

- Why am I doing this? And—if I can't come up with a good answer—is this really important?

Our final example is Warner-Lambert CEO Lodewijk J. R. de Vink. He uses self-questions as a way of gaining perspective on the details of his job—to step back and place the challenges of the day in a broader context. "Every day," de Vink says, "I ask myself, 'Where do I want to be? Am I on track to get there?' And on my way home, I ask myself, 'What did I accomplish today? What could I have done better?' "

These are great questions—ones that apply to the life and career of anyone, from an entry-level worker to a top executive. Why not begin using them yourself and make answering them a part of your daily mental regimen? Questions like these can become rungs on your personal ladder of success. That, too, is part of the power of questions.

Experts report that the average businessperson today can expect to have several distinct careers, often in widely differing industries. The niche you fill today is probably different from the one you occupied five years ago—five years in the future, you may be working in a field that does not even exist today.

This ever-changing business environment puts a premium on thinking, growth, learning, and adaptation. But even as the specific skills and technologies you apply at work change, one constant is the power of questions. Whether you are primarily focused on selling, marketing, and persuading others; on leading, guiding, and inspiring them; or on contributing through the creativity, timeliness, and focus of your thinking—asking smart questions is one of the most crucial tools you can use to boost your effectiveness and that of the people around you.

A thinking organization is a necessity in today's fast-paced world. Without thinking about the answers to focused questions, organizations will not make the right choices nor change appropriately. The success of an organization can rest upon a simple, necessary, and powerful question: Is our mission to serve our customers or our stockholders?

10

How Questions Can Draw Families Together

Once a human being has arrived on this earth, communication is the largest single factor determining what kinds of relationships he makes with others and what happens to him in the world about him.

—VIRGINIA SATIR, therapist and writer

FINDING OUR VOICES

As any parent knows, children are born into the world asking questions: "Is there really a Santa Claus? May I have a cookie? Are we there yet?" And somehow along the way—lost in the swell of our efforts to respond appropriately to children, efforts that inevitably move between patience and exhaustion— our children begin to lapse into silence or become monosyllabic.

PARENT: How was school today?
CHILD: Fine.
PARENT: Do you have much homework?
CHILD: No.

Children, especially little children, are impulsive, inquisitive, and happy to tell you all kinds of things. As one mother described her nine-year-old to me, "If it's in his head, it's on his tongue." In some, this childhood quality of perennial curiosity lingers on—in the scientist for whom achieving an answer only raises other questions; in the litigator performing a cross-examination; in the physician who is seeking to make a diagnosis.

There are several reasons why in many of us our questioning habit quiets as we age. We have seen others pass us by, people who seem smarter, more authoritative, more interesting. We are afraid of sounding silly or looking unprepared. Sometimes, particularly in new social situations, when we enter a roomful of strangers, for instance, we become shy. At times we fall silent simply because we cannot articulate, or frame clearly, the questions that race through our minds. Often, we do not even know what to ask.

Children moving through the turbulent waters of adolescence are only beginning to become aware of what adults know: that as we get older, questions, and their answers, become more complex. They have consequences. They require more thinking, more work, a process that may be demanding, or painful, or personal. And, in the egocentric, conforming social world of the teenager, there is the fear, "What are people going to think about me?"

So sometimes it is simply easier just to say nothing. As Abraham Lincoln once quipped, "Sometimes it is better to be silent and thought a fool than to open your mouth and remove all doubt."

At home, with our busy workdays and frenetic pace, it is also easier for family members to take their meals on the fly, rather than to sit down for dinner together and search for conversation. It's easier not to risk a confrontation with our teenager about friends or curfews or appropriate clothing choices; easier to separate bickering siblings than to make them work out their problems; easier to deliver a lecture to our daughter about why she has to do her homework than to find out why she avoids it. It is easier just to roll over and go to sleep than to talk into the night with our spouse about a problem at the office that needs resolving.

But each time we take that shortcut, each time we turn away an opportunity to instill in our children a questioning mind and a questioning style of communication, we lose a chance to build a self-confidence and self-direction that will last well into adulthood.

This is because families are still the most important force in our lives. They are our ground zero—the place where we learn how to communicate with others. Families establish our intellectual patterns; they shape the way we see the world—and ourselves. Every time we use questions:

- We encourage our children to think clearly for themselves.

- We give them practice in making choices and in solving problems.

- We help them develop the skills they need to make good decisions.

- We motivate them to become independent thinkers.

- We instill in them the confidence they need to become happier, more successful adults.

IQ What families have in common the world around is that they are the place where people learn who they are and how to be that way.

—Jean Illsley Clarke, family psychologist

THE SEASON OF QUESTIONS

Our religious traditions offer many teachings about the importance of questions. Iba Ezra, the Torah commentator, commented: "One who is ashamed to ask will diminish wisdom among men." Of course, we know the adage that every wise man answers a question with a question. The discipline of asking good questions allows our minds to expand and be open to the various possibilities that exist around us. Every faith has its own way of asking questions.

In Judaism, the religious faith in which I was raised, questions are the essence of the Passover experience, the spring celebration commemorating the deliverance of the Jews from bondage in Egypt. They are a wonderful way of looking at how faith, family, and questions combine to deepen one's understanding of one's religious heritage and history.

The Talmud directs parents to stimulate their children to ask questions through the night; in order to do this, certain rituals and symbols are used as prompts: the adults set their tables on the floor, and there are no chairs, just pillows. Why? "Because," explains Rabbi Matthew Gewirtz, "we want the children to come in and ask about it." The parents eat hard-boiled eggs, parsley and saltwater, bitter herbs and matzo—all to stimulate questions and discussion with the young. The youngest child at the table asks, "Why is this night different from all other nights?" Everything that follows constitutes an answer to that question. The meaning of each of the special foods is explained: the egg stands for the strength of the Jewish people; the parsley's green color symbolizes the hope of a new life in the Promised Land; the saltwater symbolizes the tears of the enslaved; the bitter herbs symbolize the bitter and cruel way the Pharaoh treated the Jewish people when they were slaves; and the matzo symbolizes that hurried departure of the slaves from Egypt.

"We get caught up in the details of family life," says Rabbi Gewirtz, "and forget that asking can restore a sense of imagination to us—the wonderful sense of imagination we possessed as children. Through the symbolic reenactment of the journey from slavery to freedom, from despair to hope, from doubt to faith, we are reminded that incredible change is possible—and of the importance of inquiry in order to learn, in order to help, in order to move forward in our lives."

IQ Sometimes the questions you ask are more important than the answers you get.

—Rabbi Matthew D. Gewirtz, Congregation Rodeph Sholom

WHO MADE GOD? AND OTHER IMPONDERABLES

Children will sometimes ask questions that are devastating in their simplicity: "If God knows everything that we do, then is God the one who kills us when it's time for us to die?"

What do we say when we do not know the answers? One thing we can do is listen, and we can keep asking. This is because some questions cannot be answered but nonetheless must be asked: How do we explain suffering in the world? the death of a child? the Holocaust?

We are deeply uncomfortable with the random nature of the world; we find it difficult to accept ambiguity. And our children will find it even more so, as the beneficiaries of the information

age. They will get factual answers to their factual questions—
more than any other generation. It is your job as a parent to
encourage your children to ask questions, including the ones
with difficult answers and some with no answers—"Why did
my father leave my mother?" or "Why do birds fly?" or "Why
do I have to go to school?"

Somewhere between the unfair and the grim, between the
imponderable and the improbable, in what Rabbi Gewirth calls
"the gray area of life," is a place where you can go when you
cannot find a concrete answer, but where you can find things
that can make you a fuller person. And that is the second thing
we can do when we don't have ready answers: We can explore
the *feelings* behind the question.

A neighbor told me how upset her son would become whenever it was time to visit her mother, an Alzheimer's patient just
now entering the final stages of her illness, in a nursing home.
"Why do we have to go?" he would yell at her, pulling the pillows off the couch and throwing them onto the floor. "Can't I
go to Jimmy's house while you visit Grandma? She doesn't even
recognize me anyway. She won't miss me."

His attitude, which at first she took as insensitive and selfish,
baffled and angered my neighbor as much as it surprised her.
Her son had always been close to his grandmother before the
disease had overtaken her. But then when she began to gently
probe his feelings, she discovered his anger was really fear—fear
that his grandmother was going to die, fear that his mother
might inherit the disease, fear that simply by touching her, he
might end up as helpless as she was. His words, "She won't miss
me," were more eloquent than he could guess. They evoked a
feeling as natural as the beating of a heart.

IQ
> Growing is about learning and learning is about adventure. Some of the greatest adventures you can ever have are when you know how to ask smart questions. The joy of understanding can only be derived from smart and sensitive questions and empathetic listening.

—Dale Moss, director of sales worldwide, British Airways

DEVELOP A QUESTIONING HABIT IN EVERYDAY LIFE

Communicating effectively with our children takes patience, and above all it takes respect for the child, no matter how young, and no matter how disrespectful an older child may sometimes seem.

Since we as parents are authority figures, we can use this authority to positive advantage by being sure that we get answers to our questions, but we have to be gentle and careful in the ways we question. Think, for instance, how humiliated you would feel if your boss berated you for asking a question. Squash your first instinct to say, "Because I said so!" You would not accept that as a reason from your child, nor should your child accept that response from you. If you do not allow children to question your motives or your reasons when they are children, they will grow up to be adults who do not question.

Parents should instill in their children's minds the fact that they have the right to know certain information. They should also teach their children that if they do not get the information they are entitled to, they should ask for it.

Are there times when explanations are not required? Yes, of course. Sometimes, instead of giving clear instructions about what has to be done—the television turned off, playroom toys put away—we feel we need to explain ourselves and convince our children to see the merit of our position or the value of a simple request. The problem with this is that everything then becomes a negotiation: getting ready for bed, getting dressed for school, finishing homework. Children should not question everything you tell them to do. They need authority and routines and they need to know that somebody is in charge—and that it's not them.

That said, children need to know that as they get older there will be more things over which they will have control. But you do not have to explain the reason something has to be done at that very moment. Simply say it needs to be done and you can come back to it and explain why later. Developing a questioning style should not be confused with a power struggle.

> **IQ** It is not the correct thing to scold children for asking questions: this is about as reasonable as to scold them for breathing or thinking.
>
> —Florence Howe Hall, writer

GROWING UP WITH THE QUESTIONING HABIT

Children learn by example: When you look at a child's behavior and then look at his or her parents' behavior, you will see many similarities. One of the most common is in communication style. The best way to develop the questioning habit in your children is to develop it in yourself. If your child does not observe you asking questions, then he or she won't ask any.

You can practice the questioning habit with your children in the following ways:

- **Ask questions you really want answered.** Children are like radar detectors; they can sense insincerity a mile away.

- **Listen to what your child has to say.** A friend tells me how her daughter caught her in the act of not listening, of stringing her along with "uh-huh, uh-huh, uh-huh." How often have you done the same?

- **Validate your child's answers with praise.** Many children grow up feeling their emotions and curiousness devalued by the adults around them. At the most influential stage of their lives, children need to learn that it is okay to ask questions. Reward them for it. Let your children know they are smart. Let them know they have good ideas, and that they make good choices and decisions.

- **Build on your child's innate talent for questioning.** When my children used to ask "why, why, why?" during those "terrible twos," I thought I would scream—until I began turning the question back to them. "What made you ask that?" I would get a much better understanding of how their minds worked and why certain things interested them.

- **Take the time to respond thoughtfully.** Children are wise to pat answers.

- **Remember that every question has a purpose.** When you ask yourself, "What am I trying to accomplish with this question? What is my goal?" you will form a better question, and you'll receive a better answer.

- **Consider the reasons behind your child's questions.** Young children will often repeat a question in spite of your best efforts to give them a well-formed answer. This is because many children ask questions to quiet their anxieties and concerns; the consistency of your response reassures them and gives them certainty. Many children will ask questions for the purpose of gleaning information, the ownership of knowledge, but others are simply seeking comfort in what can be a big and mysterious world.

- **Ask questions of others.** Children model the behaviors they observe in adults. When they see you using questions with your spouse and your peer group, they will be encouraged to do likewise. It will seem natural and automatic.

IQ ────────────────────────────────
To listen to a child means to discover his logic. Helping him means guiding him to a different viewpoint from which he can see advantages.

—Rudolf Dreikurs, child-rearing guru

HELPING YOUNG CHILDREN TO USE QUESTIONS

We question the most when we are children because this is the time when we have the least amount of information about the world around us. We want to know what everything is and why it is there. Keep your children asking about what they see around them. Little children are like sponges, so that what you teach them now will stay with them for the rest of their lives. Recognize that much of a child's self-concept comes from how we treat them; parents don't always appreciate how important this is. If you give them the message that they don't have the right to question, they will grow up to believe that.

How do we get small children started asking questions?

We model it for them. "Do you want grape juice or apple? Do you want to wear your yellow pajamas or your blue? Shall we play hide-and-seek or Candy Land?"

Asking very young children for information can sometimes be as difficult as getting it from older children, although for very different reasons, as we shall see. All children need cues, or conversation prompts. When it comes to little ones, it doesn't cue them enough if you simply ask your preschooler, "How was school today?" You have to ask specific questions: "Who sat next to you at snack?" or "Will you tell me about the story your teacher read to you today?" You have to extract chronology from them: "And then what did he say?" followed by, "And what did you do?"

IQ   Does the fairy godmother know she's make-believe?

—Laura Weinstock, age six

Reading stories to smaller children is a wonderful way to encourage them to ask questions. Ask them about the characters and story lines, using questions like: "What do you think will happen next?" or "What do you think Cinderella should do?" or "How do you think the story will end? Why do you think so?" Try using what-if questions. These encourage children to be creative and to come up with alternative story ideas. Questions such as, "What would have happened if the fairy godmother hadn't been there?" and "What would have happened if Snow White hadn't eaten that apple?" will spark a child's imagination. Follow up with plenty of what-ifs and then-whats. Participate in the creation of these alternate stories. It will also help create a strong bond between you and your child. More important, you are giving your child the tools to make better decisions as an adult.

QUESTIONS AND FEELINGS

As you and your children begin to talk—whether it is about the school day or a situation at home or even a story—it is wise to pay attention to their *emotions* as well as their words. Small children often do not have the language to convey how they feel;

school-age children are often too caught up in their confusion and upset of the moment—a fight with another child, being the object of teasing, not being invited to a birthday party—to explain themselves clearly.

Good parenting exposes feelings, but in the most gentle way so that you can be trusted and depended upon. Here is where your ability to ask questions with intelligence and sensitivity can open up a child's mind in a safe way, so that she can look deeper into herself without judgment.

None of us wants to look at our dark sides alone. This is why being in a good and loving relationship is so important, and why a parent's ability to use questions skillfully can make a difference. A child can invite a trusted parent into his frightened or saddest places without fear of judgment. But as soon as you say, "Oh, that's silly! Of course Benjy is your friend!" or "Stop it! That's ridiculous; you're a wonderful soccer player!" you are using language that immediately shuts you out.

Instead, listen first and then ask with respect, using your child's language when you can and validating your child's feelings. "I know you're afraid. I can hear that. Let's talk about it. I'm sure you have a lot to say about it. Do you need me to help you to talk about it?"

When seven-year-old Katie, for instance, came home from her first kickball game—up to which she had been counting the days—she burst into tears and declared she was never going to play *ever* again. The simple questioning approach her baffled parents took initially yielded unsatisfactory answers. With persistence, it turned out that the first time she was up, Katie kicked the ball but ran to third base instead of first. Her teammates jeered at her, "What, are you stupid? How could you not know where to run!" Katie felt humiliated because, in fact, she hadn't known where to run. No one had told her and she did not ask, "What do I do after I kick the ball?"

Only through a questioning process did she begin to understand that you can do many things without knowing all there is to know. Through questions, Katie's mother helped her to see that adults are always learning, too: Katie's mother had to learn how to use a computer; her father had just learned how to snowboard. When Katie was very small and hadn't learned to read yet, she could only look at picture books and the individual letters until she learned how to put them together. She was turning into a wonderful reader!

"When we rent a car," Katie's dad asked her, "what do I always remember to ask the attendant?"

Katie thought a moment and replied, "You ask where the spare is."

"And why do you think I do that?"

But Katie had gotten the point. Her answer made it clear she understood now that before we do some things it is a good idea to ask, "What are the important things I should know before I do this?" And, of course, the reason her father always asked about the spare tire was because once he had gotten a flat in the middle of the night and had been stuck without one.

You will have dialogues like this your entire life as a parent, and it begins early on.

IQ There is no such thing as a worthless conversation, providing you know what to listen for. And questions are the breath of life for a conversation.

—James Nathan Miller

LEARNING HOW TO CHOOSE

Anybody who has ever parented a toddler knows that beneath those last dimpled layers of baby fat is a child who could give new meaning to the expression "having a mind of his own." In truth, babies are indeed capable of expressing preferences very early on. They also know what they want! We know that young people who are in charge of their own lives—who have learned how to make decisions and choices for themselves—are healthier adults. If they have had experience with making their own choices during childhood, then they don't have to fight so hard in adolescence to become independent.

Learning to choose and how to make choices is part of a continuum. At first we ask, "Do you want the grape juice or the apple? Do you want this or that?" And then you wait. Your little one is beginning to think for herself: "What is your choice?"

As they grow, so do our questions: "What is your choice? What is your thinking? What are your thoughts about that? How did you arrive at that decision?" *I want to know how you got to that final choice.*

You are asking, "Tell me how you got to be you. How do you organize your life, your thoughts, your boundaries?"

Let me know you.

UNDERSTANDING BOUNDARIES—THEIRS AND YOURS

As children grow older the questions that you ask them need to be appropriately framed. Inviting children into the family decision-making process is important and valuable; but an open-ended question such as, "Where do we want to go this summer on our vacation?" may be asking for trouble. Picture this:

You sit down with your children to discuss the possibilities. Immediately, they begin to talk about Disney World. Unfortunately, you did not have Disney World in mind because you can't afford it. You have just set up your children for a big disappointment. When you tell them the family does not have the money to go to Disney World, they begin to whine and complain. They do not understand your fiscal constraints. All they know is that they won't be able to see Mickey and Minnie. Wherever you decide to go for vacation, your children will be upset and the vacation will be a disappointment when it should be a time of relaxation and family togetherness.

The question you should have asked was, "Where do you want to go this summer: the beach or Yellowstone Park?" This sets *your* boundaries immediately. The children know from the start what their choices are and they won't be disappointed. They may still bring up Disney World, but you already set that up as not being an option by the question you asked.

Should that not be good enough for them, you can ask, "I know that you would rather go to Disney World, but we can't afford to go there this summer. What fun things do you think we can do at the beach that we can't do at Disney World?" Keep them focused on where you can go and how much fun they can have there. As they talk about all the opportunities the sand, the waves, and the boardwalk offer, they will get increasingly excited about the choices they do have.

Asking your children's opinions on family matters is important because it makes them feel part of the decision-making process. Unfortunately, your children may not understand money or time constraints. Giving them options to choose from is safe for you and important to them. I will never forget the summer I was eleven and came home from camp to find that my mother had redone my room without even asking me if it was all right, and if there were some things in it that were important for me to keep. Instead, she gave away a desk I still loved—and chose a color for the walls and a fabric for the bedspread I did not like.

This affected me in several ways. As an adult, I learned to always question my children and involve them in areas that directly related to their domain. I began to realize in what other ways my mother had inadvertently disregarded me, my feelings, my territory, even though I knew she was a good and loving mother. It made me realize why I often gave in and didn't stand up for myself in school, with friends, in my work. It took me a long time and a lot of growing up to realize that in my mother's eyes, she had been planning a big surprise—one that she hoped would delight me and make me happy. There are always reasons why people do what they do. But in that case, my mother and I simply didn't have the questioning skills to save us both some heartache.

> **IQ** A problem that presents itself as a dilemma carries an unfortunate prescription: to argue instead of act.
>
> —Elizabeth Janeway, novelist, essayist, critic

FROM CONFLICT TO CONVERSATION: USING QUESTIONS TO SOLVE FAMILY PROBLEMS

"But you promised!"
"She started it!"
"I hate him!"

It is so easy for us as parents to be drawn into our children's battles, large or small. But when we try to impose a solution, our children lose an opportunity to learn necessary social skills, like problem-solving, conflict resolution, seeing another point of view, and empathy.

We have to squash our instinct to go in there and fix it. We know in our heart it is far more important that our squabbling children learn how to solve a problem *together* than it is to know which of them started it.

And it is important to tell them that.

When you take the approach of asking him questions, your child recognizes that in you he has a partner who will help him understand. By giving a child the power to know how he can figure it out by himself, by helping him to arrive at his own solution, he will grow. If it is your solution, he won't grow. But if it is his solution, he will flower. That you ask questions is the key.

Scenario #1: Sandy has just slammed the door on her older sister. She will not play with her anymore. "It's not fair! I hate her!" Sandy insists.

Your first instinct might be to go charging into your older daughter's room in your "protect my baby" battle gear. Or it might be to say to Sandy, "No, of course you don't hate your big sister. Sisters should love each other." Would either of these reactions solve the problem?

No. In the first instance, if you yourself make the solution, you will become a new problem: Your older child will turn against you and your younger one won't learn how to fight her own battles. And neither child will learn how to resolve disagreements. In the second instance, you will have denied Sandy the right to her feelings, and you will have dropped a moral issue into the stew.

A more constructive posture would be to help the children examine what happened, why Sandy feels as she does ("I hate her because she always makes me do it her way!"), and to help the children explore possible solutions ("What can we do about this?). By focusing on feelings—how each child feels, on what the problem is—you may discover that the older child, for example, feels that Sandy does not respect the fact that she doesn't always want to play with her. By getting them to focus on how to resolve their conflict, you avoid making digressive moral judgments and you help both children see the other's point of view.

Some of the helping questions you might ask include:

- Can you give me some examples?

- Tell me more about it. What makes you feel that way?

- How do you think your sister feels when . . . ?

- Do you think you could find a way to play fairly? to make time for each other? How?

- What could you do so both of you have fun?

- Do you suppose it might help if you could take turns choosing? How might that work?

- What would happen if . . . ?

By arriving at a solution both children can sign off on, each has an investment in making it work. But agree first that each understands that if it does not work out, this conversation will be reopened and a new solution will be explored.

Scenario #2: Every morning it is the same. Marie runs late for work because her ten-year-old-son, Joey, is slow in the morning getting up and out the door. In her exasperation—she has already been late twice this week, and Joey has been late for school—Marie tells him, "We need to talk about morning time and cooperation. I need your help here because obviously what I am doing is not working. What ideas do you have?"

Maria embraces the lesson of the first scenario; she has fought off the instinct to criticize or render judgment, which would only make Joey feel defensive and angry. Instead, she has brought him into the problem-solving process, not to control it, but to give him a chance to tell her how *together* they can be doing a better job. As this is, in effect, a persuasion technique, it is a wonderful example of using the seventh power of questions.

Marie's questions might include:

- How could we be doing a better job at this?

- How do you think it makes my boss feel when I am late for work? How do you think it makes your teacher feel when you are late for school?

- What can we do to organize our morning routine differently?

- What do you think about laying out your clothes the night before or my giving you a five-minute warning before it's time to leave?

- What actions could I take or words could I say that would get you moving faster?

- If waiting for me is a problem—and the reason you say you don't get up—and watching TV is not an option, what else could you be doing in the morning so you're not bored?

By agreeing to agree, and by focusing on coming up with a workable solution rather than on assigning blame, Marie has invested Joey in forging a successful outcome.

COMING TOGETHER: THE FAMILY MEETING

Family meetings are very much like board meetings, in that each family member has a voice and a vote. The concept of individual respect is at the heart of such a meeting. The expectation is that everybody there needs to be their most grown-up, and everyone can share their feelings in a privileged setting—meaning nothing that is said or shared about oneself, each other, or anyone outside the family leaves the meeting. A family meeting is its own kind of safe house.

A family meeting, which may be called weekly or only as needed, is where family members learn the skills of compromise. Each member has the right to ask questions and to have them answered. Each has the right be heard, to have his or her point of view respected, and to share in the responsibility of making the outcome work. Family meetings instill a feeling of competency by letting each member know the others consider him or her reliable and trustworthy.

One effective means of doing this is to give a child the challenge of facilitating these meetings, as his age allows. A facilitator learns how to draw others in so they become questioners, too. Another child might be given the job of summing up what everyone has said at a particular family meeting; in this way, she learns to distill and explain another's point of view, even one she may not agree with.

Whether a given issue concerns family relationships, household chores, sharing, homework, or problems outside the family, the discussion always returns to the question, "What can we do about it?"

This group effort at problem solving is like a mini United Nations—and it can be started when children are very young. "How would it be if we tried it this way?" or "What do you think about making a schedule for these things?" Everyone is allowed into the give-and-take of weighing ideas and options. Personal agendas are put aside as all work together to come up with the best plan for the family. And that willingness to approach a problem as a family problem, as a product of the multiple interactions that define family living, is, according to Dr. Rudolf Dreikurs, what makes family meetings so effective.

> There are times when parenthood seems like nothing but feeding the mouth that bites you.
>
> —Peter De Vries, novelist

COMMUNICATING WITH A CACTUS: A LOOK AT ADOLESCENTS

> At fourteen, you don't need sickness or death for tragedy.
>
> —Jessamyn West, novelist

In her guide for mothers of adolescent girls, *Don't Stop Loving Me*, Dr. Ann Caron likens the adolescent to his or her two-year-old self—the one who refuses your help as she struggles with her shoes. The one who wants to "do it by myself." You remember her; an adolescent now, she's back, and you have just been reacquainted. But what your adolescent wants to do for herself today—or indeed what she may be doing—is far more anxiety-provoking for you; plus, it's almost always done out of your sight.

Adolescence is often a difficult time for communication. Questions that are meant to try to understand how a person feels can sound intrusive and accusatory. Teenagers are cautious about their privacy. They are struggling with issues of identity and with establishing individuality and independence. And yet as a parent you are beginning to get more nervous about adolescent issues—real concerns like driving, alcohol, drugs, sex, eating disorders, guns, date rape, academics, and college admission—at exactly the time when your child is trying to achieve some independence. Some parents react by becoming extremely intrusive and overly controlling. They listen in on their child's phone conversations; they read diaries and search their child's room. These are dangerous stratagems, and they backfire. And yet, how can we balance our responsibilities as parents with our children's need for individuality?

IQ Children must be taught how to think, not what to think.

—Margaret Mead, anthropologist

Learning to Speak a Common Language: How Questions Can Help

As a parent you have a right to ask where your child is going and about the available adult supervision, but your child does not need to tell you his private feelings or what his friends are feeling. Beyond that, if you remind your child that he will make mistakes (but that everybody does) and that you trust him and have faith that he will make good choices, he will very likely live up to that. Your child doesn't want to disappoint you, and, his sarcasm and secrecy to the contrary, he does not think of you as public enemy number one.

How do you smooth out a sometimes rocky road? How do you keep your child an independent thinker during a time when his independence, and his commitment to the values with which you have raised him, will likely be tested and tested again? You do this by helping your child to hold on to his questioning habit—the very attitudes, prompts, and processes we have discussed. They almost always work for older children, too.

You also do this by offering protection (empathy) and challenge (expectations). You do this by listening—and by asking good questions that help your child to clarify his thinking. Some ideas to consider:

- **Timing is important.** Always detach a discussion about a problem or an issue from the emotions surrounding it. Trying to initiate a constructive conversation when one or both of you is agitated will almost certainly fail. While this moment may not be the time to ask a question, it does not mean it should never be asked. Say, "We need to talk about why you came in past your curfew last night. When do you think we can do that?" so your child is prepared to have a conversation, not a confrontation or an ambush. This approach can be seen as a genuine effort to understand your child's position or point of view as opposed to a desire to vent your annoyance at him.

- **Never ask a child to defend his feelings.** His opinions and his actions are fair game for your questions, but when you begin to challenge a child's feelings, you are showing disrespect. A teenager's feelings or point of view must be acknowledged, even if you don't share them.

- **Learn how to disagree while still preserving mutual respect.** Never argue back; ask your child for his or her reasons and be sure he understands that disagreement, even between loved ones, is natural and not dire.

- **Seek information without being intrusive or judgmental.** "Let me tell you what's going on in my mind right now and you tell me what you think about it" is a gentler, more effective method of access than, "How could you be such an idiot!" Another conversation prompt might be: "I'm concerned. Your grades on your last couple of math tests have been on my mind and I would like to share my concerns and you tell me what you think," or "I have a problem. I wonder if you can help me sort it out. . . ."

IQ   Is One Nobel Prize

too much to ask after all

I've done for you?

—Jewish haiku

- **Restate a problem in terms of a question.** Help your child focus the issue by reframing it to expedite problem solving. "So as I understand it, the question is, 'How are you going to prepare for . . . ?' "

- **Voice tone and body language matter.** "Why didn't you finish your homework?" versus, "WHY DIDN'T YOU FINISH YOUR HOMEWORK?" will elicit a different response. The second question will be ineffective because it is excuse-provoking. "Why did you wait until the last minute?" is going to get you an excuse, not a reason. How could you ask this same question in a more positive way? Try, "Are there some things I should know about why you're not getting your homework done that would help me to understand?"

It is helpful when a difficult conversation does not become personal. When asking personal information, older children are going to tense up. The best conversations, sometimes even the hardest, take place when you are both driving in a car or enjoying an activity together.

- **Do not think of yourself as a litigator, even if you are one.** Never try to nail your own child. Whatever validity there might have been to your point of view will get lost. The child will have a right to become angry and be uncooperative. And you will be left with the teenager's equivalent to pleading the Fifth—a stony silence. Rather, think of yourself as an arbitrator—between your child and your worst impulses. Instead of demanding that your child do it your way, ask him what's wrong with your idea. What are his concerns? What have you not thought about that's relevant and valid?

  Revise your ideas based on what your child has told you: "Then are you saying that if I give you the car tonight, you won't stay out late? In that case, I'll expect you home by eleven."

  When dealing with a teenager, remember that statements generate resistance but questions lead to answers.

  Regress. Become a two-year-old again. Ask "Why?" if you want to better understand your child's position; ask "Why not?" if you want your child to better understand yours.

  Do not criticize your child's point of view; try to understand it and then look for ways to change it. Putting down your child's ideas and opinions will only make her cling to them harder. "Let me ask you a question. If you continue to turn your assignments in late and earn the grades you've been getting, then what will your college options be?" This will refocus the discussion from the present to the future.

- **Let her come to her own solutions.** Let's say your daughter is purchasing a dress to wear to a school dance. She has selected three to try on and you think she looks horrible in two of them. Ask her, "What are your thoughts?" or "What do you think?" and listen to her answer. Keeping your voice even, ask her: "What do you like about that one?" and never put down what she says. The fact that she took you shopping with her means she's willing to listen to your opinion, too.

- **Never offer immediate solutions.** No child wants to be told what to do. Adolescents, when cornered, may look for the opportunity to lash out—"Don't you think I already thought of that!" or "You're trying to run my life!" or "That's the stupidest idea I've ever heard."

  If your child comes to you with a problem, ask her instead what she thinks she can do or wants to do about it. She may have some firm ideas. Ask her about her decision-making process: "How did you get to that choice?" or "Tell me more about what you would say. Pretend I'm your friend. Let me hear your words," or "What makes you feel that is the best way to fix this problem?" And when it is over, tell her, "Here's what I liked about the way you handled that." Let her enjoy the satisfaction of having figured it out, of being able to take care of herself. That's what competency is all about, and becoming an adult is all about achieving competency.

- **Always leave your teen some wiggle room.** When making a suggestion, allow your child the option of not accepting your advice. You do this by making soft suggestions: "Would you think about trying this way?" or "How would it make you feel if . . . ?" Your job is to empower your child to feel confident, not to make yourself look like a genius.

I Q Parents are the bones on which children sharpen their teeth.

—Peter Ustinov, actor

Sleight of Hand: Conversation Starters and Stoppers

The most common complaint teens have is that their parents don't understand them. And, for the most part, the teen is correct. Asking your child how school was is not a true, sincere attempt to understand him. In the 1999 movie *The Story of Us*, the character played by Bruce Willis asks his kids each night at dinner, "What was your high and what was your low today?" These two questions let your kids know that it is alright to feel down as well as up.

Some of the best conversations between parents and teens happen when the subject isn't about them. World news, national news, music, television, and movies are all conversational venues that allow you and your child to talk, and to ask questions, *together*. These conversations can also sharpen your child's critical thinking skills and help him to articulate his own thoughts and opinions.

Inevitably, when we talk about the problems of other people—real or celluloid—we are also talking about ourselves. As Rudolf Dreikurs reminds us, "No one likes to expose themselves to accusations and criticism; and so it helps when we can create a distance that promotes objectivity, as though the issues we speak about belong to someone else."

Ask your child, "What did you think about the way he/she handled that problem?" or "Was there anything else he/she might have done?" or "How would you feel if that happened to you?" or "What do you think she should do next?"

Ann Caron observes that teenage soap operas push all of today's hot-button issues and that newspaper advice columns and talk radio hosts often ask about adolescent problems. These are both excellent conversation starters: "What do you think of what Ann Landers suggests?" or "If you were Dr. Laura, what would *you* have told that girl to do?"

When does communication break down? When we deliver lectures instead of creating a dialogue. And when we attack.

Teenagers are not only cautious, they are fiercely protective—of their feelings, as we have seen, but also of their friends. If you have issues or doubts about your son's friends, tread carefully. Be sure you can keep your legitimate concern for your child's emotional and physical safety separate from your opinion about his friend. Here is how questions can guide you:

"I can tell you like hanging out with Sam. Can you tell me why you like his company? What else can you tell me so I can get to know him better?" or "Your friendship with Aaron seems to have fallen apart. Do you want to tell me about it? Does that make you sad? Is there anything you think can be done to repair it?"

> IQ It is better to know some of the questions than all the answers.
>
> —James Thurber, *New Yorker* cartoonist and humorist

THE GOLDEN RULE

In her groundbreaking book about the special problems of adolescent girls, *Reviving Ophelia*, Mary Pipher tells us, "certain kinds of homes help girls hold on to their true selves." I think the same may be said of any home where adults and children have learned how to *hear* each other.

In some homes families place a premium on conversation; family members talk about the weather, who is going to pick up more orange juice, when did the tailor say Danny's new suit would be ready, and which parent is going to take Lizzie to her soccer dinner. But they also talk about choices and consequences and risk and options, and they teach intelligent resistance. They know how to share what they do, what goes on that day at work or school; they know how to share what they know and what they don't. Every day they show each other the respect and interest that makes each of them feel valuable and worthy. And in doing all of this, parents prepare their kids for independence.

Do parents and children disagree and argue? Of course. Are there times when, if the parents don't feel beaten from exhaustion, they feel that they and their children have exhausted each other? Yes.

No one denies that raising families is one of life's holy terrors, but, thankfully, those of us who have crossed to the other side, those of us whose children are now raising their own children, will be the first to tell you that while doing so they became people who feel more deeply, hurt more deeply, question more deeply, and love more deeply. What children take from us, they give. All you have to do is ask.

11

Rediscover Questions:
Recapture and Redefine
the Essential You

If I had influence with the good fairy who is supposed to pre-side over the christening of all children I should ask that her gift to each child in the world be a sense of wonder so inde-structible that it would last throughout life, as an unfailing antidote against the boredom and disenchantment of later years, the sterile preoccupation with things that are artificial, the alienation from the sources of our strength.

—RACHEL CARSON, environmentalist

There once was a child with an infinite sense of wonder. Each day was a revelation, an opportunity to conquer one of the world's great mysteries—learning to tie a shoe, to swim, to recite the names of the planets, to solve an algebraic equation. For a long time, this child's insistent nature was a passport into this passionate, fevered thing called living, until our friend, lean and long now of limb, tumbled into that stuffy, static place called Adulthood. A world where you trade what used to be your curiosity for what others call perspective; where you give up discovery and daring for safety and serenity; and where some small part of you—because we are all in some part that child—dies.

Do you remember your own childhood?

Do you remember when you were assertive, imaginative, creative, active—and you came to these things naturally? effortlessly? Did you have an imaginary friend? Did you create elaborate games of pretend? When you wanted a new toy, were you resourceful in the ways in which you tried to get it? Were you so determined that you threatened to hold your breath until you turned blue, to run away from home if you didn't get your way? Did you not stop asking questions until you heard the answers you wanted?

How did you respond when you were asked, "What do you want to be when you grow up?" Is that what you became? What did you wish for during those years of wonder, when you blew out the candles on your birthday cake? Should you have been more careful about what you wished for? And are you still making birthday wishes now? Or have you stopped believing they can come true?

BEYOND THE BOUNDARIES

Every human being on this earth is born with a tragedy and it isn't original sin. He's born with the tragedy that he has to grow up. . . . He has to lose everything that is lovely and fight for a new loveliness of his own making. . . . A lot of people don't have the courage to do it.

—Helen Hayes, actress

I have sometimes thought that if childhood is all about discovering one's potential, adulthood is where many of us squander, bury, or lose it. *Why?*

Part of it is about programming, which comes first from home and what we see our parents do and say. We all have our stories. I can still recall my father telling me that I had better take that first awful job that was offered to me because, he said, I might not get another! How's that for confidence building? A friend recalls the report cards she used to bring home. She had worked hard for that string of A's. "Good job," her father said before turning right around to her brother. "This is what we expect from you," he told the boy. "After all, it is you who will one day have to go out and earn a living." I don't know if her brother got the message, but my friend certainly did.

We also become programmed at school. We were taught to believe that every question had only one solution; and there was not much time to ask us thoughtful questions. Seldom were we asked, "What do you think?" or "How could this have been made better?" or "What would you have done if . . . ?" Our guidance counselors were not always the most positive; and our peers, even then, influenced us as well.

Every once in a while something came along to ignite our belief system. It was sometimes as basic as a simple reading experience. A man I know read a book when he was nine about a town where the ordinary routines and rituals of life were reversed, turned inside out or upside down. Nothing ran or worked as you expected it to. Forty years later, my friend still vividly recalls the bank that gave away money ("Why leave it here where it can't do any good?" asked the teller) and the department store that paid its customers to take away the merchandise ("What are we going to do with all this stuff?"). Such explanations struck my friend as perfectly reasonable and they stimulated him to become, throughout his life, someone who asked questions, who challenged the predictable order of things, who looked at problems differently, and who sought solutions in the unexpected. And that's where he found them. A hugely successful entrepreneur today, he looked at the world in ways that others did not. He found ideas and answers in places no one else thought to look.

IF MOZART HAD A CHOICE

> It's a sad day when you find out that it's not accident or time or fortune but just yourself that kept things from you.
>
> —Lillian Hellman, writer and playwright

For many years men were raised with often impossibly high expectations; "The White House or Bust!" might have appeared on the bumper stickers of an entire generation speeding off into that proverbial sunset. So much was asked and even more expected. Their sisters, girlfriends, and future wives could only later set such great goals; back then they could aspire simply to be wives, like their mothers.

Social norms did change in the sixties and seventies, but then, in the eighties and nineties, both men and women discovered that disappointment and a sense of failure cut across the genders. The reality of burnout and midlife crisis and trying to do it all tempered, if not arrested, our rocket ride to the top. In spite of good incomes and VP titles, many of us feel mired in dissatisfaction and fear of yielding those offices with their expansive views to younger, less exhaustible executives. We coined new words like *overreaching* and *underachieving*; and we struggled to find ourselves—only to find that while our lives may be materially different from our parents', they are not necessarily more satisfying or any less of a struggle.

So we have reset our goals and learned to lower our expectations. We've learned to play the hand we've been dealt and stop asking for more. After all, isn't accepting one's limitations, one's place in the grand scheme, the essence of a steady, assured adulthood? "I'm too tired to try to change, and anyway it's too late," someone told me not long ago.

But is it?

I think that too many of us have been living in a cult—the cult of adulthood—and it is time to deprogram ourselves.

I am reminded of a wonderful Ellen Goodman essay celebrating one's sheer durability: sure, you were still learning the alphabet at the same age that Mozart was writing minuets, and, by the process of age discrimination, you're too old to ever be hailed as the next new thing. But when you think about it, by the time you have arrived at midlife, you've lived longer than Mozart or Jane Austen or George Gershwin. What are you going to do with this gift? Does it make a difference in your life that, at *their* midlife points, Paul Gauguin was still a banker, and Elizabeth Barrett Browning had not even begun to write, nor Grandma Moses to paint? And the list goes on. As Goodman so eloquently put it, you could be Mozart and dead at thirty-five, or you could be alive, with the rest of your life, with all its possibilities, ahead of you. Which way would you have it?

BELIEVE YOU CAN—AND YOU WILL

IQ Wonder and despair are two sides of a spinning coin. When you open yourself up to one, you open yourself to the other. You discover a capacity for joy that wasn't in you before. Wonder is the promise of restoration: as deeply as you dive, so may you rise.

—Christina Baldwin, writer and educator

You do not need the Sphinx to tell you why.

The happiest and most successful people *I* know are the ones who have never stopped asking more *of themselves* and *from themselves*. They are relentless. They dive into life with the exuberance of a child hitting the water for the first time in summer. They author their own lives with imagination and without apology, and do so by remaining all the while self-searching and self-knowing. They remain true to themselves even in the wake of the personal or professional turbulence called modern life. They do this by continuing to ask questions.

They know that:

- Life is full of opportunities, but we must keep our minds open or we will not see them. If we close our eyes, we see only risks. When a door closes, we must remember that a window also opens.

- To stay in tune with who we are and what we really want from life, we must constantly question ourselves.

- To build effective relationships we must constantly question our partners, children, and peers.

- To be happy in our faith, we must question and understand.

They know that if you ask for very little in life, that is exactly what you will get. They know how to say yes to life.

> A child should be allowed to take as long as she needs for knowing everything about herself, which is the same as learning to be herself. Even twenty-five years if necessary, or even forever. And it wouldn't matter ... because nothing is really important but being oneself.
>
> —Laura Riding Jackson, poet

YOU ARE WHAT YOU THINK—YOU ARE MORE THAN YOU THINK

IQ The average four-year-old asks three hundred questions a day. The average college graduate asks twenty.

—Larry Wilson, founder and vice chairman,
Pecos River Division, AON Consulting

What holds you back? Now is the time to start listening to your thoughts, your wishes and dreams and fantasies. Start believing that you can. Remember that only a *not* separates the word *can't* from *can*. Dialogue with yourself about the thoughts and feelings that keep you from seeking more. Take a personal inventory and try to map the life moments that slowly silenced you: the little put-downs; the reprimands for asking too many questions; the teachers who discouraged you from questioning too much or who thought, because your hand was always in the air, you were a smart aleck or troublemaker; the bosses who assumed you already knew the answer. Understand that you cannot change the past, but you can control how you respond to it *today*.

These are some of the things that prevent people from thinking they can make positive changes:

- *I'm too busy.* You probably are, and so you are not far off the mark if you tell yourself you have no time to pursue the things that really matter to you. But you can make time if you want to. Use questions to figure out ways to make more time for yourself: "Do I really need to do this? Can it be delegated? Can the way I do it be made more efficient? Can it be outsourced?" Set priorities.

  It's hard to put yourself ahead of a family—but I have found it useful to think about the way flight attendants explain that in an emergency, a parent is supposed to take care of himself first, before helping a child put on a life vest or oxygen mask. I think this instruction is intended to help prevent a parent from becoming panicked or disoriented, but I also find a good metaphor in it—an unhappy parent is of no good to the family. Children need to see their parents enjoying their lives, even if it means taking time away from them. Finding pleasure in your own life can be one of the most important legacies a parent can leave.

- *I'm afraid.* On our journey toward adulthood we have all found ways to protect ourselves from ridicule, from hurt, from self-exposure. We've become averse to risk. But being fully human means to put ourselves out there, every day. We are never too old to be creative and imaginative and bold and brave. Secretly, don't we all admire those who are? Keep things in perspective. Ask yourself: "What is the worst thing that could happen to me?" Then ask: "What is the worst thing that could happen *if I make this change?*" Which scares you more? Which of these choices cannot be undone?

- *I'm lazy.* Who isn't? Thinking is hard! Self-discovery is a difficult study. Why do some people seem happier and more successful than others? Because they ask questions and force themselves to answer. We answer other people's questions, but *we do not answer our own.* You can live a lifetime, Beryl Markham once said, "and at the end of it, know more about other people than you know about yourself." Do you call that living *your* life?

- *It's not the right time.* This one is a favorite. It is easy to make excuses to avoid change and, in no time at all, we begin to believe that our excuses are actually facts. My father always said he wanted to write a book but he used the excuse that he had to earn a living, and that he was just too tired to write after he came home from work—though he always found the energy for a game of tennis.

What excuses do you use? An excuse is a form of emotional paralysis. Could you take a class? join a support group? I wish my father had tried either of these. The routine of a weekly or monthly meeting would have imposed a discipline on him that he could have managed, and it would have made him less fearful. He may have believed he'd conned others that he was just too busy, but in his heart of hearts I also believe he knew otherwise. Our little self-deceptions are most harshly illuminated in our own dark corners—and most painfully felt.

IQ Questions we ask ourselves are ways of self-justification.

—Stephen Gale, social scientist

- *I don't believe I can get more—so why ask?* If you never ask, then you'll never know. By not asking, you'll already have failed. You'll only have succeeded in not getting what you already don't have! There's always a chance you may be wrong—and if you're right, and your request is denied, at least you can take consolation in having been right. You have nothing to lose by trying, and you gain nothing by not trying at all.

My father was an average achiever until he had a series of heart attacks, which caused him to begin thinking about his mortality and of all the things he had not done. Dad was a real estate appraiser, and had appraised such buildings as the Empire State Building and Grand Central Terminal. Clearly, he was good at what he did, and he enjoyed it, but he had hardly ever raised his rates, until he got sick. That became a major turning point for him. He decided he needed more money to travel, and that he wanted to spend more time with his family. So he started taking more vacation time and asking for higher consulting fees. Not only did he get higher fees, he got more than he ever expected. For the rest of his life, my father kept asking what would have happened if he had asked for these things earlier.

- *I've got tenure.* Not so. In modern life, especially working life, nothing is certain anymore. With one big corporation swallowing another, you never know when *you* are going to be downsized. Too often, we make changes based upon external circumstances. Do not wait. Be active, not reactive.

> Even if you're on the right track you'll get run over if you just sit there.
>
> —Will Rogers, actor and humorist

- *It's not my fault.* People tend to focus on the other person rather than on their own internal barometers: "Why is my boss such a jerk?" or "How come they're always doing this to me?" This kind of thinking is unhelpful. It is more effective to ask yourself, "What am I feeling now? Why am I feeling this way?" Forget what other people do or think: focus inward. The only one who matters in your game plan is you. Become the quarterback of your own life.

YES, NO, AND OTHER TURNING POINTS

Does it surprise you to realize that the important, defining moments of your life have been based on your answers to questions?

- What do I want to be when I grow up?

- Where should I go to college?

- What major shall I declare?

- Should I accept that job offer?

- Will you marry me?

Some of our questions are accompanied by painful truths:

- What is wrong with me?

- Who am I?

- How can I be happier?

- Why can't I be happier?

- How can I earn more money?

- Where do I want to live?

- What kind of lifestyle do I want?

- Am I fully using my potential to love? to learn? to earn? to grow and change?

And, finally, some of our questions may represent big turning points:

- What do I want to do with the rest of my life?

- Am I settling instead of reaching?

The challenge in answering these questions is that they require tremendous honesty, but their sheer magnitude makes us turn away from that challenge. As with any large task we undertake, it helps to break a question down into small, manageable parts. Asking a more specific question can help you solve a problem or reflect more profoundly upon it.

Let's take a look at two career-related stories.

Scenario #1: I met Marsha and Ruth, who work together as financial analysts, when they attended one of my workshops. During a break, we began to talk. I was amazed at how their fears and doubts, their *cannots* and *should nots,* were causing them to make important decisions about themselves that were far too limiting. Neither one particularly enjoyed her job, which was basically to sit all day at a computer terminal reviewing exhaustive and tedious corporate earnings reports affecting no one ultimately but groups of wealthy investors.

Ruth, the older of the two, defended her reasons for staying with a job that gave her no satisfaction by saying she was fifty years old and had made her choices. In this youth-driven culture, where was she going to go—and so that was that. Her lack of interest in her own self-development and growth surprised and saddened me, as did Marsha's. But Marsha's resistance to making changes was guided by an advantageous pension plan, and yet she was only twenty-seven years old! However well she stood to do, it would be of no consequence to her for thirty years or more!

During our conversation, Marsha spoke of how she really wanted to do something with dance or movement, and I encouraged her to follow her passion. How wonderful it would be to get up each day and be paid for doing the thing you love to do! I told her about my friend's father, who at age eighty-six still goes to his office every day. As a dancer or aerobics instructor, or as the owner of a studio, she might not still be able to go to work at that gentleman's age. But her memories, and feelings of self-worth, would be just as rich. Career decisions, including job

change, must be guided by many reasons—job security or financial security being only one component. Asking questions
allows you to come to a decision that makes good sense, but
also allows you to preserve what's good about *you*.

Scenario #2: Jim was a segment producer for the eleven o'clock
weekend news of a local television affiliate when he got caught in
a management shake-up due to poor ratings. Approximately ten
staff members lost their jobs as a result of across-the-board lay-
offs imposed by the new management team.

In Jim's market, there weren't a lot of other doors to knock
on—there were only two other local channels—and unless he
was prepared to pick up and move to a new city, he was going
to have to reevaluate his options. And he did.

Jim began by asking himself what he liked most about his
job. His top reason was unusual; it was the weekend work,
which allowed him to spend weekday time with his family. Jim
was also honest enough with himself to admit, as his second
important reason, that he liked the fact that his job had brought
him into contact with prominent, interesting, and influential
people. As he continued to evaluate his job, he recognized that
as a television producer he was less a journalist than a facilitator—and that weekend news was feel-good news. He was not
exactly covering Capitol Hill. He took direction from the
assignment editor, and then he was responsible for figuring
out who to interview and how to get the reporter and crew to
the scene, get the footage, get it edited, and get it done by air-
time.

What Jim realized from all this surprised him and led him to
his next career. What he was really doing was staging events.
Jim decided he would reinvent himself as a corporate event
planner, organizing conferences, weekend junkets, and other
business-related functions.

Today, every event is another production for his city's top
companies and their executives. After five years in the business,

planning their annual stockholders' meetings, sales conferences, corporate celebrations, and other special occasions, Jim's ratings couldn't be better!

SETTLING IS CREATIVITY'S ENEMY

Insanity, Albert Einstein once said, is doing the same thing over and over again while hoping to achieve a different result. How many of us keep forging ahead with projects, jobs, or assignments we don't believe in? How many of us spend years pursuing dead ends or circling around cul de sacs because there's nowhere else to go? Even if we know the ground we work is infertile and isn't going to produce much, we keep working at it; and yet when you keep digging a hole in the wrong place, all you're going to get is a bigger hole.

There are several ways to love your work—for the ego-building strokes it provides and/or for the actual work itself. In my work, I enjoy recruiting new clients and sending out letters and follow-up materials. I find great satisfaction in creating new workshops and speeches, training others, keynoting, coaching, managing my staff, and of course writing books! I like some of these activities more than others, and if I were to grow to *dis*-like any one of the major activities I must perform to do my job, I would eliminate that service or hire it out, a luxury newly available to us now that so many of us work for or run our own small businesses. If I were to stop loving what I do, I would figure out how to make a change.

Many of us will change jobs and even careers several times. We spend approximately ninety-six thousand hours of our lives working, while most of us aren't working at something we like to do. Years ago I had a hand knitwear company where I designed the clothes and marketed them. It was a successful business, but after a while it no longer satisfied me. I asked myself, "Do I really love this? Do I want to spend many years of my life doing this kind of work?" And the answer was a clear no, so I moved on.

In fact, as I have said, I moved on many times. I have had five careers and I never expected to be so restless as to keep changing them. But I always had a feeling inside that I could do more, and I paid attention to those signals. I did not disregard those flickers of dissatisfaction, but kept asking the tough questions. So must you.

IQ ──────────────────────────────

The person who knows "how" will always have a job.
The person who knows "why" will always be his boss.

—Diane Ravitch, educator and writer

ASK! ASK! ASK!—BE RELENTLESS!

A successful career is the combination of doing a job that makes the best use of our talents and also having one that we find exciting. You may define exciting as selling or as dealing with high-power clients. Some people will find their passion in social or environmental work or in teaching. Each of us is different and each of us must ask, "What will I find exciting?" Where our passion lies is often close to where our talents lie. When we are doing something we are good at, we feel a sense of accomplishment. When we are challenged with a task that we can accomplish with some degree of difficulty we are even more fulfilled. But finding a job that makes use of our talents and at the same time challenges us is difficult. We may follow false paths. Sometimes we go into careers thinking we will like them, only to find we do not. Often, we simply fail to ask the questions that will lead us to find out what will make us happy. Those questions might include:

- What do I like to do?

- Why do I like to do it?

- What don't I like to do?

- Why don't I like to do it?

- What jobs have I had in the past that I have found satisfying?

- What jobs have I had in the past where I have felt challenged?

- What are my talents?

- Why am I talented in those fields?

As you start discovering matches, start looking for work that encompasses those areas. For example, I feel that I do two things well—teach and entertain. Since neither one alone was sufficient for me to earn a living, I asked myself if there was a way to combine them. Five years ago I started speaking and presenting workshops that rely heavily on infotainment. I use music and all kinds of zany characters, whom I introduce with rhyme. I have a lot of fun doing this, and my audiences have fun, too.

> **IQ** When you're following your energy and doing what you want all the time, the distinction between work and play dissolves.
>
> —Shakti Gawain, *Creative Visualization*

During your job search be alert for opportunities. I encourage job seekers and, in fact, everyone to become joiners, to do volunteer work, and to become active in their places of worship and in their communities. Go to parties, talk to people online, on planes—there are opportunities everywhere.

We all hear about networking, but I believe one of the most important parts of networking is being thoughtful and helping others. I am always amused that people think that networking is passing out your business card, but it is so much more. My mother used to say to keep doing good deeds and reaching out to others, but don't necessarily expect help back in the obvious places. Do not expect tit for tat, for the people you expect to help you may not. Help often comes from the most unexpected directions.

IQ The doors of Opportunity are marked "Push" and "Pull."

—Ethel Watts Mumford, novelist and humorist

SHIFTING GEARS

If you are dissatisfied with your current job, look at it as any problem you face. First you must decide what the problem is. You cannot solve anything without first knowing what you are solving. Ask yourself:

- Do I like my job?

- Am I settling?

- Do I like the people I work with?

- Am I appreciated and valued at this company?

- Do I find this job fulfilling?

- Am I unhappy with the work I do or with the amount of money I am paid?

- Is the field or industry I am in interesting to me?

- Are the duties I perform the kind of duties I like?

- What do I like about my job?

- What do I dislike about my job?

- What are my goals for the future and is this job on the right track to fulfilling those goals?

- If I could change one thing about my job, what would that be?

The answers to these questions will help you find out what the problem is. Keep asking: "Am I settling?" If you do not feel appreciated or do not like your coworkers, but you do like your duties, it may be time to move to another company. If you find the job unfulfilling or boring, but you like the company and feel appreciated and valued, perhaps you can try moving to another department. If you like nothing about your job—not your coworkers, boss, pay, or work—it is time to try something completely different. If the problem is your compensation, ask for a raise. Whatever the problem, you must first define it by asking questions. Once you can define the problem, the solution will easily present itself.

ASK THE EXPERT

IQ "That is difficult to say exactly," said Mr. Kirkwood, enjoying, like all lawyers, making a reply to a simple question difficult.

—Agatha Christie, mystery writer

We all have doctors and dentists, lawyers and landlords, bankers and stockbrokers, insurance agents and financial planners—a bevy of experts and advisors to handle all the important aspects of our lives—our health, wealth, and general well-being. Busy, respected, highly paid, most of them have probably worked hard to get where they are, while most of us probably feel intimated by them. True, our doctors can hold our lives in their hands. Our lawyers provide crucial advice; landlords control where we live; financial advisors can make our fortunes or cause us ruin.

And yet sometimes we turn over too much authority to these people who handle our personal business. Remember, after all, they work for us! Begin by realizing that we pay *them*. When I was a young girl, I read a book called *Men Are Like Streetcars*, the gist of which is if you miss one, another one is always behind it. Do not lose your authority and perspective: we do not have to be responsible to these experts; they must be responsible to us.

The first step in taking a questioning approach with our personal businesspeople is to feel entitled to the information you are requesting. That should not be hard to do, because you *are* entitled. It is your right to leave their office or hang up the phone feeling certain you have received all the information you wanted. If you have a question to ask your architect or lawyer, ask it. We trust that *they're* the ones who have the answer. Isn't that why you have hired them?

Because many of us become flustered when we speak to people whose judgment and experience we respect, and because we are speaking to them about highly personal, and often emotional, matters, it helps to first ask yourself: "What are the things I want to know?" Make a list of these questions that naturally follow from this answer so you can be sure to ask them, and work on phrasing your questions.

Be sure to make your wording clear and concise because this will get you the answer you want—or better advice. I am reminded of a movie moment that makes this point wonderfully well. In one of the *Pink Panther* movies, Inspector Clouseau starts up the stairs and encounters a man and a dog.

"Does your dog bite?" asks the inspector.

"No," the man responds; and seconds later Clouseau is bitten in the leg.

"I thought you said your dog doesn't bite!" the exasperated inspector demands.

The man's answer? "This is not my dog."

IQ There is a law which decrees that two objects may not occupy the same place at the same time—result: two people cannot see things from the same point of view, and the slightest difference in angle changes the thing seen.

—Mildred Aldrich, writer

An important question always to ask is, "What are my options?" We feel better and more in control when we have options, and there usually are options. As I have said, when I was diagnosed with breast cancer several years ago, the first doctor I saw only gave me one option. I went searching for other doctors and other ideas. I located a doctor and a plan of treatment with which I felt more comfortable.

If you are getting a second opinion be sure that you ask the same questions of each doctor so you won't be comparing apples and oranges. For example, I asked all of the doctors to list my options, and I asked them how many cases exactly like mine they had seen. Each doctor gave different advice, but only one had thoroughly read the new research. He believed in it and I believed him. So I had the procedure and postoperative therapy he recommended, which two years later became the standard protocol for this kind of diagnosis. It was difficult to question so many well-established surgeons, but my questions helped me to make an informed choice, and they helped save my life.

Once you are aware of the options in any area, you want to ask any business professional about consequences. Ask your questions in an orderly manner and take notes. "What are the positive consequences of putting my money into municipal bonds? What are the negative?" And do this with every option. "But what about mutual funds? A Keogh?"

A second opinion is also a good idea because it allows you to tap into someone else's store of information. You may learn about something the first person you spoke to did not know or neglected to tell you. If you listen carefully to the answers of each person you talk to and take diligent notes, you will come away with all the information you need to make the decision that is right for you.

Often the information we gather from our questions can be overwhelming, especially when one's physical or financial health is involved. Some people ask, "What would you do if you were in my situation?" That is a good question. An even better one is, "If I were a close friend or loved one, what would you advise me to do?" The first question might elicit a stock response; the second, almost always, a personal one.

Often the decision-making process becomes further complicated because of the unfamiliar jargon you are hearing. "What does that mean?" is a clarifying question you should keep close by. Most professions have a vocabulary or language common to their field. Part of the reason they use their professional terminology is from habit and perhaps partly it is to gain ascendancy. Make sure that you stop them and ask what the terms mean. "What is the difference between term versus life insurance, and which will be more important in achieving my goals?" If a doctor says you have insulin resistance, ask for clarification. "Here is your prescription; take it twice daily" can mean morning and evening or before or after meals. Repeat the instructions in your own words and ask, "Is this correct?" There is no shame in asking clarifying questions; even a rocket scientist may have to ask his stockbroker what a stock option is. The only shame lies in not asking and accidentally making a damaging mistake.

LEARNING TO BE A KID AGAIN

> Wherever one cut him, with a little question, he poured, spurted fountains of ideas.
>
> —Virginia Woolf, writer

As adults we are accustomed to asking once, if at all. We do not become impatient with people who won't give us the answers we want. We have gotten used to vague answers. We do not pursue our questions. We accept other people's reasons for their actions without questioning them. We have lost our curiosity about the world. We fear what we might find out about the world, other people, and especially ourselves.

It's better not to know, the saying goes. But it's not.

Several years ago we heard about discovering our inner child. I think it's time to discover our *inner questioning, curious child*. We need to start asking questions until we are satisfied. We need to ask questions of our spouses, our partners, our doctors, our bosses, and even our friends. We need to give thought to why we choose the friends we do. How do they expand our lives? How do they enliven them? When we are together, do we always tell the same old stories? They say that friends will see us through the bad as well as the good times. How honest are your friends? Do they have the courage to call it like it is, even when you won't?

Most important, we need to ask ourselves questions.

"Today is the first day of the rest of your life," went a once popular saying. What are you going to do with yours? And what would you do today if you knew tomorrow would be the last day of your life?

We often ask ourselves questions when we find ourselves in transitional moments: after we have overcome illness, job loss, or when a relationship ends. These are good times to be asking that question, but they are not the only times we should be asking. Times change; we change. Our wants and needs and desires do not remain a steady constant from the moment we leave school to the first time we hold a grandchild in our arms. We keep growing, not evenly, not chronologically, not even logically. Our pasts and presents mingle with our futures. We do not know where our lives will take us next; that is what makes life worth living: to discover the answer to the next, the ultimate questions. What's next? We are constantly evolving, constantly changing. And as we do, like the children we once were who asked questions to make sense of our world, it is just as important for us—in getting the right information and in fulfilling our potential—to first ask a question, and then we must ask it again and again.

Just like we did when we were children.

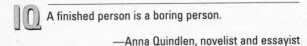

A finished person is a boring person.

—Anna Quindlen, novelist and essayist

We are happiest when we are challenged and forced to think. When we ask people to recall the best times in their lives, many will name the years they were in high school or college. This is because they were being intellectually and emotionally stimulated. Their minds were opened to different thoughts, ideas, people, cultures, and personalities. They were engaged with life.

Once that experience ends, for many of us, so does the thinking. Most of us are too busy, too tired to be challenging other people, let alone asking ourselves the big and timeless questions.

There are no teachers around here to ask us questions that make us think, but as adults that is our job. We must begin to ask the questions that force us to look in the mirror and be true to ourselves.

The questions we do not want to ask are the questions we must ask.

This is the only way to fulfill our potential.

IQ The only questions that really matter are the ones you ask yourself.

—Ursula K. LeGuin, writer and critic

FINAL JEOPARDY

"If I knew I could not fail, what would I do?" It all comes down to this.

What would you do in a universe without fear, without obstacles?

I bet you could answer this question in a flash. "I would quit my job and open a restaurant," or "I would learn to fly a plane," or "I would have a one-woman show," or "I would write a novel."

And then, if you are like most people, you would pull your thoughts back as quickly and instinctively as we pull back a hand that touches something hot. That is when the doubts rush back in. Immediately you begin with the rationalizations and the excuses and the justifications. "I can't because I would have to change my lifestyle and go back to school and, of course, I have no time. . . ." In other words, your running inner dialogue will talk you out of your plan before you even formulate it.

Fear and doubt stand in the way of most of our growth. We forgo our true desires because we are afraid of what might happen: we will fail; we will have less money; we will lose the only relationship we have, even though it's bringing no joy. We think we are risking too much.

But whether we move forward or not there is risk. Doing nothing is also a choice.

A question I ask myself a lot is, "How will I feel if I don't do this?" There are mornings when I wake up and do not want to go out running. I ask myself how I will feel if I don't go, and I know I will feel sluggish and annoyed with myself the entire day. I will be miserable if I don't go. That is when I force myself out of bed, into my sneakers, and into the park.

A man I know had a wonderful job—with travel, expensed lunches, creative and supportive colleagues—but he was bored. There is an expression people use when someone leaves a job—they ask, "Did he jump or was he pushed?" In this man's case, there was no reason for him to give up the security and status he enjoyed working at a prestigious corporation, but his soul was slowly dying. And when he asked himself, "How will I feel ten years from now if I stay in this job?" the answer came to him loud and clear. He would be miserable. He would grow to hate the good colleagues and the good life he led. He would grow, eventually, to hate himself. He took the risk and began to search out other opportunities. Was he pushed or did he jump? It does not matter. He took the risk.

When you invest your money and the market goes down, there is the risk it may go even lower, but there is always the possibility it may go right back up. This is part of the seesaw nature of life. If we do not use our potential, there is the risk that we will live our lives and at the end of it ask, "Where did it all go?"

To me, that is the saddest question of all, the one I hope you never have to ask.

IQ You realize there's more to life than a triple lutz. You don't take things for granted. You appreciate every day. When things happen like that you know you have to enjoy life. If you wake and aren't happy, you say to yourself, "I'm so lucky. What am I doing? Why am I putting myself down?" It makes me realize I'm so fortunate.

—Michelle Kwan, figure skater

HOW WILL I FEEL IF I DON'T DO THIS?

What is standing in the way of a better life for you? When there are obstacles to overcome, you must systematically break them down by asking, "What do I have to do to overcome this obstacle?" Once you have answered that question, you must then do that thing. The answer is important, but the action is even more important.

If we ask a question about our careers, our relationships at home, if we seek the counsel of specialists and experts; if we go through the process of finding out what we want to know but don't take action—of what use was the question? If we ask what we want to do with our lives, but then don't do it, why did we ask?

We can ask, and ask, and ask, and we can find the answers—good answers, right answers, achievable answers. But the answers are useless unless we *do something* with them.

Earlier in this chapter we spoke about people who play the hand they've been dealt. They remind me of a question Albert Einstein once asked. He wanted to know "Did God have any choice in the creation of the world?"

Einstein's answer does not interest me as much as his question. For what he was asking was whether our world could have looked or been organized any other way. If, in fact, God had a choice in the way our world is shaped, then *we* have a choice in the way we react to it, to those cards we have each been dealt.

As we have seen, questions can do many things. They can give us control in a conversation; they can persuade others; they can show people we care about them; they can help us to clarify our thoughts, ideas, and opinions; they can give us the information we need. But we are the ones who must take the action.

Of all the powers of questions, the final power lies with us. The power to ask the question, to listen to the responses, and to take action.

The answer is a resounding *yes*.

12

The Fifty Smartest Questions

*Job in the Bible asks God, "Why are you doing this to me?"
God basically answers him by saying, "Are you the one who
created the world? Are you the one who can do all the things
that I can do? How can you be so arrogant as to think you
understand any of this?"*

*It's one of the most famous questions in the Bible, because
of the answer, but also because of the power of the question.
A colleague once told me the reason she thinks Job "gets better" and lives a hundred and forty happy and prosperous
years after his troubles is because he is allowed to question.*

*The reason we all "get better" is the fact that we are able
to cry out to God and say, "Why me?" In the end, expressing
ourselves through questions can really save us.*

—RABBI MATTHEW D. GEWIRTZ,
Congregation Rodeph Sholom

ALL QUESTIONS ARE SMART QUESTIONS

The famous British mathematician and philosopher Alfred North Whitehead once said, "The 'silly question' is the first intimation of some totally new development." I think what he meant is that the questioning attitude is what leads to all new ideas. When we begin to question what is known, when we look at the world and our place in it with wonder and curiosity, when we refuse to simply accept things as they are, we ready ourselves for a great adventure.

That is what asking questions is all about.

We have asked hundreds of questions throughout this book. They are all smart questions, depending on how and when you use them. Because I am always asked at the end of my workshops for specific questions I think are the smartest, I have included this list.

That does not mean these are the only questions you should ask. In fact, these are more than questions, they are concepts. They are designed to get people to think, to clarify information so that there are fewer misunderstandings and miscommunications, to help people to sell themselves, and to help understand the consequences of taking certain actions.

These are just examples of the kinds of questions you might ask. Do not take their wording literally. Change them to suit the circumstance and to suit your personal style. Remember that in many situations—a job interview, going in to ask for a raise, or having an important discussion with a friend or family member—you want to go in with some question that you plan to ask based on what you are trying to accomplish. At the same time, you need to be flexible enough so that you can ask questions based on what other people say and how they answer your questions.

Here is a list of fifty questions for you to use as samples. I have divided them into six major categories.

Getting to the Specifics

These questions are meant to help you clarify, define, probe, and get to the bottom of issues and circumstances. They can be used to avoid mistakes and help you gain a greater understanding of people and situations.

Most of the mistakes we make are because we assume that we understand what the other person means. Since most people think and speak in generalities, it's important that you get the specifics. The key is to ask these questions in a nonaggressive manner so that people don't get defensive or annoyed. Let them know that you're asking because you want to be sure you genuinely understand what they are saying.

1. Can you clarify that?

2. Can you give me an example of what you mean?

3. What specifically do you mean by that?

4. Do you have any questions about what I just said?

5. What specific results are you looking for?

6. What do you plan to do with this information/report/project?

7. What is the real problem here?

Tuning In—Intellectually and Emotionally

Part of understanding another person is to be tuned in to his or her emotional state or way of thinking. We often find ourselves in situations where we want to know how the other person is feeling. We also want to know the other person's perspective, so we can meet their expectations—from their standpoint. That means knowing what is most important to them and how we might best fulfill it.

At other times it is important to tune in to our own thoughts and feelings. We go blindly into situations where we should be taking time to ask ourselves: "What's important to me here? What do I need to accomplish and how can I best do it?" We often need to define issues for ourselves so that we can better communicate them to others.

 Love is the answer, but while you are waiting for the answer, sex raises some pretty good questions.

—Woody Allen, comedian

Tuning in to Others

   8. From what standpoint are you asking?

   9. How do you feel about it?

  10. How strongly do you feel about it?

  11. What do you think about it?

  12. What's most important to you?

  13. What are your priorities?

  14. If I were in [his or her] shoes, how might I be feeling?

Tuning In to Yourself

  15. How do I feel about it?

  16. What do I think about it?

  17. What is my purpose?

  18. What assumptions am I making?

  19. What am I really trying to say with this message?

  20. What is the best way to phrase this question?

IQ No man really becomes a fool until he stops asking questions.

—Charles Steinmetz, electrical engineer and inventor

Feedback

We like to think that we are making ourselves perfectly clear at all times. The truth is, we are not always understood, and the best way to find out is to ask. The more specific you want the feedback to be, the more specific your question must be. For instance, you could ask your boss, "Have I made all the changes in this report that you requested?"

When you do get feedback, be prepared to ask clarifying questions. For instance, if your boss says, "You do not communicate well with your colleagues," ask what she means by that. Does that mean you need to write better memos? or that you need to listen more attentively? Or if your spouse says, "I could have used more help before the party," ask for specifics: "What would you have liked me to do?" or "What would be helpful for me to do next time?"

We often learn best about what we did wrong and how we can improve in the future by getting specific feedback. When I do my workshops, I always include an evaluation sheet at the end of participants' workbooks. I find these are a great help when I am planning future programs. When you do ask for feedback, don't forget to ask yourself some questions first, for instance: "Does this person have a frame of reference to provide me with sound feedback? Do I respect this person's opinion? Am I prepared to handle emotionally what he or she has to say?"

Sometimes we are asked to give feedback to others. Giving feedback can be tricky. It is not easy to give constructive criticism. Be sure you understand exactly what the other person wants from your feedback.

Getting Feedback from Others

    21. Did I understand you correctly when you said . . . ?

    22. Did I answer your question?

    23. How am I doing?

    24. Have I done what you requested?

Giving Feedback to Others

    25. What type of feedback would be most helpful to you?

    26. What do you plan to do with the feedback?

    27. Do you want me to just listen?

    28. Do you want me to ask questions and interact with you?

    29. Do you want me to give you advice?

Closing

Many people have difficulty with closing questions. In a selling or persuading situation, you will never know where the person stands unless you ask a closing question. If you do not, you will never find out what objections or obstacles lie in your way. Fear of rejection may stop you, but if you don't ask, the objections will never be addressed.

    30. Are we in agreement?

    31. Are you ready to go ahead?

    32. Is it a deal?

Consequences

Every action has an equal and opposite reaction. Every action you take has a consequence and should be considered carefully. The more important the action, the more careful consideration it deserves, and that consideration begins with you asking yourself questions.

The things that we regret in life are often those for which we did not consider the consequences. When my maternal grandfather died, he left his money equally to all his children, but he left his business to his only son. My mother's older sister, a widow, was in need of money, and my father, who had a strong sense of justice, fought to get her more money. He felt my uncle, who had been left the business, should provide for his sister. His intentions were honorable, but when he embarked on what he saw as a battle, he alienated part of our family forever. Had he stopped to think of the impact of his actions, he might have taken another course.

We often take certain actions in order to get short-term gains, and we fail to consider what will happen in the long run. Asking the following questions will reduce the possibility of that happening:

33. What if . . . ?

34. Is it worth it?

35. What will I regret not doing?

36. What might the short-term results be?

37. What might the long-term results be?

IQ The real questions are the ones that obtrude upon your consciousness whether you like it or not, the ones that make your mind start vibrating like a jackhammer, the ones that we "come to terms with" only to discover that they are still there. . . . They barge into your life at the times when it seems most important for them to stay away. They are the questions asked most frequently and answered most inadequately, the ones that reveal their true natures, slowly, reluctantly, most often against your will.

—Ingrid Bengis, poet

Personal

This list of questions is limitless. I cannot list all the questions you might ask yourself—only you can do that. The point is only that you *ask*. The easiest way to get into the asking habit is to begin by asking yourself questions. Then you can begin to ask questions of others as well. Here is a small sampling of questions to ask yourself:

38. Can you help me?

39. Can I help you?

40. Am I where I want to be?

41. What do I want to do?

42. Where do I want to spend the rest of my life?

43. And with whom?

44. What are my options?

45. What questions should I be asking?

46. What do I need to do to meet my goals?

47. What am I willing to change to get there?

48. What did I accomplish?

49. What could I have done better?

> **IQ** The important thing is not to stop questioning. Curiosity has its own reason for existing. One cannot help but be in awe when he contemplates the mysteries of eternity, of life, of the marvelous structure of reality. It is enough if one tries merely to comprehend a little of this mystery every day. Never lose a holy curiosity.
>
> —Albert Einstein

A colleague of mine once said, "I asked for very little out of life, and that's what I got." Do not settle for a little. Ask for more for yourself and others. Questions can change your life, in the smallest ways and in the largest. Ask more every day, and every day you will get more back. So remember the last and most important question of all:

50. What should I ask?

SUGGESTED READING

Bush, Barbara. *Barbara Bush: A Memoir*. New York: A Lisa Drew Book, Charles Scribner's Sons, 1994.

Caldwell, Taylor. *Listener*. Mettituck, N.Y.: Amereon, 1960.

Carnevale, Anthony P., et al. *Workplace Basics: The Skills Employers Want*. Washington, D.C.: American Society for Training and Development and U.S. Department of Labor, 1989.

Caron, Ann F. *Don't Stop Loving Me: A Reassuring Guide for Mothers of Adolescent Daughters*. New York: Henry Holt and Company, 1991.

Claxton, Guy. *Hare Brain, Tortoise Mind: How Intelligence Increases When You Think Less*. New York: Ecco Press, 1997.

Dillon, J.T. *Questioning and Teaching: A Manual of Practice*. New York: Teachers College Press, Teachers College of Columbia University, 1988.

Dreikurs, Rudolf, with Vicki Stoltz. *Children: The Challenge*. New York: Hawthorn Books, 1964.

Dreikurs, Rudolf. *Coping with Children's Misbehavior: A Parent's Guide*. New York: Hawthorn Books, 1972.

Faber, Adele, and Elaine Mazlish. *How to Talk So Kids Will Listen and Listen So Kids Will Talk*. New York: Avon Books, 1980.

Fiorina, Carly. "Making the Best of a Mess," *New York Times*, September 29, 1999.

Fisher, Roger, and William Ury. *Getting to Yes: Negotiating Agreement Without Giving In*. Boston: Houghton Mifflin, 1981.

Fisher, Ronald P., and R. Edward Geiselman. *Memory-Enhancing Techniques for Investigative Interviewing: The Cognitive Interview*. Springfield, Ill.: Charles C. Thomas Publisher, 1992.

Galinsky, Ellen and Judy David. *The Preschool Years: Family Strategies That Work: from Experts and Parents*. New York: Times Books, 1988.

Goodman, Ellen. *Close to Home*. New York: Simon and Schuster, 1979.

Hallowell, Edward M. "The Human Moment at Work," *Harvard Business Review*, January–February 1999: 58–66.

Heifetz, Ronald and Donald Laurie. "The Work of Leadership," *Harvard Business Review*, January–February 1997: 124–134.

Lebowitz, Fran. *Metropolitan Life*. New York: E.P. Dutton, 1978.

Leeds, Dorothy. *Marketing Yourself: The Ultimate Job Seeker's Guide*. New York: HarperCollins, 1991.

Leeds, Dorothy. *Smart Questions: The Essential Strategy for Successful Managers*. New York: McGraw-Hill, 1987.

Leeds, Dorothy. *Smart Questions to Ask About Your Children's Education*. New York: HaperPaperbacks, 1994.

Levin, David Michael. *The Listening Self: Personal Growth, Social Change, and the Closure of Metaphysics*. London: Routledge Publishing, 1989.

Lewin, Roger A. *Compassion: The Core Value That Animates Psychotherapy.* Northvale, N.J.: Jason Aronson, 1996.

MacFarquhar, Karissa. "The Connector," *New Yorker*, October 18 and 25, 1999: 110–32.

McConnell, John H. *AMACOM Conference Leadership Manual.* New York: AMACOM, 1973.

McInerny, Jay. "Naked on the Grass," *New Yorker,* January 18, 1999.

Mitroff, Ian. *Smart Thinking for Crazy Times: The Art of Solving the Right Problems.* San Francisco: Berrett-Koehler Publishers, 1998.

Naisbitt, John. *Megatrends: Ten New Directions Transforming Our Lives.* New York: Warner Books, 1982.

Okuda, Michael, and Denise Okuda. *Star Trek Chronology: The History of the Future.* New York: Pocket Books, 1996.

Overbye, Dennis. "Did God Have a Choice?" *New York Times Magazine,* April 18, 1999.

Payne, Stanley L. *The Art of Asking Questions.* Princeton, NJ: Princeton University Press, 1980.

Pipher, Mary. *Reviving Ophelia: Saving the Selves of Adolescent Girls.* New York: Putnam, 1994.

Postman, Neil. *Crazy Talk, Stupid Talk: How We Defeat Ourselves by the Way We Talk—and What to Do about It.* New York: Dell, 1976.

Rich, Dorothy. *MegaSkills.* Boston: Houghton Mifflin, 1992.

RoAne, Susan. *What Do I Say Next? Talking Your Way to Business and Social Success.* New York: Time Warner Books, 1997.

Robbins, Anthony. *Awaken the Giant Within.* New York: Summit Books, 1991.

Salopek, Jennifer J. "Is Anyone Listening?" *Training & Development*, September 1999: 58–59.

Schiller, David. *The Little Zen Companion.* New York: Workman, 1994.

Schoenfeld, Dr. Myron. *Strictly Confidential: How Doctors Make Decisions*. New York: Oceana Publications, 1990.

Schwartz, Tony. "Going Postal," *New York* magazine, July 19, 1999: 33–36.

Shell, Richard G. *Bargaining for Advantage: Negotiation Strategies for Reasonable People*. New York: Viking, 1999.

Steiner, George A. *A Step-by-Step Guide to Strategic Planning: What Every Manager Must Know*. New York: Free Press Paperbacks, 1979.

Taitz, Sonia. *Mothering Heights*. New York: William Morrow and Company, 1992.

Tannen, Deborah. "Listening to Men, Then and Now," *New York Times*, May 16, 1999.

"TV Looks for One Right Answer," *New York Times*, July 24, 1999.

Wahlroos, Sven. *Family Communication*. Chicago: Contemporary Books, 1995.

Walton, Douglas. *Question Reply Argumentation*. New York: Greenwood, 1989.

Wolfson, Susan J. *The Questioning Presence: Wordsworth, Keats, and the Interrogative Mode in Romantic Poetry*. Cornell, N.Y.: Cornell University Press, 1986.

Yankelovich, Daniel. *The Magic of Dialogue: Transforming Conflict into Cooperation*. New York: Simon & Schuster, 1999.

POSTSCRIPT

"Success is turning knowledge into positive action."

Dorothy Leeds's presentations—delivered with dynamic, theatrical learning techniques—will help you manage better, communicate more effectively, and improve your image and relationships. More importantly, they will help you to take your knowledge and use it.

If you want to know more about Dorothy Leeds's speeches, seminars, and audiocassette programs, please call or write to:

Dorothy Leeds
Organizational Technologies, Inc.
800 West End Avenue, Suite 10A
New York, NY 10025
Phone: 212-864-2424
Fax: 212-932-8364

If you would like an electronic adventure, visit Ms. Leeds's web site at www.dorothyleeds.com or e-mail her at dleeds@dorothyleeds.com.

Her speeches and seminars include:

"The Seven Powers of Questions: Secrets to Success in Life and at Work"

"PowerSpeak: The Complete Guide to Persuasive Public Speaking and Presenting"

"PowerWriting: How to Get Your Message Across with Ease and Authority"

"Smart Questions + Smart Listening = Dialogue Selling"

"Smart Questions: An Essential Strategy for Successful Managers"

"Marketing Yourself: The Ultimate Job Seeker's Guide"

"Assertiveness Training for Women in Business (. . . and Men, Too!)"

"Women's Unique Strengths"

and her one-woman show, "Mom, I Almost Made It!"

Her audiocassette programs are:

"PowerSpeak: The Complete Guide to Persuasive Public Speaking and Presenting"
    (6 cassettes with comprehensive workbook) $95.00 for the set

"Smart Questions: The Key to Sales Success"
    (6 cassettes with comprehensive workbook) $95.00 for the set

"Marketing Yourself: The Ultimate Job Seeker's Guide"
(6 cassettes with comprehensive workbook) $95.00
for the set

INDEX

Page numbers in italic indicate illustrations, those in bold indicate tables.

Accelerated Learning, 51
Action, taking, 269–70
Active versus reactive, 253
Activities, questioning in, 177
Adolescents, 235–43
  arbitrator versus litigator, 239–40
  body language, 238
  common language for, 236–41
  conversation starters and stoppers, 241–42
  disagreeing with respect, 238
  feelings, 237
  golden rule, 242–43
  individuality, need for, 235–36
  information seeking, 238
  listening importance, 237
  problems, restating, 238
  solutions, finding, 240
  suggestions, 240
  timing importance, 237
  voice clues, 238–39

Adulthood cult, 247–48
Aggressiveness or assertiveness, 96–97
Aldrich, Mildred, 263
Allen, Woody, 274
Althofer, Beth, 41, 162
American Management Association, 207–8
Answers
  answering reflex, 16–18
  asking questions, impact on, 20–23
  assumptive questions, 33
  closed-ended questions, 29–31, 188, 193, 200
  contaminated questions, 33
  controlling, 27–35
  general questions, 31–32
  indirect questions, 33–34
  leading questions, 33
  legal system and, 19–20
  manners and, 17–18

Answers (*cont.*)
  multiple-choice questions, 32–33
  objectives of questions, **34–35**
  open-ended questions, 30–31, 127,
    166, 188, 200, 203, 205
  polygraph tests, 22
  power of asker, 16
  programmed to answer, 18–20
  purpose of questions, 24–26, 27
  quality questions for quality
    answers, 24–26
  school and, 18–19
  self-concept from, 18
  selling and, 183–84
  specific questions, 31–32
  validation of, 224, 227
  voice clues, 22–23
  waiting for, 126
  wanting to hear, 23–24, 53–54
  wording influence on, 20–22
  See also Control from questions
Appreciation for ideas, 121
Arbitrator versus litigator, 239–40
Armstrong, Lance, 84
Art of Asking Questions, The (Payne),
  20
Asking versus telling
  leadership, 198–200, 206, 207
  organizations, 172, 174–77
  selling, 179–81, 183, 192
  thinking stimulation, 41
Assertiveness or aggressiveness, 96–97
Assumptions obstacle, 78, 81–84
Assumptive questions, 33
Atlantic Forensic Investigations and
    Consultants, 22, 128
AT&T, 186
Attention spans and listening, 140, 153
Authority, fear of questioning, 11

Bad listening, 138–44
Baldwin, Christina, 248
Barbara Bush: A Memoir (Bush), 12
Bargaining for Advantage (Shell), 64
Belief and achievements, 246–53

Believing ourselves, 159–60
Bengis, Ingrid, 278
Billings, Joe, 157
Bloomberg, Michael, 3
Body language clues
  for adolescents, 238
  for listening, 134, 155
  for opening up people, 115, 125–26,
    127–28
Bonhoeffer, Dietrich, 60
Boundaries
  essential you, 245–47
  families, 229–30
Brainstorming
  leadership and, 210–15
  thinking stimulation from, 59–60
British Airways, 184, 198
Bush, Barbara, 12–13
Business situations
  control from questions, 95
  listening importance, 138–39
  opening up people, 114–15
  See also Organizations
"Buy-in," developing, 206–7

Calacanis, Jason, 13
Caldwell, Taylor, 131
Camus, Albert, 144
Careers and essential you, 257–61
Caring questions, 122–25
Caron, Ann, 235, 242
Carroll, Lewis, 109
Carson, Rachel, 244
Change
  excuses to avoid, 251–52
  fear of, 251, 267–68
  positive changes, preventing, 250–53
  questioning, change from, 1–3
  questions, 171–73
Children
  learning to be, 265–67
  persuasion in child-rearing, 167–68
  potential of, 244–45
  questioning talent of, 216–18, 224
Children: The Challenge (Dreikurs), 167

Choosing, learning how, 228–29
Christie, Agatha, 261
Clarifying questions
  jargon, clarifying, 264
  listening and, 154
  thinking from, 48–49, 77, 81
Clarke, Jean Illsley, 219
Claxton, Guy, 55–56
Clinton, Bill, 75
Closed-ended questions
  answers and, 29–31
  leadership, 200
  selling, 188, 193
Closing questions, 192–95, 276
"C mode," 97
Coaching questions, 163–65
Comfort areas for opening up people,
  116–18
Commenting while listening, 155
Common language for adolescents,
  237–40
Compassion (Lewin), 139
Complacency danger, 197–98
Compromise, learning, 234–35
Confidence areas for opening up
  people, 116–18
Consequence finding questions, 277
Contaminated questions, 33
Control freaks, 102–3
Control from questions, 89–109
  aggressiveness or assertiveness,
    96–97
  answers, controlling, 27–35
  business situations, 95
  "C mode," 97
  control freaks, 102–3
  control meeks, 102, 103–4
  conversation steering, 92–93
  defensiveness, diffusing, 97–99
  defined, 90
  delivery of questions, 107
  demeaning questions, 105
  effective questions, 105–7
  emotional control, 91–92, 98–99

excuse-provoking questions, 104–5
"fight or flight" mode, 98
help, asking for, 99
"hot potato" exercise, 92–93
ineffective questions, 104–5
information getting questions, 106
job interviews, 93–94
journalists, 95–96
negative control, 109
positive control, 109
preparation importance, 107–9
problem solving questions, 106
reasons for wanting control,
  94–96
salespeople, 96, 184
situational control, 92–94
social situations, 94, 95
sympathy technique, 99
talking and control, 100–101
Control meeks, 102, 103–4
Conversation
  prompts, 226
  starters and stoppers, 241–42
  steering, 92–93
Creativity in organizations, 210–15

Daydreaming, 152–53
Dean, Ronda, 214
Defensiveness, diffusing, 97–99
Delivery of questions, 107
Demeaning questions, 105
Denise Calls Up, 6–7
Details before emotional questions,
  127
Detective, becoming, 66–72
de Vink, Lodewijk J.R., 38, 199,
  214–15
De Vries, Peter, 235
Dialogue Selling, 173, 186–98
Difficult questions, saving, 127
Dillon, J.T., 13–14, 63, 81
Disagreeing with respect, 237
Distractions from thinking, 57
Don't Stop Loving Me (Caron), 235
Dreikurs, Rudolf, 167, 225, 235, 241

Ears for listening, 133, 148
Edison, Thomas, 42–43
Effective questions, 105–7
Einstein, Albert, 257, 269, 279
Emotions
    control, 91–92, 98–99
    questions, 110–13
    right brain, 50–51, 50–52
    See also Feelings
Empathy from listening, 145, 146–47
Emphasis, misunderstandings from,
    86–87
Essential you, 244–70
    action, taking, 269–70
    active versus reactive, 253
    adulthood cult, 247–48
    asking (not) and failure, 252–53
    belief and achievements, 246–53
    boundaries, beyond, 245–47
    careers and, 257–61
    childhood potential, 244–45
    children, learning to be, 265–67
    excuses to avoid change, 251–52
    experts, dealing with, 261–65
    fear of change, 251, 267–68
    focusing inward, 253
    happiness questions, 258–59, 261
    honesty for, 255
    inner questioning child, 265–67
    jargon, clarifying, 264
    jobs and, 257–61
    laziness, 251
    networking, 260
    options, identifying, 263–64
    other people focus, 253
    positive changes, preventing,
        250–53
    potential, using our, 267–68
    programming, 246
    saying yes to life, 248–49
    second opinions, 264
    self-deceptions, 251–52
    settling, creativity's enemy, 257–58,
        261
    social norms and, 247

time, finding, 250–51
turning points, 254–57
Everyday life questioning habit, 222–23
Excuse-provoking questions, 104–5
Excuses to avoid change, 251–52
Expectations and listening, 137–38
Experts, dealing with, 261–65
Expression, urgency for, 141
Eyes
    for listening, 134, 148, 153
    for opening up people, 125, 127
Ezra, Iba, 219

Fact finding, 68–72, 150. See also
    Information from questions
False Evidence Appearing Real (FEAR),
    144
Families, 216–43
    boundaries, theirs and yours, 229–30
    children's questioning talent,
        216–18, 224
    choosing, learning, 228–29
    compromise, learning, 234–35
    conversation prompts, 226
    everyday life questioning, 222–23
    family meetings, 234–35
    feelings and questions, 221, 226–28
    growing up, 223–25
    imponderable questions, 220–21
    listening importance, 224
    modeling questioning, 225–26
    persuasion, 233
    power struggle or questioning,
        222–23
    problem solving, 231–33, 234
    purpose of questions, 224–25
    reassurance from questioning,
        224–25
    religious traditions and, 219–21
    responses to questions, 224
    self-concept from, 218, 225–26
    sincerity of questions, 223
    story reading for questioning, 226
    validation of answers, 224, 227
    See also Adolescents

FEAR (False Evidence Appearing Real), 144
Fear of change, 251, 267–68
Feedback
    persuasion principle, 163–65
    questions, 275–76
Feelings
    adolescents, 237
    families, 221, 226–28
    information, 73–74
    listening for, 148–49
    See also Emotions
Fergason, James L., 43, 58, 213
Fifth Discipline, The (Senge), 169
"Fight or flight" mode, 98
Fiorina, Carly, 157
Fisher, Ronald P., 81, 102
Focazio, Bob, 187
Focusing
    inward, 253
    listening, 153
    questions for, 38–41
Fry, Arthur, 36, 37

Gale, Stephen, 252
Galland, Helen, 95
Gawain, Shakti, 259
Geiselman, R. Edward, 81, 102
Generalities obstacle, 77–81
General questions, 31–32
General to specific questions, 80–81
Gewirtz, Rabbi Matthew D.
    on children and questions, 14
    on famous questions in Bible, 271
    on fear of questions, 45
    on feelings behind questions, 149
    on gray areas of life, 221
    on heart for listening, 135
    on importance of questioning, 220
Golden rule, 242–43
Golomb, David, 108
Gone With the Wind, 56
Goodman, Ellen, 248
Good Morning, America, 32

Groups, listening in, 154
Growing up, 223–25
Gutenberg, Johannes, 5
Gypsy, 23–24

Hall, Florence Howe, 223
Hallowell, Edward M., 7
Happiness questions, 258–59, 261
Harvard Business Review, 7
Hayes, Helen, 245
Hayward, Andrew, 53
Heart for listening, 135, 148
Heifetz, Ronald A., 175
Hellman, Lillian, 247
Help, asking for, 99
Hendrix, Harville, 138
Hintikka, Jaakko, 66, 67
Hiring questions, 199–201
Holtz, Lou, 65
Honesty for essential you, 255
Hopkins, Tom, 192
"Hot potato" exercise, 92–93
How questions, 72, 115
Howson, Tamar, 142, 197, 214
"Human Moment at Work, The," 7
Human touch in communication, 6–7
Hurt from opening up, 119–20

I-centered, 136, 137, 153–54
"Illusion of listening," 153
Imago Therapy, 138
Impatience and listening, 153
Implied questions, 189
Imponderable questions, 220–21
Indirect questions, 33–34
Individuality, need for, 235–36
Ineffective questions, 104–5
Information from questions, 61–88
    adolescents, 237–38
    assumptions obstacle to, 78, 81–84
    detective, becoming, 66–72
    emphasis and misunderstandings, 86–87
    facts, finding, 68–72, 150
    feeling information, 73–74

Information from questions (*cont.*)
  generalities obstacle to, 77–81
  general to specific, 80–81
  how questions, 72
  listening and missing, 142
  miscommunication, solving, 68–72
  motives, 73–74
  obstacles to right information, 74–87
  opening up people, 118
  "paper-tearing" exercise, 61–62
  perplexity resolution, 63
  pictures from words, 85–86
  purpose of questions, 81
  reasons for questions, 63
  red flag words and phrases, 79–80
  right information, lack of, 65–66
  selling, 184
  statements versus questions, 62
  success from, 64–72
  vacuum, filling, 62–63
  volunteering information obstacle to,
    75–77
  what if questions, 71
  what questions, 70–71
  when questions, 70
  where questions, 69–70
  who questions, 68–69
  why questions, 71–72
  word meanings obstacle to, 84–87
Inner questioning child, 265–67
Inner voice and listening, 144
Intelligence from listening, 147
Interview questions, 93–94
Inventions from questions, 36–37
It Takes a Prophet to Make a Profit
  (Shook), 182

Jackson, Laura Riding, 248
Janeway, Elizabeth, 230
Jargon, clarifying, 264
Job interviews, 93–94
Jobs and essential you, 257–61
Journalists, 95–96
Judaism, 219–20
Judgments from opening up, 120–21

Kant, Immanuel, 45
King, Larry, 124–25
Korda, Michael, 110
Kwan, Michelle, 269

Land, Edwin, 36, 37
Laurie, Donald L., 175
Laziness, 251
Leadership, 199–210
  asking or telling, 199–200, 206, 207
  brainstorming, 210–15
  "buy-in," developing, 206–7
  closed-ended questions, 200
  hiring questions, 199–201
  listening importance, 203, 211–12
  meetings, 206–10
  mentoring, 204–5
  needs analysis, 202–3
  open-ended questions, 200, 203, 205
  postanalysis questions, 209
  secondary brainstorming, 212–13
  start-up questions, brainstorming,
    211
  Super Probe questions, 200–201,
    205
  telling or asking, 199–200, 206, 207
  training questions, 201–5
  See also Organizations
Leading questions, 33
Learning
  organizations, 169–70
  questioning, 13–14
  what we don't know, 12–13
Lectures, problems with, 160–61, 167
Leeds, Dorothy, xiii–xvii, 9, 285–87
Left brain (rational), **50–51**, 50–52
Legal system and questioning, 19–20
LeGuin, Ursula K., 267
Leiberman, Janice, 32
"Let's talk about me" factor, 113–15
Levin, David Michael, 143
Lewin, Roger A., 139
Lewis, Anthony, 111
Lies, 128–30
Lincoln, Abraham, 217

"Listening between the lines," 148
Listening quality, 131–56
  adolescents, 237
  attention spans and, 140, 154
  bad listening, 138–44
  benefits, 144–47
  body language, 134, 155
  business situations, 138–39
  clarification, asking for, 154
  commenting while listening, 155
  daydreaming, 152–53
  ears for, 133, 148
  empathy from, 145, 146–47
  expectations and, 137–38
  expression, urgency for, 141
  eyes for, 134, 148, 153
  facts, listening for, 150
  families, 224
  FEAR (False Evidence Appearing
      Real), 144
  feelings, listening for, 148–49
  focusing, 153
  groups, listening in, 154
  heart for, 135, 148
  I-centered, 136, 137, 151
  "illusion of listening," 153
  Imago Therapy, 138
  impatience and, 153
  improving, 147–51
  information, missing from bad, 142
  inner voice and, 144
  intelligence from, 147
  leadership, 203, 211–12
  "listening between the lines," 148
  mind for, 134–35, 148
  misinterpretations from bad,
      142–43
  mistakes reduction, 142, 147, 155
  names, remembering, 154
  note taking, 155
  observation for information, 132
  opening up people, 124–25
  organizations, 175, 211–12
  others, listening to, 12–13
  others' view of our, 143
  problem identification from, 147
  purpose, listening with, 136–38
  quiz, 148, 151–56
  rewards, 139, 153
  selling, 185
  spouses, 138
  strategies, 152
  successful people and, 132–33
  tests and, 155
  time for, 140–41
  time spent listening, 132
  training for, 139–40
  tuning in and out, 154
  value feeling from, 146–47
  vocal variety technique, 148–49
  voice clues, 149
  who is speaking, 150–51
  work of, 139

MacFarquhar, Karissa, 13
Magic of Dialogue, The (Yankelovich),
    55
Manners and questioning, 17–18
Marketplace knowledge, 195–98
Market research cautions, 195–97
Markham, Beryl, 251
Mason, Perry, 19
McInerny, Jay, 130
McKennirey, Peter, 181
Mead, Margaret, 236
Meetings
  business, 206–10
  family, 234–35
Melton, Douglas W., 197
Memory-Enhancing Techniques for
    Investigative Interviewing (Fisher
    and Geiselman), 81
Men as reticent speakers, 117–18
Mentoring, 204–6
Message, conveying, 113
Mind for listening, 134–35, 148
Miscommunication, solving, 68–72
Misinterpretations and listening,
    142–43
Misperceptions and selling, 182–83

Mistake reduction from listening, 142, 147, 155
Mitroff, Ian, 59
Mizner, Wilson, 136
Modeling questioning
  in families, 225–26
  in organizations, 177
Moss, Dale, 184, 198, 222
Motives, 73–74
Multiple-choice questions, 32–33
Mumford, Ethel Watts, 260
Murphy, Jim, 128
Murray, Mamie, 22, 128–29

Naisbitt, John, 7
Names, remembering, 154
National Association of Purchasing Managers, 123
NBC, 67–68
Needs analysis, 202–3
Needs versus wants, 187
Negative
  control, 109
  questions, 1–2, 39, 40, 44–45
Networking, 260
New Yorker, 13
New York Times, 68, 111, 117
Note taking, listening, 155

Objections as unanswered questions, 190–92
Objectives of questions, 34–35
Observation for information, 132
Obstacles to right information, 74–87
Omissions, 129
Open-ended questions
  answers and, 30–31
  leadership, 200, 203, 205
  opening up people, 126–27
  persuasion, 166
  selling, 188
Opening up people, 110–30
  answers, waiting for, 126
  appreciation for ideas, 121

body language, 115, 125–26, 127–28
business situations, 114–15
caring questions, 122–24
comfort areas for, 116–18
confidence areas for, 116–18
details before emotions, 127
difficult questions, saving, 127
emotional questions, 110–13
eye contact for, 125, 127
how questions, 115
hurt from, 119–20
information from, 118
judgments from, 120–21
"Let's talk about me" factor, 113–15
lies, 128–30
listening importance, 124
men as reticent speakers, 117–18
message, conveying, 113
omissions, 129
open-ended questions for, 126–27
penalty from truth, 120
problem solving from, 118, 119
rapport, developing for, 126
reasons for, 118, 119–21
reluctant talkers, 116–21
selling, 185
silence, uncomfortableness, 113–14
social situations, 114
stalling tactics, 130
talking about ourselves, 113–15
techniques for, 126–28
telemarketers, 123
truth, 128–30
unburdening by talking, 113
voice clues, 115, 125–26
why questions, 115
women as intuitive, 117
word choice, 129
Options, identifying, 263–64
Organizational Technologies, 178
Organizations, 169–215
  activities, questioning in, 177
  asking or telling, 172, 174–76
  brainstorming, 210–15

change questions, 171–73
creativity, 210–15
learning organizations, 169–70
listening importance, 176, 211–12
modeling questioning culture, 177
platforms for questioning, 177–78
questioning culture, building, 177–79
sales department breakthrough,
    173–74
secondary brainstorming, 212–13
self-questioning, 213–15
start-up questions, brainstorming, 211
telling or asking, 172, 174–77,
    180–81, 183, 192, 199–200, 206,
    207
thinking organizations, 169–71
virtuous cycle of feedback, 170
See also Business situations;
    Leadership; Selling
Original thinking, rewards from, 54
Other(s)
listening, others' view of, 143
people focus, 253
questions for, 38, 40
Ourselves, questions for, 37–38, 39–40

"Paper-tearing" exercise, 61–62
Parke-Davis Women's Healthcare, 214
Patterns, being stuck in, 46–47
Payne, Stanley L., 20–21
Penalty from truth, 120
Perplexity resolution, 63
Personal questions, 278–79
Persuasion, 157–68
believing ourselves, 159–60
child-rearing, persuasion in, 167–68
coaching questions, 163–65
families, 233
feedback principle, 163–65
lectures, problems with, 160–61, 167
open-ended questions for, 166
secret of, 157–59
self-discovery process, 161–63
selling, persuasion, 165–67, 185–87
Picasso, Pablo, 5

Pictures from words, 85–86
Piper, Mary, 242
Platforms for questioning, 177–78
Polygraph tests, 22
Positive
changes, preventing, 250–53
control, 109
questions, thinking, 40, 43–46
Postanalysis questions, 209
Postman, Neil, 5, 35
Potential, using our, 267–68
Power of asker, 16
Power struggle or questioning,
    222–23
Preparation importance, 107–9
Probing questions, 49–50
Problem solving
families, 231–33, 234
listening for, 147
opening up people for, 118, 119
questions for control, 106
restating problems, 238
thinking and, 58–60
Productiveness from thinking,
    54–55
Programmed to answer, 18–20
Programming and essential you, 246
Purpose, listening with, 136–38
Purpose of questions
answers and, 24–26, 27
families, 224–25
information finding, 81

Qualifying prospects, 187–89
Quality questions for quality answers,
    24–26
Questioning and Teaching: A Manual
    of Practice (Dillon), 13–14
Questioning culture, building, 177–79
Questioning Presence: Wordsworth,
    Keats, and the Interrogative Mode
    in Romantic Poetry, The
    (Wolfson), 16–17
Question-Reply Argumentation
    (Walton), 145

Questions, power of, 1–14, 271–79
  answers, asking impact on, 20–23
  authority, fear of questioning, 11
  change from, 1–3
  closing questions, 276
  communication tool, 2, 4–5
  consequence finding questions, 277
  failure from not asking, 252–53
  feedback questions, 275–76
  human touch in communication, 6–7
  learning to ask, 13–14
  learning what we don't know, 12–13
  listening to others, 12–13
  negative questions, 1–2, 39, 40, 44–55
  personal questions, 278–79
  power of, 8–10
  rude, fear of being, 13
  specifics (getting to) questions, 273
  success from, 6, 64–72, 132–33
  tuning in questions, 273–74
  turning points, 3–4, 254–57
  vulnerability and, 11–12
  See also Answers; Control from
    questions; Essential you; Families;
    Information from questions;
    Listening quality; Opening up
    people; Organizations; Persuasion;
    Thinking stimulation
Question/thought continuum, 41,
  41–42, 44
Quindlen, Anna, 266
Quiz, listening, 148, 151–56

Rapport, developing, 126
Rational (left brain), 50–51, 50–52
Ravitch, Diane, 258
Reassurance from questioning, 224–25
Red flag words and phrases, 79–80
Reilly, D., 19
Relationship building, selling, 195
Religious traditions and questioning,
  219–21
Reluctant
  talkers, 116–21
  thinkers, 52–58

Responses to questions, 224
Reviving Ophelia (Piper), 242
Rewards, listening, 139, 153
Right brain (emotional), 50–51,
  50–52
Right information, lack of, 65–66
RoAne, Susan, 143
Robbins, Anthony, 3
Rogers, Carl, 138
Roosevelt, Eleanor, 83
Rude, fear of being, 13

Sapir, Avinoam, 76
Satir, Virginia, 216
Saying yes to life, 248–49
Schoenfeld, Myron R., 88
School
  questioning in, 18–19
  thinking after graduation, 56–57
Secondary brainstorming, 212–13
Second opinions, 264
Select Appointments North America,
  138
Self-concept
  from answers, 18
  from questioning, 218, 225–26
  from thinking, 57–58
Self-deceptions, 251–52
Self-discovery process, 161–63
Self-questioning, 42–43, 213–15
Selling, 179–98
  answering questions, 183–84
  asking or telling, 180–81, 183, 192
  benefits of questions, 181–82
  closed-ended questions, 188, 193
  closing questions, 192–95
  complacency danger, 197–98
  control from questions, 96, 184
  defined, 179–82
  Dialogue Selling, 173, 186–98
  implied questions, 189
  information from questions, 184
  listening quality, 185
  marketplace knowledge, 195–98
  market research cautions, 195–97

misperceptions, 182–83
needs versus wants, 187
objections as unanswered questions, 190–92
open-ended questions, 188
opening up people, 185
persuasion in, 165–67, 185–87
qualifying prospects, 187–90
relationship building, 195
sales department breakthrough, 173–74
Super Probe questions, 188–90
telling or asking, 180–81, 183, 192
test closing questions, 194
thinking from questioning, 184
wants versus needs, 187
See also Organizations
Senge, Peter, 169
Settling, creativity's enemy, 257–58, 261
Shell, G. Richard, 64
Shook, Robert L., 124, 182
Silence, uncomfortableness with, 113–14
Sincerity of questions, 223
Situational control, 92–94
Smart Questions: The Essential Strategy for Successful Managers (Leeds), 9
Smart Thinking for Crazy Times (Mitroff), 59
SmithKline Beecham, 142, 197, 214
Social norms and essential you, 247
Social situations
controlling, 94, 95
opening up people, 114
Solutions, finding, 58–60, 240
Specific questions, 31–32
Specifics (getting to) questions, 273
Spouses and listening, 138
Stalling tactics, 130
Star Trek, 1, 89
Start-up questions, brainstorming, 211
Statements versus questions, 62
Steiner, George A., 179

Story of Us, The, 241
Story reading for questioning, 226
Strauss, Jon, 162
Success from questioning, 6, 64–72, 132–33
Suggestions, soft, 240
Super Probe questions, 188–90, 200–201, 205
Sutherland, Donald, 26
Sympathy technique, 99

Talking
control, 100–101
ourselves, talking about, 113–15
See also Telling versus asking
Talmud, 219–20
Tannen, Deborah, 117
Telemarketers, 123
Telling versus asking
leadership, 199–200, 206, 207
organizations, 172, 174–76
selling, 180–81, 183, 192
thinking stimulation, 41
Test closing questions, 194
Tests and listening, 154–55
Theater for Learning, 178
Thinking organizations, 169–71
Thinking stimulation, 36–60
Accelerated Learning, 51
answers, not wanting to know, 53–54
asking or telling, 41
brainstorming, 59–60
clarifying questions, 48–49, 77, 81
distractions from, 57
focusing from questions, 38–41
inventions from questions, 36–37
left brain (rational), 50–51, 50–52
negative questions, 39, 40, 44–45
original thinking, rewards from, 54
others, questions for, 38, 40
ourselves, questions for, 37–38, 39–40
patterns, being stuck in, 46–47
positive questions, 40, 43–46
probing questions, 49–50

Thinking stimulation, (*cont.*)
  problems and, 58–60
  productiveness from, 54–55
  question/thought continuum, *41,*
    41–42, 44
  reluctant thinkers, 52–58
  right brain (emotional), **50–51**, 50–52
  school and, 56–57
  self-concept from, 57–58
  self-questioning, 42–43
  selling, 184
  solutions, finding, 58–60
  telling or asking, 41
  time and energy for, 55–56
  working backward, 59
  worry from, 44–45
Thurber, James, 242
Time
  adolescents, timing importance, 237
  essential you and, 250–51
  listening time, 132, 140–41
  thinking time, 55–56
Tomlin, Lily, 77
Training
  listening, 139–40
  questions, 201–5
Training & Development, 139
Truth, 128–30
Tuning in and out, 154
Tuning in questions, 273–74
Turning points, 3–4, 254–57

Unburdening by talking, 113
U.S. Department of Labor, 132
Ustinov, Peter, 241

Vacuum, filling, 62–63
Validation of answers, 224, 227
Value feeling from listening, 146–47
Virtuous cycle of feedback, 170
Vocal variety technique, 148–49

Voice clues
  for adolescents, 239
  for listening, 149
  for opening up people, 115, 125–26
  for questioning, 22–23
Voltaire, 36
Volunteering information obstacle,
  75–77
Vulnerability and questioning, 11–12

Walters, Barbara, 110–11, 124–25
Walton, Douglas N., 145
Wanting to hear answers, 23–24, 53–54
Wants versus needs, 187
Webster, S. Tobin, 24
Weinstock, Laura, 226
West, Jessamyn, 235
What Do I Say Next? (RoAne), 143
What if questions, 71
What questions, 70–71
When questions, 70
Where questions, 69–70
Whitehead, Alfred North, 80, 272
Who is speaking, 150–51
Who questions, 68–69
Why questions, 71–72, 115
Wilson, Larry, 8, 83, 212, 250
Wolfson, Susan J., 16–17
Women as intuitive, 117
Woolf, Virginia, 265
Word(s)
  meanings obstacle, 84–87
  opening up people and, 129
  questions and influence of, 20–22
Working backward, 59
Work of listening, 139
Worry from thinking, 44–45

Yankelovich, Daniel, 55, 146

Zuckerman, Laurence, 122

Dorothy Leeds, a much-in-demand motivational speaker, is also a communications consultant who has trained more than half a million executives for major corporations including ITT, Merck, Merrill Lynch, and IBM. The author of *Smart Questions: The Essential Strategy for Successful Managers* among other books on persuasion and the art of speaking in business, Ms. Leeds has written and been featured in articles in the *New York Times*, *Forbes*, *BusinessWeek*, and *Money* magazine, as well as appearing frequently on the *Today Show*, *Good Morning America*, *Smart Money*, and *MoneyTalk*. A native New Yorker, Ms. Leeds holds a graduate degree from Columbia University and continues to reside in New York City when she is not on tour lecturing or promoting her many books. Dorothy prides herself on knowing more about asking questions than anyone on the planet.